A HACKER'S MIND

A
HACKER'S
MIND

HOW THE POWERFUL
BEND SOCIETY'S RULES,
AND HOW TO
BEND THEM BACK

Bruce Schneier

W. W. NORTON & COMPANY
Celebrating a Century of Independent Publishing

For information about permission to reproduce selections from this book, write to
Permissions, W. W. Norton & Company, Inc., 500 Fifth Avenue, New York, NY 10110

For information about special discounts for bulk purchases, please contact
W. W. Norton Special Sales at specialsales@wwnorton.com or 800-233-4830

Manufacturing by Lake Book Manufacturing
Book design by Daniel Lagin
Production manager: Lauren Abbate

ISBN 978-0-393-86666-7

W. W. Norton & Company, Inc., 500 Fifth Avenue, New York, N.Y. 10110
www.wwnorton.com

W. W. Norton & Company Ltd., 15 Carlisle Street, London W1D 3BS

1 2 3 4 5 6 7 8 9 0

To Tammy

Contents

A HACKER'S MIND

Introduction

They say that water, it never runs uphill.
It never has, and it never will.
But if you get enough money involved,
There's bound to be a loophole in the natural law.
And water, is gonna flow uphill.

–"Water Never Runs Uphill," Jim Fitting, Session Americana

A company called Uncle Milton Industries has been selling ant farms to children since 1956. The farms consist of two vertical sheets of clear plastic about a quarter inch apart, sealed at the sides, and with a top you can open up. The idea is that you fill the space with sand and put ants into the two-dimensional environment. Then, you can watch them dig tunnels.

The box doesn't come with any ants. It would be hard to keep them alive while it sat on the store shelf, and there's probably some child safety regulation about insects and toys. Instead, the box comes with a card where you can write your address, send it to the company, and receive back a tube of ants in the mail.

When most people look at this card, they often marvel that the company would send a customer a tube of ants. When I first looked at the card, I thought: "Wow, I can have this company send a tube of ants to anyone I want."

Security technologists look at the world differently than most people. When most people look at a system, they focus on how it works. When security technologists look at the same system, they can't help but focus on how it can be made to fail: how that failure can be used to force the system to behave in a way it shouldn't, in order to do something it shouldn't be able to do—and then how to use that behavior to gain an advantage of some kind.

That's what a hack is: an activity allowed by the system that subverts the goal or intent of the system. Just like using Uncle Milton's system to send tubes of ants to people who don't want them.

I teach cybersecurity policy at the Harvard Kennedy School. At the end of the first class, I announce a surprise quiz for the next time we meet. I tell the students that they will be expected to write down the first hundred digits of pi from memory. "I understand that it is not realistic to expect you to memorize a hundred random digits in two days," I tell them. "So I expect you to cheat. Don't get caught."

Two days later the room is buzzing with excitement. Most of the students don't have any new ideas. They've written the digits on a tiny scrap of paper, which they hide somewhere. Or they record themselves reading the digits, and try to conceal their earbuds. But some are incredibly creative. One student used an invisible ink and wore glasses that made the digits visible. One student wrote them out in Chinese, which I don't read. Another encoded the digits in different-colored beads and strung them on a necklace. A fourth memorized the first few and the last few and wrote random digits in the middle, assuming that my grading would be sloppy. My favorite hack was from a few years ago. Near as I could tell, Jan was just writing the digits down in order—albeit very slowly. He was the last one to finish. I remember staring at him, having no idea what he might be doing. I remember the other students staring at him. "Is he actually calculating the infinite series in his head?" I wondered. No. He programmed the phone in his pocket to vibrate each digit in Morse code.

The point of this exercise isn't to turn my class into cheaters. I always remind them that actually cheating at Harvard is grounds for expulsion. The point is that if they are going to make public policy around cybersecurity, they have to think like people who cheat. They need to cultivate a hacking mentality.

This book tells the story of hacking—one that's very different from what's depicted in movies and TV shows, and in the press. It's not the story you'll find in books teaching you how to hack computers or how to defend yourself against computer hackers. It tells the story of something much more endemic, something fundamentally human, and something far older than the invention of computers. It's a story that involves money and power.

Kids are natural hackers. They do it instinctively, because they don't fully understand the rules and their intent. (So are artificial intelligence systems—we'll get to that at the end of the book.) But so are the wealthy. Unlike children or artificial intelligences, they understand the rules and their context. But, like children, many wealthy individuals don't accept that the rules apply to them. Or, at least, they believe that their own self-interest takes precedence. The result is that they hack systems all the time.

In my story, hacking isn't just something bored teenagers or rival governments do to computer systems or that less ethical students do when they don't want to study. It isn't countercultural misbehavior by the less powerful. A hacker is more likely to be working for a hedge fund, finding a loophole in financial regulations that lets her siphon extra profits out of the system. He's more likely in a corporate office. Or an elected official. Hacking is integral to the job of every government lobbyist. It's how social media systems keep us on their platforms.

In my story, hacking is something that the rich and powerful do, something that reinforces existing power structures.

One example is Peter Thiel. The Roth IRA is a retirement account allowed by a 1997 law. It's intended for middle-class investors, and has limits on both the investor's income level and the amount that can be invested. But billionaire Peter Thiel found a hack. Because he was one of the founders of PayPal, he was able to use a $2,000 investment to buy 1.7 million shares of the company at $0.001 per share, turning it into $5 billion—all forever tax free.

Hacking is the key to why we often feel that government is unable to protect us against powerful corporate interests, or wealthy personal interests. It's one of the reasons we feel powerless against state authority. Hacking is how the rich and powerful subvert the rules to increase both their wealth and power. They work to find novel hacks, and also to make sure their hacks remain so they can continue to profit from them. That's the important point. It's not that the wealthy and powerful are better at hacking, it's that they're less likely to be punished for doing so. Indeed, their hacks often become just a normal part of how society works. Fixing this is going to require institutional change. Which is hard, because institutional leaders are the very people stacking the deck against us.

All systems can be hacked. Many systems are currently being hacked—and it's getting worse. If we don't learn how to control this process, our economic, political, and social systems will begin to fail. They'll fail because they'll no longer effectively serve their purpose, and they'll fail because people will start losing their faith and trust in them. This is already happening. How do you feel knowing that Peter Thiel got away with not paying $1 billion in capital gains taxes?

But, as I will demonstrate, hacking is not always destructive. Harnessed properly, it's one of the ways systems can evolve and improve. It's how society advances. Or, more specifically, it's how people advance society without having to completely destroy what came before. Hacking can be a force for good. The trick is figuring out how to encourage the good hacks while stopping the bad ones, and knowing the difference between the two.

Hacking will become even more disruptive as we increasingly implement artificial intelligence (AI) and autonomous systems. These are computer systems, which means they will inevitably be hacked in the same ways that all computer systems are. They affect social systems—already AI systems make loan, hiring, and parole decisions—which means those hacks will consequently affect our economic and political systems. More significantly, machine-learning processes that underpin all of modern AI will result in the *computers* performing the hacks.

Extrapolating further, AI systems will soon start discovering new hacks. This will change everything. Up until now, hacking has been a uniquely human endeavor. Hackers are human, and hacks have shared human limitations. Those limitations are about to be removed. AI will start hacking not just our computers, but our governments, our markets, and even our minds. AI will hack systems with a speed and skill that will put human hackers to shame. Keep the concept of AI hackers in mind as you read; I will culminate the book with that in the final part.

That's why this book is important right now. If there's any time when we need to understand how to recognize and defend against hacks, it's now. And this is where security technologists can help.

Once—I wish I could remember where—I heard this quote about mathematical literacy. "It's not that math can solve the world's problems. It's just that the world's problems would be easier to solve if everyone just knew a little bit more math." I think the same holds true for thinking about security. It's not that the security mindset, or a hacking mentality, will solve the world's problems. It's that the world's problems would be easier to solve if everyone just understood a little more about security.

So let's go.

PART 1

HACKING
101

What Is Hacking?

"Hack," "hacking," "hacker"—these terms are overloaded with meaning and innuendo. My definition is neither precise nor canonical. I'm fine with that. My goal is to demonstrate that thinking in terms of hacking is a useful tool to understand a broad array of systems, how they fail, and how to make them more resilient.

> Def: **Hack** /hak/ (noun) -
>
> 1. A clever, unintended exploitation of a system that (a) subverts the rules or norms of the system, (b) at the expense of someone else affected by the system.
>
> 2. Something that a system allows but which is unintended and unanticipated by its designers.

Hacking is not the same as cheating. A hack could also be a cheat, but it's more likely not. When someone cheats, they're doing something against the rules—something the system explicitly prohibits. Typing someone else's name and password into a website without their permission, not disclosing all of your income on your tax return, or copying someone else's answers on a test are all cheating. None of those are hacking.

Hacks are not the same as improvements, enhancements, or innovations. Practicing your tennis serve and returning as a better player is improving. When Apple adds a new feature to its iPhone, it's an enhancement. Figuring out a clever new way to use a spreadsheet can be an innovation. Sometimes a hack is also an innovation or an enhancement—like when you jailbreak your iPhone to add features that Apple doesn't approve of—but it's not necessarily one.

Hacking targets a system and turns it against itself without breaking it. If I smash your car window and hotwire the ignition, that's not a hack. If I figure out how to trick the car's keyless entry system into unlocking the car door and starting the ignition, that's a hack.

Notice the difference. The hacker isn't just outsmarting her victim. She's found a flaw in the rules of the system. She's doing something she shouldn't be allowed to do, but is. She's outsmarting the system. And, by extension, she's outsmarting the system's designers.

Hacking subverts the intent of a system by subverting its rules or norms. It's "gaming the system." It occupies a middle ground between cheating and innovation.

"Hack" is a subjective term. There's a lot of "I know it when I see it" when it comes to hacking. Some things are obviously hacks. Some things are just as obviously not hacks. And some things are in the grey area between the two. Speedreading—not a hack. Hiding a microdot in a period on a page of printed text—definitely a hack. Cliff Notes—maybe; I'm not sure.

Hacks are clever. A hack results in grudging admiration (possibly in addition to righteous anger), and has some element of "Cool—I wish I'd thought of that," even if it is something you would never do. This is true even if the hack is done by evil, murderous people. In my 2003 book, *Beyond Fear*, I opened with a long explanation of why the 9/11 terrorist attacks were "amazing." Those terrorists broke the unwritten rules of airplane hijacking. Before them, hijackings involved forcing a plane to fly *to* somewhere, some number of political demands, negotiations with governments and police, and generally peaceful resolutions. What the 9/11 terrorists did was awful and horrific, but I also recognized the ingenuity of their hack. They only used weapons that were allowed through airport security, transformed civilian jets into guided missiles, and unilaterally rewrote the norms around airplane terrorism.

Hackers and their work force us to think differently about the systems in our world. They expose what we assume or take for granted, often to the embarrassment of the powerful and sometimes at terrible cost.

Terrorism aside, people love hacks because they're clever. MacGyver was a hacker. Prison break and caper movies are filled with clever hacks: *Rififi, The Great Escape, Papillon, Mission Impossible, The Italian Job, Ocean's 11, 12, 13,* and *8.*

Hacks are novel. "Is that allowed?" and "I didn't know you could do that!" are both common reactions to hacks. What is and isn't a hack also changes over time. Rules and norms change. "Common knowledge" changes. Because hacks tend to be eventually either forbidden or allowed, things that were once hacks no longer are. You once had to jailbreak your smartphone to turn it into a wireless hotspot; now hotspots are standard features in both iOS and Android. Hiding a metal file in a cake sent to a jailed confederate was initially a hack, but now it's a movie trope that prisons will be on guard against.

In 2019, someone used a drone to deliver a cell phone and marijuana into an Ohio prison. At the time, I would have called that a hack. Today, flying a drone near a prison is expressly illegal in some states, and I don't think it's a hack anymore. I recently read about someone using a fishing rod to cast contraband over a prison's wall. And also about a cat, who was caught carrying drugs and phone SIM cards at a Sri Lanka prison (but later escaped). Definitely a hack.

Hacks are often legal. Because they follow the letter of the rules but evade the spirit, they are only illegal if there is some overarching rule that forbids them. When an accountant finds a loophole in the tax rules, it's probably legal if there is no more general law that prohibits it.

There's even a word for this sort of thing in Italian: *furbizia,* the ingenuity that Italians deploy towards getting around bureaucracy and inconvenient laws. Hindi has a similar word, *jugaad,* which emphasizes the cleverness and resourcefulness of making do. In Brazilian Portuguese, the equivalent is *gambiarra.*

Hacks are sometimes moral. Some assume that just because a certain activity or behavior is legal, it's automatically moral, but of course the world is more complicated than that. Just as there are immoral laws, there are moral crimes. Most of the hacks we'll be discussing in this book are technically legal, but contravene the spirit of the laws. (And systems of laws are only one type of system that can be hacked.)

The word "hack" traces its origins to the MIT Tech Model Railroad Club in 1955, and quickly migrated to the nascent field of computers. Originally it described a way of problem solving, implying cleverness or innovation or resourcefulness, without any criminal or even adversarial qualities. But by the 1980s, "hacking" most often described breaking computer security systems. It wasn't just getting a computer to do something new, it was forcing it to do something it wasn't supposed to do.

In my way of thinking, it's just one short step from hacking computers to hacking economic, political, and social systems. All of those systems are just sets of rules, or sometimes norms. They are just as vulnerable to hacking as computer systems.

This isn't new. We've been hacking society's systems throughout history.

2

Hacking Systems

Hacks can be perpetrated on any system, but comparisons between these different types of systems can be useful in highlighting more features of how hacks operate—for example, the tax code versus computer code.

The tax code isn't software. It doesn't run on a computer. But you can still think of it as "code" in the computer sense of the term. It's a series of algorithms that takes an input—financial information for the year—and produces an output: the amount of tax owed.

The tax code is incredibly complex. Maybe not for most of us as individuals, but there are a bazillion details and exceptions and special cases for rich people and businesses of various kinds. It consists of government laws, administrative rulings, judicial decisions, and legal opinions. It also includes the laws and regulations governing corporations and various types of partnerships. Credible estimates of the size of it all are hard to come by; even experts had no idea when I asked. The tax laws themselves occupy about 2,600 pages. IRS regulations and tax rulings increase that to about 70,000 pages. The laws involving corporate structures and partnerships are equally complicated, so I'm going to wave my hands and assume a total of 100,000 pages—or 3 million lines—for the US tax code. Microsoft Windows 10 takes up about 50 million lines of code. It's hard to compare lines of text to lines of computer code, but the comparison is still useful. In both examples, much of that complexity is related to how different parts of the code interact with each other.

All computer code contains bugs. These are mistakes: mistakes in specification, mistakes in programming, mistakes that occur somewhere in the process of creating the software, mistakes as pedestrian as a typographic error or misspelling. Modern software applications generally have hundreds if not thousands of bugs. These bugs are in all the software that you're currently using: in your computer, on your phone, in whatever "Internet of Things" (IoT) devices you have around your home and work. That all of this software works perfectly well most of the time speaks to how obscure and inconsequential these bugs tend to be. You're unlikely to encounter them in normal operations, but they're there (like so many parts of the tax code that you never encounter).

Some of those bugs introduce security holes. By this I mean something very specific: an attacker can deliberately trigger the bug to achieve some effect undesired by the code's designers and programmers. In computer security language, we call these bugs "vulnerabilities."

The tax code also has bugs. They might be mistakes in how the tax laws were written: errors in the actual words that Congress voted on and the president signed into law. They might be mistakes in how the tax code is interpreted. They might be oversights in how parts of the law were conceived, or unintended omissions of some sort or another. They might arise from the huge number of ways different parts of the tax code interact with each other.

A recent example comes from the 2017 Tax Cuts and Jobs Act. That law was drafted in haste and in secret, and passed without any time for review by legislators—or even proofreading. Parts of it were handwritten, and it's pretty much inconceivable that anyone who voted either for or against it knew precisely what was in it. The text contained an error that accidentally categorized military death benefits as earned income. The practical effect of that mistake was that surviving family members were hit with surprise tax bills of $10,000 or more. That's a bug.

It's not a vulnerability, though, because no one can take advantage of it to reduce their tax bill. But some bugs in the tax code are also vulnerabilities. For example, there was a corporate tax trick called the "Double

Irish with a Dutch Sandwich." It's a vulnerability that arose from the interactions of tax laws in multiple countries, finally patched by the Irish.

Here's how it worked: The US company transfers assets to an Irish subsidiary. That subsidiary charges the US company huge royalties from sales to US customers. This dramatically lowers the company's US taxes, and Irish taxes on royalties are designed to be low. Then, using a loophole in Irish tax law, the company can shift the profits to entities in tax havens like Bermuda, Belize, Mauritius, or the Cayman Islands—to ensure that these profits remain untaxed. Next, add a second Irish company, this time for sales to European customers, also taxed at a low rate. Finally, use another vulnerability, this one involving a Dutch intermediary company, to transfer the profits back to the first Irish company and on to the offshore tax haven. Tech companies are particularly well-suited to exploit this vulnerability; they can assign intellectual property rights to subsidiary companies abroad, who then transfer cash assets to tax havens.

That's how companies like Google and Apple have avoided paying their fair share of US taxes despite being US companies. It's definitely an unintended and unanticipated use of the tax laws in three countries, although Ireland purposely pursued lax tax rules in order to attract American companies. And it can be very profitable for the hackers. Estimates are that US companies avoided paying nearly $200 billion in US taxes in 2017 alone, at the expense of everyone else.

In the tax world, bugs and vulnerabilities are called loopholes. Attackers take advantage of these; it's called tax avoidance. And there are thousands of what we in the computer security world would call "black-hat researchers," who examine every line of the tax code looking for vulnerabilities they can exploit: tax attorneys and tax accountants.

We know how to fix vulnerabilities in computer code. First, we can employ a variety of tools to detect them before the code is finished. Second, and after the code is out in the world, there are various ways we can find them and—most important of all—quickly patch them.

We can employ these same methods with the tax code. The 2017 tax law capped income tax deductions for property taxes. This provision didn't come into force until 2018, so someone came up with the clever hack to prepay 2018 property taxes in 2017. Just before the end of the year, the

IRS ruled about when that was legal and when it wasn't, patching the tax code against this exploit. Short answer: most of the time, it wasn't.

It's often not this easy. Some hacks are written into the law, or can't be ruled away. Passing any tax legislation is a big deal, especially in the US, where the issue is so partisan and contentious. It wasn't until 2021 that the earned income tax bug for military families started getting fixed. Congress didn't fix the actual 2017 bug; they fixed an even older bug that interacted with the 2017 bug. And its fix won't be complete until 2023. (And that's an easy one; everyone acknowledges it was a mistake.) We don't have the ability to patch the tax code with anywhere near the same agility that we have to patch software.

There's another option: that the vulnerability isn't patched and slowly becomes part of the normal way of doing things. Lots of tax loopholes end up like this. Sometimes the IRS accepts them. Sometimes the courts affirm their legality. They might not reflect the intent of the tax law, but the words of the law allow them. Sometimes they're even retroactively legalized by Congress after a constituency gets behind them. This process is how systems evolve.

A hack subverts the intent of a system. Whatever governing system has jurisdiction either blocks or allows it. Sometimes it explicitly allows it, and other times it does nothing and implicitly allows it.

3

What Is a System?

A hack follows the letter of a system's rules, but violates their spirit and intent.

In order for there to be a hack, there must be a system of rules to be hacked. So I need to step back and define more precisely what the word "system" means, at least as I'm using it.

> Def: **System** /ˈsis-ˌtəm/ (noun) -
>
> A complex process, constrained by a set of rules or norms, intended to produce one or more desired outcomes.

The word processor I wrote this paragraph on is a system: a collection of electronic signals constrained by a set of software rules specific to producing writing such that these words appear on the screen—my desired outcome. The creation of this book is the product—outcome—of another system, with processes that include designing the pages, printing them, binding them together in order, putting on a dust jacket, and boxing them for shipment. Each of those processes is completed according to a set of rules. And those two systems, plus several others, result in the paper book you are holding in your hand, the electronic file that you are read-

ing on your e-reader, or the different electronic file that is being played
on whatever audiobook system you're using. This idea is true whether the
elements of the system are housed under one roof or distributed around
the world. It is even true whether the outcome is real or virtual, free or
overpriced, poorly produced, or unreliably available. One or more systems are always involved.

Systems have rules. Usually rules of law, but also rules of a game,
informal rules of a group or process, or unspoken rules of society. Cognitive systems follow laws, too—natural laws.

Note that the hacks are something the system allows. And by "allows,"
I mean something very specific. It's not that it's legal, or permitted, socially
acceptable or even ethical—although it might be any or all of those. It's
that the system, as constructed, does not prevent the hack from occurring
within the confines of that system. The system doesn't allow these hacks
deliberately, but only incidentally and accidentally because of the way it
was designed. In technical systems, this generally means that the software permits the hack to occur. In social systems, it generally means that
the rules—often laws—controlling the system do not expressly prohibit
the hack. This is why we sometimes use the word "loophole" to describe
these hacks.

What this means is that hacks are conducted against systems in which
participants have agreed in advance—either explicitly or implicitly—to
abide by a common set of rules. Sometimes the rules of the system aren't
the same as the laws that govern the system. I get that that's confusing, so let's explain it by example. A computer is controlled by a set of
rules consisting of the software running on that computer. Hacking the
computer means subverting that software. But there are also laws that
potentially govern what someone can legally do. In the US, for example, the Computer Fraud and Abuse Act makes most forms of hacking
a felony. (Notice what's going on here. The computer system is what's
being hacked, but a more general legal system is protecting it.) There
are a lot of problems with how general the law is, but precisely because
of that generality it has become a catch-all that declares all computer
hacking illegal.

Professional sports are hacked all the time, because they are governed by explicit sets of rules. The law is often hacked, because law is nothing but rules.

In some systems, of course, the laws *are* the rules or, at least, provide many of them. As we'll see when we discuss hacking finances or the legal system itself, simple typos or confusing language in a bill, contract, or judicial opinion can open the door to endless exploits that were never intended by the original drafters or judges themselves.

Note something very important: the rules don't have to be explicit. There are lots of systems in our world, particularly social systems, that are constrained by norms. Norms are less formal than rules; often unwritten, they nevertheless guide behavior. We are constrained by social norms all the time, different norms in different situations. Even politics is governed by norms as much as by law, something we repeatedly learned in the US in recent years as norm after norm was broken.

My definition of system includes the word "intended." This implies a designer: someone who determines the desired outcome of a system. This is an important part of the definition, but really it's only sometimes correct.

With computers, the systems being hacked are deliberately created by a person or organization, which means the hacker is outsmarting the system's designers. This is also true for systems of rules established by some governing body: corporate procedures, rules of a sport, or UN treaties.

Many of the systems we'll be discussing in this book don't have individual designers. No one person designed market capitalism; many people had their hand in its evolution over time. The same applies to the democratic process; in the US, it's a combination of the Constitution, legislation, judicial rulings, and social norms. And when someone hacks social, political, or economic systems, they're outsmarting some combination of the designers of the system, the social process by which the system evolved, and the societal norms that govern the system.

Our cognitive systems have also evolved over time, with absolutely no designer involved. This evolution is a normal part of biologically based systems: new uses for existing systems emerge, old systems get repurposed, unneeded systems atrophy. But we do speak about the "purpose" of a biological system: the purpose of the spleen or the purpose of the amygdala. Evolution is a way for a system to "design" itself without a designer.

For those systems, we'll start with a system's function within a body or ecosystem—even if there was no one designing that purpose.

Hacking is a natural outgrowth of systems thinking. Systems permeate much of our lives. These systems underpin most of complex society, and are becoming increasingly complex as society becomes more complex. And the exploitation of these systems—hacking—becomes ever more important. Basically, if you understand a system well and deeply, you don't have to play by the same rules as everyone else. You can look for flaws and omissions in the rules. You notice where the constraints the system places on you don't work. You naturally hack the system. And if you're rich and powerful, you'll likely get away with it.

4

The Hacking Life Cycle

In computer security speak, a hack consists of two parts: a vulnerability and an exploit.

A vulnerability is a feature in a system that allows a hack to occur. In a computer system, it's a flaw. It's either an error or an oversight: in the design, the specification, or the code itself. It could be something as minor as a missing parenthesis—or as major as a property of the software architecture. It's the underlying reason that the hack works. An exploit is the mechanism to make use of the vulnerability.

If you're logging into a website that allows your username and password to be transmitted unencrypted over the Internet—that's a vulnerability. The exploit would be a software program that eavesdrops on Internet connections, records your username and password, and then uses it to access your account. If a piece of software enables you to see the private files of another user, that's a vulnerability. The exploit would be the software program that allows me to see them. If a door lock can be opened without a key, that's also a vulnerability. The exploit would be whatever physical shim or tool is required to pry it open.

Let's take a computer example: EternalBlue. That's the NSA code name for an exploit against the Windows operating system, used by the NSA for at least five years before 2017, when the Russians stole it from that agency. EternalBlue exploits a vulnerability in Microsoft's implementation of the Server Message Block (SMB) protocol, which controls client–server communication. Because of the manner in which the SMB was coded, sending a carefully crafted data packet over the Internet to a Windows computer allowed an attacker to execute arbitrary code on the receiving computer, and thereby gain control over it. Basically, the NSA was able to exploit EternalBlue to remotely commandeer any Windows computer on the Internet.

Several types of people—each with different skill sets—can be involved with a hack, and the term "hacker" can confusingly refer to all of them. First, there's the creative hacker, who uses her curiosity and expertise to discover the hack and create the exploit. In the case of EternalBlue, it was a computer scientist at the NSA who discovered it. In the case of the Double Irish tax loophole, it was some international tax expert who painstakingly studied the different laws and how they interact.

Second, there is the person who uses the resultant exploit in practice. In the NSA, it was an employee who deployed the exploit against a target. In an accounting firm, it was whichever accountant applied Irish and Dutch tax laws to a particular corporation's tax avoidance strategy. The hacker who performs that sort of hack makes use of someone else's creativity. In the computer world, we derisively call them "script kiddies." They're not smart or creative enough to unearth new hacks, but they can run computer programs—scripts—that automatically unleash the results of someone else's creativity.

And finally, there is the organization or person in whose service this is all being done. So we can speak of the NSA hacking a foreign network, or Russia hacking the US, or of Google hacking the tax code.

This is all important, because we're going to be talking repeatedly about how the rich and powerful hack systems. I'm not saying that wealth and power makes someone a better technical hacker, it just gives that person better access. Like the US or Russia or Google, it enables them to hire the technical expertise needed to successfully hack systems.

Hacks are both invented and discovered. More specifically, the underlying vulnerability is discovered, then the exploit is invented. Both words are used, but I prefer "discovered" since it reinforces the notion that the capability is latent in the system even before anyone realizes that it's there.

What happens once hacks are discovered depends on who discovers them. Generally, the person or organization that figures out the hack uses it to their advantage. In a computer system, this might be a criminal hacker or a national intelligence agency like the NSA—or anything in between. Depending on who starts using it and how, others may or may not learn about it, or others may independently discover it. The process might take weeks, months, or years.

In other systems, the utility of a hack depends on how often and how publicly it's used. An obscure vulnerability in a banking system might be occasionally used by criminals, and remain undetected by the bank for years. A good hack of the tax code will proliferate simply because whoever owns the discovery is likely selling their knowledge of it. A clever psychological manipulation might become public once enough people talk about it—or it might be obscure and unknown for generations.

Eventually, the system reacts. The hack can be neutralized if the underlying vulnerability is patched. By this I mean that someone updates the system in order to remove the vulnerability or otherwise render it unusable. No vulnerability, no hack. It's as simple as that.

This all implies that there's someone who controls the target system and is in charge of whatever processes update it. This is obvious if the system is the Microsoft Windows operating system or any other large software package; the developer is behind it. Companies like Microsoft and Apple have become very good about patching their systems.

This also works for open-source and public-domain software; there's usually a person or organization behind it, and the code is there for all to see. It works less well for low-cost IoT software, much of which is designed abroad, at a minimal profit margin, by software teams that have long since disbanded. Even worse, many IoT devices can't be patched at all. This isn't a matter of not knowing how; many IoT devices embed their computer code in hardware and not software, and are thus inherently unpatchable. This problem worsens as production lines are disbanded and companies go out of business, leaving millions of orphaned Internet-connected devices behind.

In technical systems, hacks are often patched as soon as they're discovered. This process doesn't work nearly as well with the social systems

I'm discussing in this book. Updating the tax code, for example, requires a years-long legislative process. The people benefiting from the hack might lobby against any change in the law. There might be legitimate disagreement about whether the hack benefits society or not. And, as we'll see in much of the rest of the book, the wealthy and powerful have an outsized say in what is nominally the democratic process of figuring it out.

If the system isn't patched, then the hack becomes integrated into the system's rules. It becomes the new normal. So what starts out as a hack can quickly become business as usual. That's the trajectory for many of the nontechnical hacks I'll talk about in this book.

5

The Ubiquity of Hacking

No matter how locked-down a system is, vulnerabilities will always remain, and hacks will always be possible. In 1930, the Austro-Hungarian mathematician Kurt Gödel proved that all mathematical systems are either incomplete or inconsistent. I have a theory that this is true more generally. All systems will have ambiguities, inconsistencies, and oversights, and they will always be exploitable. Systems of rules, in particular, have to thread the fine line between being complete and being comprehensible, within the many limits of human language and understanding. Combine this with the natural human need to push against constraints and test limits, and with the inevitability of vulnerabilities, and you get everything being hacked all the time.

Club Penguin was a Disney online kid's game that operated from 2005 to 2017. Children talking to strangers online is always a worry, so Disney created an "Ultimate Safe Chat" mode that prohibited free-form text by restricting players to a list of pre-scripted messages. The idea was to keep kids safe from unscripted chatting with real or imagined child predators. Kids being kids, they wanted to talk with each other. They hacked this restriction by using their avatars' body positions to communicate things like letters and numbers.

Children are natural hackers. They don't understand intent and, as a result, don't see system limitations in the same way adults do. They look at problems holistically, and can stumble onto hacks without realizing what they're doing. They aren't as constrained by norms, and they certainly don't understand laws in the same way. Testing the rules is a sign of independence.

Like Club Penguin, many online games for children have tried to place restrictions on speech, to prevent bullying, harassment, and predators. Kids have hacked them all. Tricks to evade moderators and swear filters include deliberate misspellings like "phuq," separating out key information over several utterances so that no single utterance breaks the rules, and acrostics. Some sites prohibited users from typing numbers; kids responded by using words: "won" for one, "too" for two, "tree" for three, and so on. Same with insults: "lose her" for loser, "stew putt" for stupid.

Schools have tried to restrict the ways students use school-provided computers, and students have responded by hacking them. They pass successful hacks around to their friends. After one district limited the websites students were allowed to visit, students realized that if they used a VPN, the restrictions couldn't be detected or enforced. After another district blocked chat apps, the students figured out that they could chat using a shared Google Doc.

That hack wasn't new. It even has a name: foldering. In separate incidents, it was used by General Petraeus, Paul Manafort, and the 9/11 terrorists. They all realized that they could evade communications surveillance if they shared an email account with their co-conspirators and wrote messages to each other, keeping them as email drafts and never sending them.

I remember hacks to get around phone system rules from my childhood. If you're too young to remember how this works, I'll explain. The caller would call a human operator and tell the operator who they were and that they wanted to make a collect call. The operator would place the call, and ask whoever picked up the phone on the other end if they wanted to accept the collect call from the sender. Collect calls had a hefty surcharge. But because the operator initiated the call, information could be transmitted before anything was charged. So, we would call collect, the operator asking the other party—generally our parents—if they would accept a collect call from us. Our parents would say no and then return the call at standard, less expensive, rates. This kind of thing could be made more efficient. Some families had a list of names to tell the operator; they were all coded messages of some sort: "Bruce" meant "arrived safely," "Steve" meant "call back," and so on. (The operator had no idea what the caller's real name was.) Even today, people have phone hacks to get around billing rules. In Nigeria, it's called "flashing": calling someone and hanging up before they can pick up. This was also huge in India in the early 2010s, because costs for cellular and landline calls were so different. All of these hacks are intended to subvert the phone systems in order to exchange information without paying for the privilege.

Homeschooling during the COVID-19 pandemic brought out the hacker in many students. One student renamed himself "Reconnecting . . ." and turned his video off, so it looked like he was having connectivity problems. In March 2020, during the early months of the pandemic, the Chinese city of Wuhan went into lockdown. Schools started holding classes remotely, and students tried to flood the DingTalk homework app with one-star reviews, hoping that it would be removed from app stores. (It didn't work.)

Systems tend to be rigid and rule-bound. Systems limit what we can do, and, invariably, some of us want to do something else. So we hack. Once you're familiar with what systems are and how they operate, you'll see them everywhere. And then you'll see hacking everywhere.

This doesn't imply that all systems are broken. Recall Gödel. There's a saying among lawyers: "All contracts are incomplete." A contract works not because it rigidly prevents the parties from subverting its intent; it works because most loopholes are filled with trust and good intention— and there's a system of arbitration and adjudication available if things go badly. It might sound naive and idealistic, but systems of trust are what make society work. We don't demand airtight protection in our agreements, because (1) that's impossible to achieve, (2) any attempt will be too long and unwieldy, and (3) we don't really need it.

It's the same with more general systems. What makes a system work is not its presumed invulnerability. It's that same combination of trust and adjudication. Even though I'm going to be talking about hacks and hacking, they are all largely exceptions. Most people don't hack systems, and those systems work pretty well most of the time. We rightly trust that most people don't hack systems. And we have systems to deal with hacks when they occur. This is resilience. This is what makes society work. It's how we humans have dealt with hacking for millennia.

Not all systems are equally hackable. As we move through the book, we'll see various characteristics of systems that make them more or less vulnerable to hacking. Complex systems with many rules are particularly vulnerable, simply because there are more possibilities for unanticipated and unintended consequences. This is certainly true for computer systems—I've written in the past that complexity is the worst enemy of security—and it's also true for systems like the tax code, financial regulations, and artificial intelligence. Human systems constrained by more flexible social norms and rules are more vulnerable to hacking, because they leave themselves more open to interpretation and therefore have more loopholes.

On the other hand, systems that are less critical, smaller-scale, and marginal—and possibly more experimental and ill-defined—will cause less harm if they're disrupted, and it's probably better to let those systems evolve through more hacking than to worry about what might go wrong.

There's not much value, and a lot of danger, in letting people hack the process of designing and building a bridge. Getting it wrong would be catastrophic. There's a lot more to be said for allowing the kind of hacking that results in wonderful, unanticipated ways to use the Internet.

Hacking is a natural part of the human condition. It's ubiquitous and, as we'll see, an evolutionary process: constant, unending, and capable of creating, as Darwin would say, "forms most beautiful and most wonderful"—or most strange and terrible.

PART 2

BASIC HACKS
AND DEFENSES

6

ATM Hacks

To start with, we'll look at a variety of hacks against obviously constrained systems. It'll be an essential foundation for understanding
hacks against broader political, social, economic, and cognitive systems.

An ATM is just a computer with money inside. It's connected to the
banking network by the Internet—a couple of decades ago it was a phone
connection and a modem—and runs on the Windows operating system.
Of course, it can be hacked.

In 2011, an Australian bartender named Don Saunders figured out
how to get free money from ATMs. He stumbled into the hack late one
night. (It makes a better story if we imagine he was drunk at the time.)
He noticed a way that he could transfer money he didn't have from one
account to another, then withdraw the cash without the system recording the transaction. The bonanza resulted from a vulnerability in the
ATM's software used to record transfers between accounts, combined
with another vulnerability in the time lag in how the various accounts
credited and debited when the ATMs went offline for the night. Saunders
didn't understand any of that, though. He found it by accident, and realized that he could reproduce the result.

Over the next five months, Saunders withdrew $1.6 million
Australian—that's roughly $1.1 million US. And he wasn't so much caught
as he eventually stopped doing it, felt guilty about it, went into therapy

over it, and then publicly confessed. The bank had never figured out how it was losing so much money.

Let's pause for a second and talk about what's being hacked here. Stealing money from a bank is always illegal. The hack isn't of the banking system; the hack is of the ATM system and the bank's software. Saunders found an unintended and unanticipated way to use those systems—to do things that the systems allowed—in a way that subverted their intent. That's the hack.

The decades-long evolution of ATM attacks and resultant security countermeasures nicely illustrates the arms race between hackers and defenders. More than that, it illustrates several themes that we'll return to throughout the book. Systems never exist in isolation. They're made up of smaller systems, and they're part of larger systems. ATMs are computer software, yes. But they're also physical objects. Their use involves customers, and a remote banking network. Hackers can target any of those aspects of ATMs.

The first ATM attacks were crude, more basic thievery than hacking. Criminals would glue the cash dispenser doors shut, then pry them open after a frustrated customer gave up and left. They would find a way to "trap" cards in the slot, then pull them out and use them later. They would rip entire machines out of walls and cart them away, opening them up later in some safe location—as seen on the television show *Breaking Bad*. Defenders responded. Subsequent ATM designs didn't have doors on the cash dispensers, so there was nothing to glue shut. They were better secured to the wall, and their store of cash was refilled more often so there was less money inside to steal. (Smart attackers responded to that by targeting machines the evening before a long holiday weekend, when there was more money inside.) Modern ATMs have their own camera systems, not to prevent these sorts of attacks, but to better identify and hopefully arrest criminals who perpetrate them.

Other attacks directly targeted the customer's perceptions of authority. Here's one example. A criminal dressed in a suit or company uniform interrupts a customer using an ATM. "This machine is out of order. Use that one over there." The customer obediently moves to the next machine, leaving the criminal to put an "out of order" sign on the first machine.

The customer completes his transaction and leaves, and the criminal completes the customer's interrupted transaction on that first machine to withdraw money.

A string of thefts along those lines led to several more changes in ATM design. Initially, the machine would hold a customer's card until the end of the transaction, ensuring that the customer couldn't be interrupted by official-looking strangers. Eventually, the back end was reengineered to prevent multiple simultaneous ATM transactions. That didn't prevent all hacks of authority. A cruder version, reported in Indonesia, involved a fake bank manager convincing a customer to give him his ATM card after he pretended to call the bank and cancel it.

Another family of hacks involves stealing information in order to create and use a duplicate card. This is called "skimming," and has become widespread and sophisticated over the years. The canonical hack involves placing a second magnetic-stripe reading device over a card slot, so that the customer unwittingly slides his card through the malicious reader along with the ATM's real reader. Add a hidden camera or a sensor on the keypad, and a criminal can steal the PIN as well. A variant involves putting a fake free-standing ATM in a public location, like a shopping center. It looks like a legitimate ATM, but all it does is skim magnetic-stripe information and collect PINs—displaying an "out of order" message afterwards to shoo the cashless customers away.

These hacks exploit several vulnerabilities. First, the customer doesn't have enough expertise to notice a skimmer or a fake ATM. Second, a magnetic-stripe ATM card is easily duplicated. And third, the ATM authentication system—possession of the ATM card and knowledge of the PIN—just isn't that secure.

Other ATM hacks target the software. In the hacking literature this is known as "jackpotting": making the ATM spit bills out like coins from a slot machine, no stolen card or PIN required. A 2016 attack of this sort was hatched in Taiwan and then quickly spread across Asia, Europe, and Central America, resulting in losses in the tens of millions of dollars. Another attack, exploiting a different software vulnerability, started in Europe in 2020 and is still spreading worldwide.

Jackpotting has several steps. The first is figuring out the technical details, almost certainly involving having access to a used ATM to disassemble and study. That's not hard; eBay has many for sale. Once the hackers figure out the details, they go after operational ATMs: opening a panel on the machine, connecting to a USB port, downloading malware onto the ATM computer, and installing software to allow for remote access. Dressing the part helps; a criminal who looks like a technician can do this without arousing suspicion. Then, with all of that in place, this individual can retreat to a safe location and have a compatriot approach the machine with a bag while the hackers remotely instruct the machine to disgorge all of its cash.

There's no good data on how much money is stolen this way—banks are loath to make details of this sort of thing public—but the US Secret Service began warning financial institutions about jackpotting in 2018. And that's eight years after security researcher Barnaby Jack demonstrated jackpotting at the DEF CON hacker conference in 2010. His attacks didn't require anyone to physically tamper with the ATM; he found software vulnerabilities that he could remotely exploit to accomplish the same result.

7

Casino Hacks

Richard Harris worked for the Nevada Gaming Control Board, where he inspected new slot machines before they were installed on the casino floor. Because he had access to the innards of the machines, he was able to replace the software chips with his own. His modified software was programmed to pay the jackpot when coins were inserted into a machine in a specified sequence. He modified over thirty machines between 1993 and 1995, and won hundreds of thousands of dollars through a group of associates that played his machines. Finally, one of his associates got sloppy and was caught.

Like an ATM, a slot machine is also just a computer with money inside. It was a mechanical device when invented in 1895, but since the 1980s, a computer controls the result and the wheels only serve a psychological function. Many slot machines don't even have real wheels; it's all simulated on a computer display.

And they've been hacked since the beginning. Some older machines could be physically jostled to change where the results landed. Other machines could be fooled into spinning by a coin on a string. Many machines count the coins they dispense with an optical sensor; obscuring that sensor by slipping a device inside the machine up from the coin tray resulted in bigger payouts.

Every game on the casino floor has been hacked. Some of these hacks are now normal. I don't mean that they're allowed, but that we've all heard about them and don't consider them innovative or even interesting. Card counting in blackjack used to be a hack; now there are books on how to do it and rules against doing it successfully.

The idea of predicting the outcome of roulette dates from the 1950s. The wheel spins at a constant rate, the croupier tends to spin the ball the same way, and with enough computation you can figure out which numbers the ball is more likely to land on.

A 1960s cheating technique involved a wearable computer with toe switches and an earpiece. The wearer would input data with his toes: information that would enable the computer to calculate the speed of the wheel, the speed with which the croupier habitually flicked the ball, and so on. The earpiece would tell the wearer which numbers were more likely to come up. Later designs improved on the data input and speed, and in the 1970s a group of University of California, Santa Cruz, graduate students managed to turn a profit with their shoe computer.

Their hack wasn't illegal. It wasn't until 1985 that Nevada banned the use of devices to predict the outcome of casino games. The real defense was to modify the rules of the game so that croupiers stopped taking bets earlier.

As hacks go, card counting in blackjack is a tough one to pull off for those without the requisite savant skills. Basically, players have an advantage when there are more tens remaining in the deck, and the house has an advantage when there are fewer. So a card counter tracks that information and bets more when he or she has an advantage. It's only a slight advantage—about 1% over the house—but it's real. And it requires a lot of concentration on the part of the player.

Casinos have responded in two different ways. The first is to make card counting more difficult. Many casinos shuffle six decks of cards together—automatic shufflers do the work—and only deal two-thirds of the way through the decks to reduce the player's probabilistic advantage. Or they shuffle after every hand. In both Las Vegas and Atlantic City, pit bosses are known to come around and engage suspected card counters in conversation to both distract and intimidate them.

Casinos tried making card counting illegal, but the regulators weren't convinced that the strategy equaled cheating. (Laws were passed banning card-counting devices.) All casinos can do is catch card counters and ban them from the casino. Formerly, they did this by instructing casino staff to be alert for typical card-counting behavior. More recently, casino cameras that track the movement of every card do this automatically. Since casinos are private business, they generally can (depending on the state) deny service to whomever they want, as long as they don't illegally discriminate while doing so.

The other response to card counting is to accept it as a cost of doing business. More people think they can count cards than actually can. Casinos actually benefit from the popular impression that blackjack is the one game where players can beat the house, and they make more money from wannabe card counters than they lose from actual ones. As an enticement, some casinos even advertise the fact that they deal blackjack from a single deck.

There are exceptions, of course. In the 1980s, a group of MIT and Harvard academics invented an innovative card-counting hack. Casinos know how to detect card counters; they look for people who (1) consistently win and (2) change their betting patterns in a way that implies strategic knowledge. The MIT group divided the different card-counting tasks among different players to better avoid detection. The counters sat at the tables and never changed their betting patterns. The large-money bettors also never changed their betting patterns and were steered to "hot tables" by compatriots who received signals from the counters. The group made an estimated $10 million before they gave up the business. Indeed a great hack.

8

Airline Frequent-Flier Hacks

In 1999, David Phillips bought over 12,000 Healthy Choice pudding cups. Why? To hack an airline frequent-flier program.

Airline frequent-flier plans became popular in 1981, when American, United, and Delta unveiled their programs. Now, everyone has one. They're loyalty programs, rewarding customers who consistently fly an airline and making them less likely to switch to another one. Before COVID-19, I flew all the time. I know all the ins and outs of those programs. They've all been hacked since the beginning.

One of the early hacks was called "mileage runs." Miles, which fliers earn on the basis of the distance traveled, are basically a private currency that can be redeemed for tickets. A clever hacker will look for ways to arbitrage the two currencies: instances where you can get a lot of miles for not a lot of money. So, for example, flying nonstop from New York to Amsterdam is 3,630 miles, but connecting through Istanbul is 6,370 miles. If the two tickets cost the same, and you have nothing better to do with your time, that's a great deal.

Mileage runs were definitely an unanticipated subversion of these plans. Then the hacks got weirder. The programs include reward tiers, which means that flying—for example—at least 50,000 miles in a year is valuable to a frequent traveler. Travelers would sometimes fly complicated yet cheap round-trip itineraries, with six or more stops, just to accrue the miles. They wouldn't even bother leaving the airports.

Airlines ignored these hacks for years. But in 2015, airlines started changing their frequent-flier programs to make mileage runs less useful. They imposed minimum spending requirements for elite statuses, and eventually changed the definition of "frequent-flier mile" so that it depended on dollars spent rather than miles flown.

Other hacks involved ways to accrue points other than by flying. Airlines have long had affiliations with credit cards. These cards offer miles with every purchase, but often also large mileage bonuses when signing up. The hack is obvious: sign up for a lot of credit cards, and cancel before any fees accrue. One man opened a credit card and immediately bought $3,000 worth of Amazon gift cards to qualify for a sign-up bonus. Another filled his garage with blenders for a promotion offering extra points on appliances. A third boasted that she had "taken out over forty-six credit cards in five years and earned 2.6 million miles just in sign-up bonuses."

The harm, of course, is that the banks end up paying billions of dollars in flights and other rewards for customers who are not paying fees or interest on their cards, and that these costs are passed on to consumers as higher ticket prices. Some credit cards have tried to clamp down on these hacks. In 2016, Chase instituted a rule that a consumer won't be approved for most Chase credit cards if that person has opened five or more credit card accounts across all banks in the past twenty-four months. American Express now revokes miles of people who have "engaged in abuse, misuse or gaming in connection with earning or using points," giving it a broad ability to penalize customers it believes have abused the system.

Which brings us back to the Pudding Guy. Infamous among airline-program hackers, Phillips found a vulnerability not in any particular airline's program but in a 1999 Healthy Choice tie-in. By then, most airlines had affiliate programs, where companies could buy frequent-flier miles in bulk and offer them to their customers as a reward. In this particular program, customers could earn miles on the airline of their choice for buying Healthy Choice products. Phillips searched for the cheapest qualifying product he could find, and ended up buying 12,150 single pudding cups at

25 cents each, giving him 1.2 million miles for $3,150—and lifetime Gold frequent-flier status on American Airlines. (Then he donated the pudding to charity for an additional $815 tax write-off.) Definitely not the outcome Healthy Choice was expecting, but since Phillips didn't break any rules, the company paid up.

9

Sports Hacks

Sports are hacked all the time. I think it's a combination of the intense pressure—and, at the professional level, money—and the necessarily incomplete rulebooks.

Some random stories:

American baseball, 1951. The St. Louis Browns snuck a 3-foot 7-inch tall player named Ed Gaedel onto their roster. He made one appearance at bat. It was a walk, of course, because his strike zone was so small it was impossible to throw accurately. The league had no official height requirement, so the hack was technically legal. Even so, the league president voided the player's contract the next day.

Basketball, 1976. It was double overtime in the NBA finals. The Phoenix Suns were down by one point, and there was less than a second on the clock. The Suns had the ball at the far end of the court, with no time to get it to the basket and shoot. At that moment Suns player Paul Westphal hacked the rules. He called a time-out, even though his team had none remaining. The refs called a foul, which meant that the Boston Celtics got a free throw. But the extra Boston point made no difference. What was important was that the Suns would get the ball midcourt after the free throw, which gave them a chance to score a two-point basket and force a third overtime. Which they did. The next year, the NBA changed the rules, preventing a team from advancing the ball to midcourt by causing a technical foul.

Swimming, 1988. Both America's David Berkoff and Japan's Daichi Suzuki hacked the backstroke, swimming most of the length of the pool underwater and clocking amazingly fast times. This technique was soon adopted by other top-flight swimmers, until the International Swimming Federation stepped in and limited the distance a backstroke swimmer could remain submerged.

American football, 2015. The New England Patriots used a novel hack against the Baltimore Ravens, shifting players around at the scrimmage line to manipulate the complicated rules governing which players were eligible receivers. Two months later, the league amended its rules to make the hack illegal.

It doesn't always go this way. Many hacks aren't declared illegal; they're incorporated into the game because they improve it. Many aspects of sports that are normal today were once hacks. In football, the forward pass was once a hack. So was the run-and-shoot offense, and the fast snap while the other team is changing players. In baseball, the sacrifice fly and the intentional walk were once hacks. None of those were against the rules. It's just that the players and teams didn't think of them. Once someone did, they became part of the game.

The process isn't always smooth. In basketball, dunking was once a hack. No one imagined that someone could jump high enough to push the ball into the basket. In the early decades of basketball, the move was both hailed and decried. Various leagues tried to ban dunking, but it's been a mainstay of the sport since the mid-1970s because the fans liked it.

In cricket, unlike baseball, you can score by hitting the ball in a 360-degree circle from the batter. For over a century, the conventional way to score has been to hit the ball back roughly towards the bowler, like in baseball, or to glance the ball off the edge of the bat at an angle behind the batter. In the early 2000s, a few cricketers realized they could perilously "scoop" or "ramp" the ball over their own head. This shot was entirely within the rules, requiring only extra courage and the hacker mentality (one claimed to have developed it playing on narrow Sri Lankan streets).

Some famous victories were won using this technique in exhilarating fashion, and it is now a standard shot in the game.

Sign stealing is allowed in baseball, with numerous restrictions and caveats in response to continued hacks of this system. The second baseman and the third-base coach are allowed to try to read the catcher's signs. The batter is not. Cameras in the outfield are prohibited. When the Houston Astros stole signs with a camera in 2017 and 2018, they were cheating rather than hacking, since that rule was already in place.

Most sports hacks are obvious after they're used. There's no hiding swimming underwater, or scooping the cricket ball over your head. As soon as the first player or team does it, everyone knows about it. Exceptions involve sports where things can be hidden. Two areas where this occurs are varieties of mechanical racing (automobile, yacht, and so on) and doping (of both humans and animals).

Formula One racing is full of hacks. First, members of one team find a loophole in the existing regulations to enhance their car's efficiency. Then, the other teams eventually learn about it and either copy the idea or protest the innovation. Finally, the Fédération Internationale de l'Automobile (FIA) steps in and either bans the hack or incorporates it into the next season's engineering specifications.

For example, in 1975, the Tyrell team built a six-wheeled car: two in the back and four in the front. The hack increased performance but decreased reliability. Other teams built prototypes in response, but in 1983 the FIA ruled that all cars could have no more—and no fewer, just to be on the safe side—than four wheels. In 1978, the Brabham team skirted the rule that no car could have movable aerodynamic features like fans by putting one near the radiator and calling it a cooling device. That car was voluntarily withdrawn from competition, and no rules were changed as a result. In 1997, the McLaren team developed a car with two brake pedals, the second controlling the rear wheels only. I don't know enough about automobile racing to understand the details, but it gave the driver an advantage. This was initially allowed, but then banned after other teams complained.

In 2010, McLaren hacked the ban on movable aerodynamic features by adding a hole in the cockpit that the driver could cover or uncover with his leg. The argument was made that there were no moving parts involved with the hole, so it was allowed by the rules. But the driver moving his leg had the same effect, and the technique was promptly banned. In 2014, Mercedes redesigned its Formula One engine's turbocharger, splitting the turbine and compressor and locating them on either side of the engine. The design tweak was never declared illegal, and its use is the reason why the Mercedes team dominated the sport for the next six years. In 2020, Mercedes added a feature to the steering wheel: pushing or pulling on the column changed the alignment of the front wheels. It's against the rules to add any functionality to the steering wheel; the legality of that particular hack depends on the precise definition of a steering system, and whether the feature is viewed as a steering aid or a suspension device. The FIA closed this loophole in 2021.

One final example, which we will return to elsewhere in the book. Hockey sticks used to be flat. Then someone discovered that with a curved stick, players could hit slap shots at speeds not possible before. Now curved sticks are the norm, and there are precise limits on stick curvature. During a 1993 championship game, Los Angeles Kings player Marty McSorley was famously caught with an illegally curved stick.

10

Hacks Are Parasitical

A SARS-CoV-2 virion is about 80 nanometers wide. It attaches itself to a protein called ACE2, which occurs on the surface of many of our body's cells: in the heart, gut, lungs, and nasal passages. Normally, ACE2 plays a role in regulating blood pressure, inflammation, and wound healing. But the virus has a tip that can grab it, thereby fusing together the membranes around the cell and the virus, and allowing the virus's RNA to enter the cell. The virus then subverts the host cell's protein-making machinery, hijacking the process to make new copies of itself, which go on to infect other cells. Other parts of the virus's RNA create different proteins that stay in the host cell. One prevents the host cell from sending out signals to the immune system that it's under attack. Another encourages the host cell to release the newly created virions. And a third helps the virus resist the host cell's innate immunity. The result is the disease that has dominated our lives since 2020: COVID-19.

COVID-19 is a hacker. Like all viruses, SARS-CoV-2 is a clever exploitation of our body's immune system, subverting the normal operation of that system at the expense of our general health and the lives of over 6 million people worldwide. HIV is another hacker. It infects T-helper white blood cells in our body, inserting its own DNA into the cell's normal DNA, and then replicating inside the cell. Eventually the infected

cell releases more HIV into the bloodstream, continuing the multiplica-
tion process.

In general, hacking is parasitical. Both HIV and SARS-CoV-2 are
parasites: hosted by another species and benefiting from that arrange-
ment, usually at the host's expense. A system exists to further a set of
goals, usually put forth by the system's designers. A hacker hijacks the
same system for a different set of goals, one that may be contrary to the
original ones.

This is obvious in the hacks of ATMs, casino games, consumer reward
plans, and long-distance calling plans. The goal of whoever managed the
ATM is to dispense cash to account holders and deduct the appropriate money from their accounts. The goal of the hacker is to receive cash
without having money deducted from their account (or without even having to have an account at all). Similarly, the goal of a casino is to be fair
(which means equal opportunity between players, not equal opportunity
between players and the house). The goal of the hacker is to tilt that
advantage in their favor.

It's less obvious in sports and online games. The goals of a sports
league might be to make money, entertain and satisfy fans, highlight
human competition, be fair in some sense of that term, and provide a
"good game"—whatever that means. The goal of the athlete is to win the
games they play in, either individually or as a team, at the expense of
fairness—and possibly to make money.

The goals of Club Penguin were to provide a safe and entertaining
experience for its users, follow all applicable laws, and enhance the Disney
Corporation's bottom line. The goal of the Club Penguin hacker was to
communicate more freely with other players—and this was true whether
the hacker was a six-year-old wanting to have a conversation or a child
predator trolling for victims. Both of those hackers were parasites, albeit
drastically different kinds.

Spam is an email hack. No one thought of it, let alone tried to prohibit it, when setting up the Internet protocols and the email system (even
though junk snail mail is a long-standing American tradition). Sending
unsolicited emails, and especially commercial unsolicited emails, just
hadn't been done. The idea of spam started in the 1990s, both in email

and in the then-popular Usenet messaging service, and became a serious problem in the early 2000s. In those years, an estimated 90% of all email was spam. It's a parasitical hack of a communication system.

Not all parasitical relationships come at the expense of the host, and not all hackers are evil. Usually they're behaving rationally, in their own self-interest. They might be acting in their financial self-interest, like most of the examples in this book. But they could also be acting in their emotional, moral, ethical, or political interests; they might be trying to better the world through their hacking. Sometimes they're just looking for opportunities. Sometimes, if the systems are stacked against them, they're acting out of necessity—just trying to survive. Think of someone trying to get healthcare or food for himself or his family.

Like any parasite, hacking can't be too effective at subverting a system; it needs the system to exist in order to work. So while ATM hacking can be a profitable criminal enterprise, it depends on there being ATMs to hack. If ATM hacking were too successful, banks would stop installing these oh-so-convenient cash machines. If too many people had hacked Club Penguin to have conversations that ran afoul of local child safety laws, Disney would have shut the system down earlier than it did. Spam would have destroyed email if it weren't for anti-spam programs. A hack that is too effective can end up making itself obsolete, by destroying the underlying system it depends on.

11

Defending against Hacks

Spectre and Meltdown are two hardware vulnerabilities in Intel and other microprocessors; they were discovered in 2017 and announced in 2018. Basically, some of the performance optimizations adopted over the years turned out to have security vulnerabilities. Defending against the vulnerabilities was hard because they were in hardware rather than software. While software patches had been developed to fix some of the vulnerabilities, often with considerable performance penalties, there were none for others. Replacing vulnerable systems wasn't a viable option: the computer chips in question are found in something like 100 million computers. And while future microprocessors can be designed without these vulnerabilities, existing microprocessors can't be retroactively fixed. Probably the best defense was the difficulty of exploiting the vulnerabilities. Many computers were vulnerable, but in ways that weren't obviously useful to hackers.

Defending against hacks can be hard. Countermeasures range from patching to secure systems design, and we'll talk about each of them in turn.

I'll be first to admit that my taxonomy is sloppy. Passing a law that makes card counting in blackjack illegal renders the tactic ineffective, but only if you get caught. Does that remove the vulnerability, or does it reduce the hack's effectiveness? Similarly, an anti-theft dye tag attached to an expensive dress makes the stolen garment less useful (reducing the attack's effectiveness) while also making the theft less likely (disincentivizing the thief). I'm okay with these ambiguities. In general, I am less concerned with precise categories of defenses, and more with establishing a working knowledge of the different defenses that we can employ against hacks and hackers.

The first and most obvious defense is to *remove the enabling vulnerability.*

In the computer world, the primary defense against hacking is patching. It's a straightforward technique: update the computer code to eliminate the vulnerability. No vulnerability, no exploit. No exploit, no hacking.

How well patching actually works depends a lot on the type of system we're talking about. Systems that are owned or controlled by a singular entity can, if they want to—that is, if it makes economic sense for them to—be quickly patched in the face of hacks.

Issuing the patch is just the first step of the process; next, the patch needs to be installed on the vulnerable systems. Historically, there has been a large disconnect between companies issuing patches and users installing them. Software vendors would issue patches, and users would install them or not, and if they did install them they would take weeks or months to get around to it. These unpatched systems would still be vulnerable, of course.

This scenario assumes that the singular owning entity has the ability to write the patch and cares enough to do so, and that the system can be patched. If that company has enough engineers on staff to write patches, and if there is an update system to quickly push the new software out to every user, then patching can be a very effective security technique. If one of those two things doesn't exist, then it isn't. (Remember that there are many IoT devices whose code is in firmware and can't be patched.) That's why your computer and phone are constantly patched, and generally stay secure despite all the hacking out there. That's also why your home router is rarely patched, despite its vulnerabilities.

Lots of high-profile hacks have occurred because of unpatched systems. China hacked Equifax in 2017 through a vulnerability in the Apache

Struts web-application software. Apache patched the vulnerability in March; Equifax failed to promptly update its software and was successfully attacked in May.

Also in 2017, the WannaCry worm spread to over 200,000 computers worldwide and caused as much as $4 billion in damage, all to networks that hadn't yet installed the patch for a Microsoft Windows vulnerability.

This illustrates a major downside of patching: it occurs after the fact. The vulnerability is already in the system. Hackers may be actively exploiting it at the time of the patch. And even if they aren't, the very act of patching calls attention to the vulnerability and exposes all of the systems that have not yet been patched.

For most individual users of computers and mobile devices, patching usually happens automatically. Your Microsoft computer is likely configured to automatically update itself once a month on Patch Tuesday, which can include patches for over 100 different vulnerabilities every month. Your iPhone nags you with increasingly dire warnings if you don't install your patches. (If you have not yet internalized this lesson, let me say it explicitly: Turn automatic updates on for both your computer and phone. Patch everything else as soon as you get an update. Always.)

Large organizational networks have to deal with patching in a slower, cautious manner. Because a bad patch can cause all sorts of problems by the way it interacts with other critical software, patches are generally installed deliberately and methodically. This often means that they're installed late, or not at all. We can blame Equifax for not patching Apache Struts, but that software had a reputation for buggy patches that were incompatible with other software built around Struts. Lots of organizations take great care when applying those patches.

Patching works differently with social systems than with technological systems. With the latter, the patch makes the latest hack no longer possible. This is obviously true for software, but extends to other technological systems as well. ATM manufacturers can patch their machines so that a particular jackpotting hack simply doesn't work anymore. A casino can deal blackjack from a six-deck shoe that continuously shuffles the cards. Financial exchanges can restrict trading to ten-second intervals, making hacks like high-frequency trading impossible. We can do this because the technology effectively determines the affordances of the system.

With social, economic, or political systems that don't directly involve computers, it's not as clean. When we talk about "patching" the tax code or the rules of a game, what we mean is changing the laws or rules of the system so that a particular attack is no longer permitted. So while it still might be possible to use a computer to predict roulette or to curve your hockey stick more than three-quarters of an inch, anyone caught doing it will experience the consequences. The only "installation" necessary is education: making sure that every casino pit boss and hockey referee knows the new rules and how to spot cheaters—and then punish them accordingly. Similarly, a legal tax avoidance strategy becomes illegal tax evasion, and is prosecuted if discovered (or so one would hope).

This points to another problem: cheaters can be tough to spot. Recall that roulette was vulnerable until the betting system was changed so that the hacks were no longer effective. This problem will come up repeatedly in the systems we talk about in this book. If you update computer code, the hack is no longer possible. If you update the tax code, the hack is still possible—it's just no longer a legal loophole (and by my definition, no longer a hack). That means you have to update the detection system as well, so that the now-illegal cheaters get caught and prosecuted.

Patching is also less effective when the governing body functions slowly, or when the governing body doesn't have a unified vision of whether a patch is even necessary. That is, when the system doesn't have a clear goal. What, for example, does it mean to "patch" the tax code? In most cases, it means passing another law that closes the vulnerabilities from the original law. That's a process that can take years, because the tax code is created in the political realm, which is characterized by competing visions of what public policy should accomplish. Also, the very people who take advantage of the vulnerability will attempt to hack the legislative systems to ensure that the law continues to permit their actions. Imagine if blackjack card counters were in charge of casino rules. Blackjack card counting would be celebrated as a clever, honest way to win the game in the same way tax avoidance is celebrated as smart.

In the absence of legislative patches, a court can quickly target a very specific patch. In the computer world, this is known as a hotfix: a fast software update designed to fix a particular bug or vulnerability. The term comes from the fact that, traditionally, these updates were applied to systems that were up and running: hence "hot." It's more risky; the software could crash, with whatever problems could result from that. Hotfixes are normal today—updates to your operating systems are applied while they are running, and a lot of stuff is running in the cloud—but when the term was coined, that wasn't the case.

12

More Subtle Hacking Defenses

Reducing a hack's effectiveness is a second defense.

Business email compromise is a social engineering attack, in that it exploits a vulnerability in people rather than a vulnerability in technology. In this scam, the victim receives an email from a normally trusted source, making a normally legitimate request but asking him or her to do it differently than usual, often against established protocol. So, a bookkeeper might receive an email from a vendor who asks to be paid into a new bank account. Or a home buyer might receive an email from his title company, with instructions on how to wire a down payment. Or the financial head of a company might receive an email from the CEO, asking for an emergency multimillion-dollar wire transfer to a specific account. The receiving accounts are owned by the scammer, and the victim often never sees his money again. These types of scams cost billions.

Sometimes email accounts of legitimate vendors are hacked in this scam, which increases the likelihood that the target will trust the sender. More often, the scam emails are slight variations of legitimate addresses: person@c0mpanyname.com instead of person@companyname.com, for example. (If you can't tell or are listening to this as an audiobook, the "o" in "companyname" is actually a zero.) The vulnerability here is human inattentiveness, or misplaced trust.

There are many reasons why a vulnerability can't be patched. In the policy world, the legislative process that needs to patch the vulnerability may not be functional. Or there may be no governing body that can mandate the patch. In the case of the social engineering hack I just described, the hacks subvert how the human brain works—and that isn't patchable at anything shorter than evolutionary time.

When we can't patch a vulnerability, we have three options. The first is to redesign the system so that the hack is too difficult, too expensive, less profitable, or generally less damaging. This also works when outlawing a hack isn't enough, and we want to make it harder as well.

The second is foreknowledge. If I can teach you about business email compromise and how it works, you will become better able to recognize when you are being targeted by it, and—hopefully—less likely to fall for it. This is how we defend against email and phone scams that slip through automated filters. This is how potential victims can resist effective "cognitive hacks" that play on universal human biases like fear and deference to authority.

The final option is to employ an additional system to somehow secure the vulnerable system. For business email compromise, a company might institute a requirement that any large wire transfers have two people approve them. This means that even if the hack is successful and the employee is fooled, the hacker can't profit from the successful deception.

This option is often discussed as a solution to the problem of insecure IoT devices. The worry is that in a few years, we will have all sorts of vulnerable IoT devices in our homes and on our networks, with no way to secure them. One solution is to have systems on networks that detect the presence of these devices and limit their behavior in ways that reduce the hacking threat. So you could imagine your home router being smart enough to recognize IoT devices and block them when they try to do things they're not supposed to do—like when your refrigerator starts sending spam emails, mining cryptocurrency, or participating in a denial-of-service attack.

A third defense is *detecting and recovering from a hack* after the fact.

In 2020, the Russian SVR—that's its foreign intelligence service—hacked the update servers belonging to a network management software developer named SolarWinds. SolarWinds boasted over 300,000 customers worldwide, including most of the Fortune 500 and much of the US government. The SVR installed a backdoor into an update to one of the company's products, Orion, and then waited.

Stop for a second. Just a few pages ago I explained that the computer industry's primary defense against hacking is patching. The SVR hacked the company's patching process, and then slipped a backdoor into one of the product's updates. Over 17,000 Orion customers downloaded and installed the hacked update, giving the SVR access to their systems. The SVR subverted the very process we expect everyone to trust to improve their security. This is akin to hiding combat troops in Red Cross vehicles during wartime, although not as universally condemned (and prohibited by international law).

The hack was not discovered by the NSA or any part of the US government. Instead, the security company FireEye found it during a detailed audit of its own systems.

Once the SolarWinds hack was discovered, it became immediately clear how disastrous (or successful, depending on your point of view) this operation was. The Russians breached the US State Department, Treasury Department, the Department of Homeland Security, Los Alamos and Sandia National Laboratories, and the National Institutes of Health. They breached Microsoft, Intel, and Cisco. They breached networks in Canada, Mexico, Belgium, Spain, the UK, Israel, and the UAE.

After getting into all of these systems, SVR agents were able to establish new means of access unrelated to the SolarWinds vulnerability. So even after target companies patched their software and fixed the problems in their update process that allowed the Russians to introduce the vulnerability in the first place, all of those penetrated networks were still vulnerable in probably multiple unknown ways. The only way to really regain security would have been to throw away all the hardware and software and start again from scratch. No organization did that, and my guess is that those networks can still be manipulated from Moscow.

There are a bunch of lessons here. First, detection can be hard. Sometimes you can detect hacks while they're happening, but mostly you detect them after the fact during things like audits. Second, the hack can be so devastating that no response will suffice. And finally, it can be impossible to recover from a particular hack, in which case recovery primarily involves securing the system from the next hack.

Now for a final defense: finding vulnerabilities before they're used.

Red-teaming means hacking your own systems. There are companies that specialize in this sort of analysis; or a development team can do it themselves as part of the quality control process. The red team approaches the system as if they were external hackers. They find a bunch of vulnerabilities—in the computer world, they always do—and then patch them before the software is released.

This concept comes from the military. Traditionally, the red team was the pretend enemy in military exercises. The cybersecurity community has generalized the term to mean a group of people trained to think like the enemy and find vulnerabilities in systems. This broader definition has been incorporated into military planning, and is now part of the military's strategic thinking and systems design. The US Department of Defense—particularly the national security sector—has long integrated red-teaming into its planning process. The Defense Science Board wrote:

> We argue that red teaming is especially important now for the DoD. . . . Aggressive red teams are needed to challenge emerging operational concepts in order to discover weaknesses before real adversaries do.

Unless you red-team, you have to rely on your enemies to find vulnerabilities in your systems. And if others are finding the vulnerabilities for you, how do you ensure that those vulnerabilities get fixed and not exploited? In the computer world, the primary means of ensuring that hackers will refrain from using the fruits of their efforts is by making computer hacking a crime. If you're a hacker and you discover a new vulnerability, you can use it, but you're risking jail time. But you can also sell it to other criminals, either on the black market or the grey market.

The counterincentive is bug bounties, which are rewards paid by software companies to people who discover vulnerabilities in their products. The idea is that those researchers will then inform the company, which can then patch the vulnerability. Bug bounties can work well, although a hacker can often make a lot more money selling vulnerabilities in widely used computer systems to either criminals or cyberweapons manufacturers.

In either case, finding new vulnerabilities is easier the more you know about a system, especially if you have access to the human-readable source code and not just to the computer-readable object code. Similarly, it's easier to find vulnerabilities in a rule book if you have a copy of the rule book to read, and not just information about rulings.

13

Removing Potential Hacks
in the Design Phase

AutoRun was a feature introduced in Windows 95. Before AutoRun, you would buy software on a CD-ROM, then manually run an installation script to install it on your computer. With AutoRun, you could just pop the disk into your computer, and the system would automatically search for and run the install script. This made software installation much easier for the average, technically naive user.

Unfortunately, the feature was also used by virus writers to install malware onto systems. The virus would reside on an innocuous CD-ROM or—in later years—a USB thumb drive, and would automatically execute as soon as an unsuspecting user inserted it into his computer. This is where that old security warning against plugging random USB sticks into your computer came from.

Notice that the vulnerability isn't due to a mistake. It was an attempt to balance security with usability, and was a design trade-off that might have been smart in 1995 but was not so smart a decade later. Responding to mushrooming reports of bad system behavior enabled by AutoRun, Microsoft finally redesigned the system in 2011 for Windows Vista, disabling AutoRun for thumb drives, network drives, and other media—and only enabled it for increasingly obsolete media like DVDs.

The point here is that the design process can't perfectly defend against hacks, because (1) security is only one of the properties that a system design has to optimize for, and (2) the techniques hackers use and their targets and motivations are constantly evolving as society and technology change. Designers need to revisit their basic assumptions about how they organize and run systems. Good design today is bad design tomorrow, and hackers will always find ways to exploit bad design.

Better than finding vulnerabilities in a system before they're hacked, we can deliberately try to create systems with fewer vulnerabilities; that is, *make sure vulnerabilities don't exist in the first place*. In computer security, this is called secure systems design, or security by design.

This is much easier said than done. Computer code is complex, and it's impossible to find all of the vulnerabilities that lurk within it. Mere mortals can't produce bug-free, or even vulnerability-free, software. We don't have a theory of secure software design, let alone a secure design methodology. But the main reason we don't do a lot better is that writing secure and reliable code is slow, hard, and expensive, and there mostly isn't the economic incentive to do it. With notable exceptions like airplane avionics and the Space Shuttle, most software is written quickly and shoddily. Still, we have design principles that minimize both the number of vulnerabilities and their exploitability.

Simplicity: The more complex a system, the more vulnerable it is. The reasons for this are myriad, but basically, a complex system has more things that can go wrong. There are more potential vulnerabilities in a large office building than in a single-family house, for example. The antidote for this is simplicity. Of course, many systems are naturally complex, but the simpler a system can be designed, the more secure it is likely to be.

Defense in Depth: The basic idea is that one vulnerability shouldn't destroy the whole system. In computer systems, the place you encounter this the most is multifactor authentication. Instead of just a username and a password—a single point of failure—better systems also employ multiple methods of authentication. My email, for example, is additionally secured by Google Authenticator. This is an app tied to something I own and carry with me wherever I go: my smartphone. I have to unlock the phone, open the app, and type an additional time-varying code to access my account. Other multifactor systems might include a biometric such as a fingerprint, or a small USB device you have to plug into your computer.

For noncomputer systems, defense in depth is anything that prevents a single vulnerability from becoming a successful hack. It might be a deadbolt on your door in addition to the lock on the door handle, or two barbed-wire fences surrounding a military base, or a requirement that financial transactions over a certain amount must be approved by two people. A hack that overcomes one of those defenses is not likely to overcome the other as well.

Compartmentalization (isolation/separation of duties): Smart terrorist organizations divide themselves up into individual cells. Each cell has limited knowledge of the others, so if one cell is compromised the others remain secure. This is compartmentalization, which limits the effects of any particular attack. It's the same idea behind different offices having their own key, or different accounts having their own password. You'll sometimes hear this called "the principle of least privilege": giving people only the access and privileges necessary to complete their job. It's why you don't have a master key to all the offices in your building: you don't need it.

In computer networks, this is called "segmentation," and involves separating parts of the network from each other, so a hack against one part doesn't result in a hack against the entire network—just like the protective measures taken by terrorist cells. Segmentation is the first thing an attacker tries to violate once they penetrate a network. For example, good segmentation would have prevented the Russian SVR from using its initial access in the SolarWinds hack to access different parts of the network and install additional malware and backdoors.

This concept easily extends to social systems. It's reflected in the idea that government regulators should not have any financial interest in the industries they oversee (a principle regularly violated in the US via the revolving door between the government and industry). Or that election districts shouldn't be created by elected officials who could benefit from gerrymandering them.

Fail-Safe/Fail Secure: All systems fail, whether due to accident, error, or attack. What we want is for them to fail as safely and securely as possible. Sometimes this is as simple as a dead man's switch on a train: if the driver becomes incapacitated, the train stops accelerating and eventually coasts to a stop. Sometimes this is complex: nuclear missile launch facilities have all sorts of fail-safe mechanisms to ensure that warheads are never accidentally launched.

Social systems can have fail-safes as well. Many of our laws have something to that effect. Murder is illegal, regardless of the means used; it doesn't matter if you figure out some clever way to hack a system to accomplish it. The US Alternative Minimum Tax (AMT) was supposed to serve as a fail-safe as well: a minimum tax that a citizen is required to pay, no matter what sort or how many loopholes they've discovered. (That the AMT didn't work as intended is a demonstration about how hard this can be.)

Of course, all of these countermeasures also reduce a hack's effectiveness.

Nothing in these chapters is new. I covered much of this terrain in my 2000 book, *Secrets and Lies*. Others have written about it before me, and since. But understanding the tenets of secure design is critical to limiting the effectiveness of hacking. The more you can incorporate fundamental security principles into your system design, the more secure you will be from hacking.

Whether companies use those techniques or not depends on the economics of their industry. You'd imagine that a company like Apple or Microsoft would spend a lot more money on the security of its software than would a developer that makes a game for your phone. Similarly, you'd expect a company that makes software for airplanes, cars, and medical devices to spend significantly more money and effort on security than does a company that makes software for programmable toys. And while there are exceptions, that intuition is largely correct.

14

The Economics of Defense

In 1971, someone who bought a ticket under the name "Dan Cooper" hacked the Boeing 727, using the aft staircase in a clever and unintended way: to parachute out of a flying airplane with $200,000 in cash after a successful hijacking—never to be seen again. Many copycats followed, and Boeing eventually redesigned the 727 to remove those under-tail stairs and thereby eliminate the possibility of jumping out of a commercial aircraft in flight. This was an effective, but expensive, patching of the vulnerability. But why did the vulnerability exist in the first place? Boeing might not have anticipated the threat, or it may have thought the threat was too remote to defend against.

Threat modeling is a systems design term for enumerating all the threats to a system. If the system were your home, you might start by listing everything of value in the house: expensive electronics, family heirlooms, an original Picasso, the people who live there. Then you would list all the ways someone could break in: an unlocked door, an open window, a closed window. You would consider all the types of people who might want to break in: a professional burglar, a neighborhood kid, a stalker, a serial killer. You would consider threats from people who don't have to break in: intimate partner violence is an example. And finally you would use all of that information to build a model detailing which threats are worth worrying about and which can be ignored, how much effort to spend mitigating particular threats, and so on. Your home security will be specific to the threat of art theft if you own an original Picasso. It will be different if you are the president of a country. It will be different if you live in a war zone.

Economic considerations like these are essential to understanding how to think about hacking defenses. Determine the cost of a hack. Determine the cost and effectiveness of a particular defense. And perform cost-benefit analysis to decide whether the defense is worth it. In some cases it isn't. For instance, many ATM security measures can reduce hacking and fraud, but are not implemented because they annoy legitimate customers. They could require fingerprint scans or employ facial recognition, which many customers would find invasive. If the measures sufficiently reduce the rate at which people use ATMs, they would be less profitable even though they would be more secure.

Another concept from economics that is essential to understanding hacking and defenses against it is that of an "externality." In economics, an externality is an effect of an action not borne by the person deciding to perform it. Think of a factory owner deciding to pollute a river. People downstream might get sick, but she doesn't live there so she doesn't care.

Of course, this isn't precisely true. The owner's employees might live downstream. Her customers might live downstream. Environmental activists might expose her pollution, the press might write critical articles about it, and public opinion might turn against her. Still, in our systems way of thinking, river pollution is an externality of the factory.

Hacking causes externalities. It has a cost, but that cost is borne by the rest of society. It's a lot like shoplifting: everyone has to pay higher prices to compensate for losses or to pay for antitheft measures at stores.

We know how to solve problems caused by externalities: we need to convert them into problems that affect the person who owns the system and is making the decision. To do this, we impose rules from outside the system to bring those costs inside the system.

In an ideal world this works well. In reality, it depends on enforcement and penalties. It depends on lawyers and on the outcome of litigation. It depends on the actions of regulatory agencies, which are shaped by the people in charge, by lobbyists seeking to water down regulations, and by campaign donors and their agendas. It depends on the results of research funded by industry and academia, which may or may not skew the policy debate. It depends on citizens knowing that the costs exist, knowing who to blame for the cost, and knowing how to make them pay for it.

Technical systems become insecure when the threat model changes. Basically, a system is designed according to the realities of the time. Then, something changes at some point during its use. Whatever the reason, the old security assumptions are no longer true and the system drifts into insecurity. Vulnerabilities that were once unimportant or irrelevant become critical. Vulnerabilities that used to be critical become unimportant. Hacks become easier or harder, more or less profitable, more or less common.

Maybe the most obvious example of this is the Internet itself. As ridiculous as it sounds today, the Internet was never designed with security in mind. But back in the late 1970s and early 1980s, it wasn't used for anything important—ever—and you had to be a member of a research institution in order to get access to it. And the multiuser mainframe computers that were connected to the Internet had their own security. For those reasons, the original designers of the Internet deliberately ignored security in favor of simpler protocol design, and left security considerations to the endpoints.

We all know how this story ends. Things changed. More specifically, single-user personal computers with no security started being connected to the Internet, and the network designers assumed that these computers had the same level of multiuser security that the old mainframes did. Then, everything about use of the Internet changed. Its speed changed. Its scale changed. Its scope changed. Its centrality changed. Hacks that weren't even worth thinking about back then suddenly became critical. The threat model changed. And that meant any cost-benefit analysis changed.

In computer security, we know all about dynamic environments. Every few years, it seems, things change—and security has to change with it. Email spam is a problem in a way that paper junk mail is not because the economics of each is different: it's much cheaper to send someone email than paper.

Maintaining security in this dynamic environment requires staying ahead of hackers. That's why we engage in research on computer security: conferences, journals, graduate programs, hacking competitions. We exchange information on what hackers are doing, and the best ways to defend ourselves. We try to understand where new vulnerabilities will appear before they do, and how hackers will respond.

If laws are to keep up with hackers, they need to be general rules that give regulators the flexibility to prohibit new hacks and punish new hackers. The Computer Fraud and Abuse Act was passed in 1986, an outcome of concern that existing laws were insufficiently broad enough to cover all computer-related crimes. For example, it makes it a crime, among other things, to access another's computer system without authorization or to exceed one's existing authorized access. That broad language covers a large swath of computer-related hacks, so broad that the US Supreme Court scaled it back in 2021. But the point of the law is to allow the prosecution to say: "Yes, the system allowed it. But give me a break. It might have been permitted by the system, but it was obviously not intended and you knew it was wrong. And therefore it's illegal."

Many of our social systems have both the ability to patch systems and these more general rules, at least to some degree. It's an open question: How do we perform life-cycle management of noncomputer systems? How often should we review something like our democratic institutions and check that they're still fit for purpose? And what do we do if they're not? Every few years we buy a new laptop and smartphone, and those newer devices are more secure. How can we do the same for social institutions?

15

Resilience

Systems of norms are different from systems of rules. It is in the nature of a norm that you aren't supposed to hack it; hacking a norm is just another term for violating a norm. On the other hand, because norms are informal and not codified, there's more room for interpretation. This translates into a greater potential for a motivated person to push against the boundaries of the norms or optimize their actions for a certain outcome. And because those systems require humans to respond in order to defend against attacks, it is easier for the norms to evolve to allow the hacks.

Recent politics serves as an example of this, in the way Donald Trump was able to successfully push against social and political norms. I have largely avoided using him as an example in this book, because he's so politically charged. But the example he provides here is too illustrative to ignore. Society has a mechanisms to repair soft violations of its norms—public shaming, political pushback, journalism, and transparency—and they largely work. Trump overwhelmed those mechanisms. Too many scandals emerged too quickly. The mechanisms that might have reinforced the norms of behavior for public servants were ineffective in the face of a candidate like Trump. Norms only work if there are consequences for violations, and society couldn't keep pace with the onslaught.

Trump was thereby able to push the boundaries in many directions all at once. And in many cases, it destroyed the underlying norms.

On the other hand, challenges to systems of norms can also make them resilient. Norms are implicit and flexible, and the easiest system to change. A system of norms doesn't require money, legal knowledge, or technology to challenge and change, though all those things help; our social behaviors and implicit expectations can be contested by anyone who's willing to speak up about them—and has the platform to do so. And that challenge provides more input to help those norms bend and improve instead of breaking.

Resilience is an important concept, one that applies to everything from the human body to the planetary ecosystem, from organizational systems to computer systems. It's the ability of a system to recover from perturbations, including hacks.

Resilience is why suspension bridges are built from stranded cables and not solid rods: solid rods fail suddenly and catastrophically, while stranded cables fail slowly and noisily. It's why our brains and bodies have so many different ways to adapt to whatever circumstances we find ourselves in, and why good taxi drivers know four different ways to drive between popular landmarks. It's why Orange County, California, has a functioning county government, even after it was forced to declare bankruptcy in 1994.

In security, resilience is an emergent property of a system, one that can combine such aspects of properties as impenetrability, homeostasis, redundancy, agility, mitigation, and recovery. Resilient systems are more secure than fragile ones. Many of the security measures we discussed in the previous few chapters are all about increasing a system's resilience from hacking.

There's one more point that's worth mentioning here. We've been talking about hacking defenses largely in the abstract; however, any discussion of defense needs to address the question, who is defending against whom? Who gets to decide whether the hack is beneficial or not? And—most importantly—who is in charge of defense, and how much defense is worth the effort and expense?

The examples I've provided have been pretty straightforward so far. There is some person or organization in charge of the system, and they're in charge of defense. For example, Microsoft's management gets to decide whether a particular Windows hack is a problem, and how to mitigate it. Mostly, they patch. If they can't easily patch, they live with the vulnerability for a while. (AutoRun is an example of that.) We have examples of hacks being quickly patched. We have examples of hacks never being patched. And we have examples of hacks being allowed to persist because defending against them is too expensive. If losses due to the fraud are less than the cost to patch the system, the credit card companies will allow the fraud to persist. Stores often allow shoplifters to walk out with stolen goods because retail staff who try to stop them may be physically harmed, and because falsely accusing people of shoplifting could lead to expensive lawsuits.

As we try to build social and political systems that can defend themselves against hacks, we should think about the balance between having lawmakers write laws and having regulators implement them. On the one hand, regulators are not directly accountable to the people in the same way that legislators are. On the other hand, we don't want legislators to have to consider all the implementation details before passing needed laws. The more legislatures can delegate the implementation of laws to regulators, the more agile the resultant system will be against hacking— and the more resilient.

Defending society's systems against hacking isn't just an issue for the designers of a particular system. It's an issue for society itself, and for those who care about social change and progress more generally.

PART 3

HACKING FINANCIAL SYSTEMS

16

Hacking Heaven

One of the central tenets of medieval Catholicism was penance and redemption. The idea was that if you sinned, you could atone and receive forgiveness. Big sins required not only contrition but also big acts of penance that were out of the reach of many. If the only road to atonement for a lifetime of sin involved a pilgrimage to Jerusalem, most people just wouldn't be able to achieve absolution. The next logical step was to donate money so that others could do the work on your behalf. It was a reasonable compromise, and a means for the Church to encourage charitable giving. So if the city church needed a new roof, a wealthy sinner could be directed to pay for roof repairs as penance. In exchange, the sinner received forgiveness in the form of an "indulgence," basically a document that attested before God and man that the sin was absolved. So far, so good.

The vulnerability in this scheme lay in the fact that indulgences are a limitless commodity; the exploit was that people in the Church started using that commodity as currency. The whole system was loosely regulated, which meant that no one could effectively limit the manner in which indulgences were sold. The Church could print as many indulgences as it could sell, and the wealthy realized that they could buy as much forgiveness as they needed. Middlemen appeared, paying corrupt bishops for the right to resell indulgences. What started as a system of redemption became a system of profit and power. In 1517, the practice of selling indulgences led Martin Luther to post his "Ninety-five Theses," or *Disputation on the Power and Efficacy of Indulgences*, on the door of the Castle Church in Wittenberg, Germany, kicking off the Protestant Reformation and sparking over a century of religious warfare.

Wherever there's money to be made, there's hacking. And those who can figure out profitable hacks can make a lot of money. This makes financial systems uniquely suitable—that is, profitable—to be hacked. Johann Tetzel, a Dominican friar of the early sixteenth century, invented two innovative indulgence products. First, he marketed the idea that you could buy indulgences for deceased friends, "upgrading" their status in the afterlife from purgatory to heaven. And second, he sold indulgences that purported to offer absolution for future sins and not just sins of the past. Kind of like a "get out of hell free" card.

Despite substantial protests from Catholic theologians and reformers like Martin Luther, the Vatican was unable to clamp down on the practice. The Church came to depend on the enormous profits that resulted from the sale and resale of indulgences, and that paralyzed any response. Tetzel's indulgence sales were a significant source of funding for St. Peter's Basilica, for example.

Many of the hacks we've already discussed were disabled by whoever governed the system. Airlines updated the rules to their frequent-flier plans. Sports updated the rules to the game. But once in a while, a hack was allowed—declared legal, even—by the governing system. A curved hockey stick makes for a more exciting game. The lure of card counting is profitable for casinos, even if competent card counters are not.

This normalization of a hack is common in the financial world. Sometimes new hacks are shut down by regulators, but more often they're permitted—and even codified into law after the fact. This is one of the mechanisms by which financial systems innovate. Instead of new ideas coming from the regulators in the form of new permissions, they come from actual users in the form of hacks.

While the obvious solution is to patch the system, it's often not politically possible. Power and money translate into lobbyist muscle, which tilts the board. This doesn't mean that hacks of financial systems are never patched, just that it might take a while. It wasn't until 1567 that Pope Pius V revoked permission to grant any indulgences that involved financial transactions, patching the system and eliminating the hack.

The moneyed are powerful hackers, and profit is a powerful motivation for hacking—and for normalizing hacking.

17

Hacking Banking

Many procedures we recognize as a normal part of banking today started out as hacks, as various powerful players tried to skirt regulations that limited their behavior and their profit. This isn't meant as a criticism; hacking is a way of forcing government to review and update new regulations.

For most of the twentieth century, the Federal Reserve regulated banking in the US through something called Regulation Q. First promulgated in 1933 after the Great Depression, Regulation Q controlled things like interest rates on different sorts of accounts, and rates for individual and corporate customers.

Regulation Q is a security measure. Prior to its enactment, banks competed with one another to offer the highest interest rates on customer deposits. This competition encouraged banks to engage in risky behaviors to make good on those rates. Regulation Q's limitations were designed to reduce systemic banking risk.

This worked for over forty years. As interest rates ballooned in the 1970s, banks desperately wanted to bypass Regulation Q and offer higher interest rates to compete with other investments. One early 1970s hack was the NOW account. NOW stands for "Negotiable Order of Withdrawal," a product designed to exploit the distinction between demand deposit accounts, which allow the account holder to withdraw their money at will, and term deposit accounts, which tie up the account holder's money for a predetermined period of time. NOW accounts looked for all the world like interest-bearing demand deposit accounts, but were technically term deposit accounts.

We know the hacker who invented the NOW account: Ronald Haselton, president and CEO of the Consumer Savings Bank in Worcester, Massachusetts. Haselton is said to have overheard a customer asking why she couldn't write checks from her savings account. He began to wonder the same thing, and hacked the Regulation Q rules to create what was in effect the first interest-bearing checking account.

Modern certificates of deposit, or CDs, were another example of an innovative banking hack. The hack involved recruiting a securities dealer to create a secondary market in CDs and thereby make them attractive to corporate accounts. The hackers who dreamed up the scheme were employed by First National City Bank, now Citicorp. In 1961, the bank introduced negotiable certificates of deposit, which paid a higher interest rate than that allowed for interest-bearing accounts, and five years later introduced them to the London market. Shortly thereafter, First National City Bank reorganized as a holding company in order to avoid bank regulations that would prevent it from issuing CDs at higher rates. Congress fixed the hack by amending the Bank Holding Company Act of 1956, which put the Federal Reserve Board in charge of oversight and regulation of bank holding companies.

Other banking hacks of the mid-twentieth century include money market funds and Eurodollar accounts, both designed to circumvent regulatory limits on interest rates offered on more traditional accounts.

These hacks all became normalized, either by regulators deciding not to close the loopholes through which they were created or by Congress expressly legalizing them once regulators' complaints began to pile up. For example, NOW accounts were legalized, first in Massachusetts and New Hampshire, then in New England in general, and finally nationwide in 1980. Many of the other limitations imposed by the Bank Holding Company Act were repealed with the passage of the Riegle-Neal Interstate Banking and Branching Efficiency Act of 1994. This was all part of a huge wave of banking deregulation that continued well into the 2000s.

That's the basic model, and we'll see it again and again. The government constrains bankers through regulation to limit the amount of damage they can do to the economy. Those regulations also reduce the profit bankers can make, so they chafe against them. They hack those regulations with tricks that the regulators didn't anticipate and didn't specifically prohibit and build profitable businesses around them. Then they do whatever they can to influence regulators—and government itself—not to patch the regulations, but instead to permit and normalize their hacks. A side effect is expensive financial crises that affect the populace as a whole.

The hacking continues today. The 2010 Dodd-Frank Wall Street Reform and Consumer Protection Act was passed in the wake of the 2008 Global Financial Crisis, and was intended to be a sweeping overhaul of the financial regulatory system. Dodd-Frank included a variety of banking regulations intended to create more transparency, reduce systemic risks, and avoid another financial meltdown. Specifically, the act regulated derivatives, which were often abused and were a major contributing factor to the 2008 financial crisis.

Dodd-Frank was filled with vulnerabilities. Banks immediately set their lawyers to work searching for hacks that could bypass the intent of the law—risk to the economy be damned. First, they seized on the specific wording that exempted foreign activities unless they had "a direct and significant connection with activities in, or commerce of" the United States. Once that vulnerability was closed, they split hairs on the definition of an overseas "branch" versus an overseas "affiliate." That didn't work for long, either. Finally, they zeroed in on the word "guarantee." Basically, all of these foreign derivatives were guaranteed by the US parent company, meaning they would cover the losses if something happened to the overseas affiliates. By simply removing the word "guarantee" and other equivalent terms from their contracts, they could avoid regulation.

By the end of 2014, banks had moved 95% of their swap trades offshore, to more lenient jurisdictions, in another hack to escape Dodd-Frank regulation. The Commodities Futures Trading Commission tried to close this loophole in 2016. It ruled that swaps couldn't be sent abroad to evade Dodd-Frank, and that both guaranteed and nonguaranteed swaps would be covered by the parent company. But the new rule wasn't finalized before President Trump came into office, and his appointed chair to the commission never bothered.

Other hacks centered around the Volcker Rule, another part of Dodd-Frank that prohibits banks from carrying out certain investment activities with their own accounts and simultaneously limits their interactions with hedge funds and private equity funds. Banks quickly realized they could flout this rule if the money didn't originate from their own accounts. This meant they could establish various partnerships and invest through them. This rule was rescinded during the Trump administration—making many of the hacks no longer necessary. Finally, banks realized that they could avoid all of the Dodd-Frank rules around "trading accounts" by claiming they were for something called "liquidity management."

Banking hacks illustrate another thing we'll see repeatedly. Banks and regulators play an unending game of cat and mouse. Regulators are tasked with limiting irresponsible, aggressive, corrupt behavior. Banks are motivated to make as much money as possible. Those two goals are opposed to each other, so banks hack the regulatory system wherever and whenever possible. Any bank that chooses not to do so will be overtaken by those that do.

The obvious security fix—patching—is stymied by the industry's aggressive push for normalization. This is accomplished through lobbying and also through regulatory capture: the common tendency for a regulatory agency to become dominated by the industry it is regulating, and to begin functioning in ways that benefit the industry rather than the public interest. The banking industry also does this by hacking the legislative process itself. The financial services industry spent $7.4 billion on lobbying between 1998 and 2016, with banks alone spending at least $1.2 billion.

If patching isn't a viable solution, we have to find vulnerabilities before they're hacked—and, more importantly, before they become entrenched in the underlying system and lobbyists start pushing for them to be normalized. In financial systems, government agencies could engage in red-teaming by hiring accountants and attorneys to study the systems as they evolve, and to improve regulations while they are still in draft.

Some countries—including the United States, at least for some agencies at some times—already do this sort of thing, with public comment processes for proposed regulations. The idea is to look for ways in which the rules can be hacked or ways in which near-term technological advancements could change how the rules could be hacked, then patch the text right away. This doesn't completely eliminate the problems of regulatory capture or legislative lobbying, but at least these powerful hackers aren't losing something when a loophole is closed.

On the other hand, lobbyists can abuse the comment process to pressure regulators to leave loopholes alone, or even to create new loopholes where there weren't any before. Creating a governing system like the comment process just shifts hackers' attention from the target itself to the target's governing system, which must be wary and nimble to avoid becoming just another soft underbelly for attackers to exploit.

18

Hacking Financial Exchanges

S tock markets, commodities exchanges, and other financial trading systems are also ripe for hacking. This has been true since their beginning, and it's even more so as those systems have become computerized and automated.

Hackers in this domain target information. When a financial exchange is working properly, traders with better information get better results because they buy lower and sell higher. Hacks subvert this mechanism in two basic ways. First, they leverage not-yet-public information to make lucrative trades before anyone else. Second, they disseminate false information that drives the market, then make profitable trades before everyone else realizes that they're being duped. Both of these hacks subvert market fairness: the notion that investors have equal access to information about the market.

The most obvious hack of the first type is insider trading, illegal for so long that it's not even a hack anymore. Generally, insider trading involves buying or selling a security on the basis of nonpublic information. The trader could be a CFO who knows his company's sales figures before they're disclosed, the PR person writing the financial report, or the printer who reads that report before it's published. The harms of insider trading are twofold: (1) it comes at the expense of everyone else who doesn't have the critical information, and (2) it leads people to mistrust the fairness of the market system.

In the US, insider trading was criminalized by the Securities Exchange Act of 1934, affirmed and refined over the years in US Supreme Court rulings. In 2021, three people were charged with insider trading for buying stock in the Long Island Iced Tea Co. just before it changed its name to the Long Blockchain Co. for no other reason than to ride the then-frenetic blockchain hype. A rule that has lasted for this long is a clear example of a successful systems patch.

It's actually impressive that these prohibitions have survived almost ninety years of hacking and regulatory inertia. If there's a general lesson here, it's that a broad rule enables a more robust, adaptable, and resilient regulatory regime. The simplicity of a rule minimizes vulnerabilities in the law's design. (We saw how vulnerable the complex Dodd-Frank law is.) According to former Securities and Exchange Commission (SEC) chairman Arthur Levitt, "greater specificity would give the legal fraternity various ways of getting around those specifics. [The SEC and Justice Department] want these laws purposely vague to see to it they have the maximum leverage in terms of bringing cases." The insider trading rules are deliberately broad to prevent further hacking attempts.

Front running is yet another hack that leverages secret information. If you're a broker, and you know about a big trade that's about to happen, you can make a smaller trade for yourself immediately beforehand. Then you execute your client's trade. It moves the market, and you make an instant profit for yourself. Like insider trading, this has been declared illegal.

Some hacking of financial markets and networks will target informational systems surrounding those networks. For example, in 2015, the SEC indicted two Ukrainian hackers who broke into Business Wire and PRNewswire's networks and stole more than 100,000 unreleased press releases for publicly traded companies. These were then distributed to a network of traders, who used the advance knowledge to place informed bets on the authoring companies' stocks, much like an insider trading scheme.

The second type of hack involves the creation of disinformation. An old example is the pump-and-dump. Perpetrators buy a stock, preferably an obscure one. (The penny stock market is notorious for pump-and-dumping.) Then, they recommend the stock to others, using false and misleading statements about the potential profit to be made. If others fall for the scam and purchase the stock, it inflates the price and the perpetrators sell. Traditionally, this scheme involved calling potential investors on the telephone. Today, it more often involves online trading message boards, social media groups, and spam emails. Whether it's ringleaders on the Reddit finance forum r/WallStreetBets pushing retail investors to send GameStop's price "to the moon" or Elon Musk tweeting about his bitcoin buys to millions of online followers, investors can use online communications to manipulate investor expectations and produce asset bubbles for their own profit (and others' loss) with unprecedented speed and scale. The advent of online trading has made this particular hack even more profitable. Mostly, pump-and-dump is illegal, and there are heavy fines if you get caught. On the other hand, prosecution can be difficult. Neither Musk nor anyone involved with the 2021 GameStop trading frenzy has been prosecuted.

Spoofing is another hack that involves the dissemination of disinformation. Here, a trader places millions of dollars of orders, then cancels them after other traders have noticed and reacted to them. This, too, is illegal, and a few people have been convicted of it.

Fake news—that is, deliberately deceptive reports masquerading as journalism—is another increasingly prevalent method of hacking the market through disinformation. This hack is most often used to misrepresent companies' valuation, allowing hackers to profit from fluctuations in their share prices. In 2015, for example, a fake version of Bloomberg.com was used to spread news of a $31 billion offer to buy Twitter, causing Twitter's stock to surge as the story spread, and hackers in the know sold Twitter shares at artificially inflated prices. The fake site was designed similarly to the real Bloomberg.com site, and used a similar URL. Fake press releases, fake reporters, fake tweets, and even fake SEC filings have also been used with similar success. The SEC views all of this behavior as illegal.

If you stop to think about it, disinformation is less a hack of the financial network and more a hack of other traders. It's an attempt to influence behavior. These are really hacks of our cognitive systems.

Other hacks of financial changes involve finding new ways to reduce risk, often involving loopholes in financial regulations. Hedge funds have been doing this since their inception in the 1960s, first by "hedging"—or offsetting—risks against each other, then by using diverse investment strategies, then by engaging in computer-assisted trading.

The very existence of hedge funds relies on hacking the financial regulatory system. Since their inception, hedge funds have been protected by a series of legislative loopholes that exempt them from SEC oversight. Because they only accept high-net-worth and institutional investors as clients, hedge funds are exempt from oversight under the Securities Act of 1933, which is designed to protect individual buyers in the market. By toeing the line on criteria outlined in the Investment Company Act of 1940, hedge funds exempt themselves from bans on investment techniques that are applied to registered investment companies—most notably, shorting. In 2010, the Dodd-Frank Act brought hedge funds under the oversight of the SEC, but they remain largely unregulated. Hedge funds have become a normal part of the financial system.

Over the decades, hedge funds have taken advantage of one legal loophole after another. Sometimes the loopholes are closed after their discoverer makes a lot of money. Sometimes the rules are changed to legitimize the hack. Most of the time they are just used, and eventually accepted as normal. The people who run hedge funds aren't necessarily smarter than everyone else. They just understand the system better, and are able to find vulnerabilities and craft exploits to take advantage of them. Since the people who understand the system best are the people profiting from the hacks, it's unlikely there will be much patching done anytime soon.

This is all relatively complex hacking, against multiple systems at multiple levels of generality. Some hacks operate at the technical level: spoofing and front running are hacks that make use of computer speed and automation. Some operate at the level of the financial markets. Some operate at the legislative level: vulnerabilities in securities laws, for example. This is all a microcosm of the hacks that will be described in chapters to come.

19

Hacking Computerized Financial Exchanges

Today, financial exchanges are all computerized, and the rise of computerization has led to all sorts of novel hacks. Front running, for example, is now much easier to implement and much harder to detect. Tying automated trading to "sentiment analysis"—so that trading programs buy when a stock becomes a meme or sell when bad news goes viral—can make pump-and-dumps and smear campaigns much more profitable. But the most virulent of all modern exchange hacks is high-frequency trading, or HFT. Instead of making use of true, albeit secret, information or disseminating disinformation, HFT exploits public information at lightning speed.

HFT is a form of algorithmic trading that exploits the price differentials that occur when large trade orders are placed, usually by pension funds or insurance companies. (These massive orders can have a significant impact on stock prices.) HFT algorithms detect these orders, as well other events that are likely to affect stock prices, and then profit from them. These trades are called "high frequency" because they try to "buy low and sell high" on minuscule price fluctuations at lightning speed. Often trades are made in milliseconds or microseconds, and firms vie for server space physically close to exchanges to maximize Internet speed. Just as dogs can hear frequencies that are too high for humans to hear, high-frequency trading algorithms can recognize and react to patterns far too subtle for humans to notice.

This is a hack. If we assume that the intent of a market is for buyers and sellers to exchange money and goods at prices each finds individually beneficial, then HFT hacks that intent. If we believe that all agents in a market should have equal access to market information in order to make their investment decisions, then HFT is a hack. Basically, HFT uses inhuman reflexes to make tiny bits of money on the random noise of the system as it operates. It's an artifact of the computer systems used to facilitate trading. It is definitely unintended and unanticipated by the market's designers. It definitely subverts the goals of the system for private gain. It is definitely parasitical.

Even worse than its inherent unfairness, HFT introduces new risks and new volatility into the system. In 2010, the US stock markets crashed rapidly, losing over a trillion dollars in value over the course of thirty-six minutes before rebounding. No cause was ever discovered, but the magnitude of the crash was exacerbated by HFT. In 2012, the Knight Capital Group lost $440 million through a flaw in new software that controlled HFT. As these events show, HFT and autonomous trading systems can be more risky than typical trading by human traders simply because of their speed and volume. And HFT clearly disadvantages those who don't have access to algorithmic trading systems.

Unlike some of the other hacks in this section, and in spite of its gross unfairness, HFT has been normalized. In the US, the Financial Industry Regulatory Authority has imposed some basic regulations designed to increase disclosure of the methods underlying algorithmic trading systems; the EU has similar rules. Neither is doing much to slow the practice. At its high point in 2009–2010, 60% to 70% of US trading was attributed to high-frequency trading. And while individual humans can contract with an HFT broker to have their own computer algorithms run for them, professional HFT traders will do it faster and better—to the disadvantage of others. HFT firms can pay extra to see pending orders a split second before the rest of the market does—another unfair advantage.

Taking advantage of typos is yet another market hack that operates at computer speeds. Typos are not uncommon in computerized trading systems. The large failures make the news, like the time that a Japanese company, Mizuho Securities Co., lost $225 million on a stock trade when an employee accidentally made a "transposition error," listing 610,000 shares at 1 yen apiece instead of one share for 610,000 yen. Or the time a junior trader at Deutsche Bank accidentally sent a hedge fund $6 billion in what's known as a "fat-finger error." Or the time that a trader on the Tokyo Stock Exchange lost $617 billion in stocks by pressing the wrong button and canceling forty-two separate transactions at once—more fat fingers at work.

None of those are hacks; they're just mistakes. The hack lies in deliberately placing crazy buy and sell orders in the hope of profiting from others' clerical errors. It costs nothing to make an offer, so a hack might involve continually flooding the market systems with wildly unrealistic offers. Almost all of them will expire unfulfilled, but once in a very great while one gets paired with someone else's mistake, resulting in an enormous profit.

Okay, so what about defenses? The flexibility of financial rules means that patching is a viable solution. That's because financial rules are deliberately drafted broadly and provide a lot of room for enforcement discretion. Courts and regulators can quickly and easily ban or regulate new practices just by reinterpreting or clarifying existing law. Even so, the ability of hackers to normalize their practices limits patching's effectiveness.

Here is probably a good place to employ secure systems design. We can design our financial systems to reduce the volatility that comes from high-frequency trading. Already many markets have "circuit breakers" that automatically halt trading temporarily if stock prices change by a certain percentage. We could do a lot more. For example, we could require all trades to be executed once per second—or ten seconds—and all at the same time. Or we could build systems that automatically detect dangerous HFT trades, and either delay their execution or cancel them entirely. But any design changes require regulators to go against what powerful investors want. It took fifty years for the pope to redesign indulgences after Martin Luther's theses; surely we don't have to wait that long.

20

Luxury Real Estate

In London, New York, Vancouver, and many other major cities world-wide, the luxury real estate market doesn't behave like it used to. It's not about rich people buying homes, or even second homes. It's a money-laundering machine.

Here's the hack: If you've got millions of shady dollars (or rubles), you can't just deposit it in a checking or investment account. The government requires those institutions to ask you too many nosy questions and to file a Suspicious Activity Report if your answers don't make sense. But there's a vulnerability, and that's in real estate. In many countries, regulations surrounding real estate purchases are nowhere near as onerous as those pertaining to banks and financial markets. Banks are required to screen customers to help prevent fraud and money laundering, but those rules don't apply to foreign shell corporations that engage in real estate transac-tions. Brokers and sellers don't question your questionable cash, because the government doesn't require it. Once you notice the vulnerability, the hack is obvious.

First, you purchase a superexpensive condo in a city where you have no intention of living. You make the purchase through a shell company to obscure your personal involvement (technically called "beneficial owner-ship"). You then use that property as collateral to qualify for bank loans. The money you borrow is clean, and you can invest it more conventionally, in the stock market or elsewhere, without running afoul of the regulations surrounding those systems. You really don't care if the condo appreciates, since you didn't buy it for that purpose. Still, it's a plus if prices rise, since that creates more against which to borrow. You don't rent the property, since that would devalue the property, no matter how good your tenants might turn out to be.

This is how Andrey Borodin, having fled Russia on charges of defrauding his own bank, ended up owning a £140 million flat in London. He's not alone. A 2015 report from Transparency International identified 160 UK properties, together worth £4.4 billion, all owned by what they called "high-corruption-risk individuals." Cities like New York and Miami are filled with untenanted luxury condominiums. One luxury building examined by the *New York Times* had 80% of its units owned by shell corporations in 2014.

This same trick works even if you're not trying to launder your money, albeit not as well. Real estate is still a good way to park money and acquire collateral, and rising real estate prices still increase the property owner's borrowing power.

All of this explains a seemingly odd feature of the luxury real estate market: why so many sellers choose to not sell their properties instead of lowering their asking prices to something the market can more reasonably bear. As long as there's no actual sale at the lower price, the asset doesn't have to be devalued. Pretty much everyone involved in luxury real estate prefers that outcome.

This directly damages the real estate market for people who want to live in the neighborhoods where this is prevalent. It also destroys the commercial real estate market in these neighborhoods, because there are fewer people around. Retail stores in neighborhoods like Mayfair in London have collapsed, because 30% of the homes are vacant due to offshore money launderers.

The fixes are as obvious as the vulnerability: regulatory changes that bring real estate in line with other financial systems. In 2016, the US Treasury Department implemented a pilot program in twelve cities (known as a "geographic targeting order") requiring LLCs to reveal their beneficial owners when they are created. This resulted in a 70% drop in cash purchases of real estate by LLCs. This requirement could be made permanent and nationwide; in fact, geographic targeting orders have recently been renewed and expanded to encompass new real estate markets. The federal government could extend the banking "Know Your Customer Rule" to include shell companies' beneficial owners. And the federal government could get rid of the "temporary exemption" from detailed customer scrutiny for real estate that lobbyists were able to insert into the 2001 PATRIOT ACT, as it now seems to be permanent.

There is, however, no political appetite to change the regulations—although Russia's invasion of Ukraine may change that in the UK. The reason for inertia in this field, of course, is power. There are a whole slew of industries—real estate development, construction, and so on—that benefit from the unregulated sale of luxury real estate. And there are few people in power who would benefit from the change. Raising tax revenue, improving housing affordability, increasing available stock of existing housing, and reducing money-laundering capability: those are all things the rest of us want.

Today, money laundering through real estate is so much business-as-usual that it barely qualifies as a hack anymore. And I could tell a similar story about expensive art. There's a hack that involves buying a piece of art cheaply, getting it appraised very highly, then donating it to a museum for the tax write-off. And society is harmed by the loss in tax revenue.

Societal Hacks Are Often Normalized

When we think of hacks, we imagine that they're quickly blocked—that is, patched—by the system designers. This is what generally happens with computer hacks. I'm writing this paragraph in May 2022, and here are three vulnerabilities that recently appeared in the press:

- Cisco announced multiple vulnerabilities in its Enterprise NFV Infrastructure Software. One vulnerability could allow an attacker to jump from a guest virtual machine to the host machine, and thereby compromise the entire host network.
- Cloud security company F5 warned its customers of forty-three vulnerabilities affecting four of its products. One "may allow an unauthenticated attacker with network access to the BIG-IP system through the management port and/or self IP addresses to execute arbitrary system commands, create or delete files, or disable services."
- AVG Corporation announced details of two high-severity vulnerabilities in its antivirus products that had been lurking in the code since 2012. Both flaws could enable attackers to disable security software or tamper with a client's operating system.

In every case, the vulnerability was discovered by researchers or the manufacturer itself, privately disclosed to the system designers, patched by the designers, and only afterwards published along with the fact that the system was no longer vulnerable.

In computer security, we have a name for this: "responsible disclosure." The opposite of that is a "zero-day vulnerability." This is a vulnerability that is first discovered in secret, by criminals, governments, or hackers that sell to criminals or governments—and the organization in charge of the system doesn't learn about it until it's used in the wild. No one receives any advance warning in those cases.

There was no responsible disclosure with any of the hacks we discussed in preceding chapters, nor with most of the other examples throughout this book. In noncomputer systems, that's more normal. When a hedge fund manager discovers a profitable hack against a financial system, he doesn't alert the regulator so it can get fixed. He uses it to his advantage until a government body forces him not to.

This is the process more generally. First, a vulnerability is discovered, and used in an exploit to hack the system. Eventually, it becomes more popular. This can happen slowly or quickly, depending on the hack and what it does and how profitable it can be, the pervasiveness of the system being hacked, how quickly knowledge of the hack spreads, and so on. At some point, the system's governing body learns about the hack. That governing body can do one of two things. One, it can modify the rules of the system to prevent the hack, patching the system. Or two, it can incorporate the hack into the system, essentially normalizing it. After normalization, the hack sometimes dies a natural death once everyone does it and any competitive advantage is lost.

The history of financial hacks is a history of normalization. Someone invents a hack and makes a huge amount of money. Others copy that individual and also reap windfalls. Then the regulators notice and step in. Sometimes they declare the hack illegal and convict the hackers. But most of the time, they retroactively approve the hacks. At that point, they're no longer hacks but just a normal part of finance. That normalization process doesn't always happen deliberately. As with hedge funds, some hacks are just ignored and, through inaction, passively normalized.

This can be a positive—some of these hacks, like NOW accounts and CDs, are innovations in finance—but there is a cost. Many hacks in the

preceding chapters subvert the fairness of the market by targeting information, choice, or agency. They're not so much innovative as subversive.
Their normalization testifies to the power of wealthy individuals to have
their way at the expense of everyone else.

Normalization isn't a new phenomenon, and neither is the cat-and-
mouse game between hackers and regulators. In the Middle Ages, both
Catholic and secular authorities had very strict restrictions on interest-
bearing loans because they were regarded as sinful. As banking developed as a profession, wealthy bankers avoided those restrictions through
a series of increasingly sophisticated methods. This included fudging the
record books, misleadingly classifying a prohibited usurious loan as a
permitted one, and disguising the interest on a loan as a gift from the
borrower. One hack was a "dry sea loan," which turned a prohibited loan
into an allowed "sea loan" by linking it to arbitrary sea voyages.

The response to those medieval usury hacks echoes everything in
this chapter. Between the twelfth and fourteenth centuries, the Catholic
Church updated its usury regulations to combat new financial innovations
such as the dry sea loan, created more sophisticated enforcement mechanisms, and increased the prescribed punishments for convicted usurers.
But the rich have a way of protecting their profit sources. Wealthy guilds
had the resources and expertise to create financial products that successfully evaded Church scrutiny. And a form of regulatory capture took
place, whereby the Church would accept donations and financial restitu-
tion from usury violators, incentivizing a conditional acceptance of usury.
Modern banking was essentially born in 1517 at the Fifth Lateran Council, an example of normalizing a beneficial hack. If you've ever bought a
house through a mortgage, financed a college education, or started a business with a loan, you have this normalization to thank. (The council also
legalized pawn shops, in case you've benefited from that system as well.)

Normalization seems to be common today. I'm sure most high-
frequency trading hacks would have been declared illegal if they had
been invented a hundred years ago. I'm equally certain insider trading
would be legal if it had been invented in recent decades.

22

Hacking the Market

From 2010 to 2014, Goldman Sachs owned an aluminum storage company with twenty-seven industrial warehouses in the Detroit area. Several times a day, trucks would shuffle 1,500-pound bars of the metal among the warehouses, loading it at one warehouse and unloading it at another. Every day.

It was a hack, of course. The way the spot price for aluminum is calculated depends in part on the amount of time customers have to wait between purchase and delivery. This continual shuffling of aluminum affected that price, and since those twenty-seven warehouses stored over a quarter of the country's aluminum supply, Goldman Sachs's legal dance let it manipulate the price to its own advantage.

This is a hack that is simply not available to people without the wealth of a Goldman Sachs. Money is what primes a market economy for hacking, and it's the wealthy that benefit from it.

Market hacks exploit vulnerabilities in the process by which we make and sell goods and services; that is, the normal logic of supply and demand, consumer choice, how businesses enter and leave the market, and what kinds of products get offered in the first place.

Market capitalism—the free market—is an economic system with unique advantages over the mercantile system it replaced. In contrast to central planning systems like communism, market capitalism is not controlled by any one entity. Individuals make individual decisions in their own best interest, capital flows where it can be used most profitably, and out of that chaos an efficient market emerges, at least in a perfect world.

The fundamental mechanism that makes this all work is self-interested buyers making intelligent decisions among competing sellers. The rules of the market are intended to keep that basic mechanism functioning and to prevent the system from causing greater damage. These include laws you would expect, like prohibitions against deceptive trade practices and unsafe working conditions, as well as laws you might not immediately think of, like contract enforcement, national currencies, civil courts for dispute resolution, and so on.

Markets need three things to be successful: information, choice, and agency. Buyers need information about products and services in order to make intelligent buying decisions: their merits and problems, their prices, their specs, and so on. Buyers need to have multiple sellers from which to choose, otherwise there is no competition to control prices and spur innovation. And buyers need the agency to use their knowledge about different buyers and to choose between them. All three of these market elements have been successfully hacked:

- Complex product offerings obscure information. Just try, for example, to compare prices of different cell phone programs, credit cards, or stock prospectuses. The obfuscation, and resultant confusion, makes it harder for buyers to intelligently choose between alternatives. To some extent this arises from the natural complexity of our high-tech world, but to another extent it is a deliberate hack designed to impede users' access to accurate information.
- Monopolies eliminate choice. Monopolies aren't new, and pre-capitalism they weren't a hack. But in a market system composed of sellers competing for buyers, they subvert the market mechanism. Adam Smith wrote about this in 1776, explaining that the economic interests of businessmen are often misaligned with public interests. The goal of businessmen—and, of course, business enterprises—is to maximize profits. The goal of the public is to (more or less) maximize product quantity, quality, variety, and innovation, and minimize

prices. Lack of competition means that sellers no longer fear losing buyers, and thus have no incentive to provide any of those things the public wants.

- Lock-in reduces our agency to freely choose among competing products. Someone might drink a Coke today, and if it doesn't appeal to him, he can drink a Pepsi tomorrow. But if that same person has a bad experience today with his cell phone plan, or email provider, or credit card, he's probably still going to have the same cell phone plan, email provider, and credit card tomorrow. The cost to switch, in money, time, convenience, or learning, is just higher. That's lock-in. And the hack part comes from all the different ways of enforcing lock-in: proprietary file formats that make it much more expensive to switch audio players or book readers, customizations that make it harder for you to switch business applications, social networking sites that won't let you continue to access your friends' accounts if you delete your own, or apps that don't let you take your data with you when you leave.

The result of all this is greater profits for the companies, at our expense, through hacks of the market system.

Regulation can be used to limit these market failures. Deregulation, by its nature, removes impediments to action. It allows for more hacks, by basically preapproving them before anyone can see them or their effects. This is, of course, both good and bad. It's good in that innovations can quickly be implemented. And it's bad in that subversions can be implemented just as quickly.

Historically, at least in the US, we have prioritized innovation and the minimalist regulatory structure that enables that. This has largely worked, simply because the amount of damage a bad hack could cause was contained. Today, due to both the power of technology and the global nature of our economies, that's no longer true. An economic system based on greed and self-interest only works when those properties can't destroy the underlying system. And "Move fast and break things"—Mark Zuckerberg's famous motto for Facebook—is only okay when it's your own things you're putting at risk. When someone else's things are involved, then maybe you should think twice—or be forced to fix what you've broken.

23

"Too Big to Fail"

The phrase "too big to fail" captures a critical vulnerability in our market economy. If you are so large that your failure is a systemic risk to the economy, you are free to take bigger risks because you know you won't be allowed to fail. The idea is captured in an old quote widely attributed to J. Paul Getty (though probably first said by John Maynard Keynes): "If you owe the bank $100, that's your problem. If you owe the bank $100 million, that's the bank's problem." That's "too big to fail" in a nutshell.

In more detail: some corporations are too critical to the functioning of our economy to be allowed to fail. They have become too large and too essential, and if they become too unprofitable, it is cheaper for the government to bail them out than to allow them to fail.

Recall that the overarching mechanism of the market is sellers competing for buyers; successful sellers thrive and unsuccessful ones wither. Imagine an ordinary businessperson or organization considering a risky decision. They must weigh the benefits of success with the costs of failure, and their eventual decision will consider both. Directors of an enterprise deemed too crucial to fail, on the other hand, know that the inevitable costs of any poor decisions they might make will be paid by taxpayers: that is, by society as a whole. This creates moral hazard and incentivizes risky decision-making. If they're successful, they'll win. And if they're unsuccessful, they're protected from loss. "Too big to fail" is an insurance policy against bad bets. It drastically perturbs our market system. It's a distortion fueled by money and power. And it's a hack.

In the aftermath of the 2008 financial crisis, the US government bailed out several major Wall Street banks and other financial institutions after their managers made years of bad business decisions. This was done through the Troubled Asset Relief Program, which authorized the government to purchase floundering companies' assets and stock, including mortgage-backed securities. It was thought that the $700 billion bailout was essential to protect the overall US economy. The fear was that absent a bailout, it would all collapse. And it would have cost the government far more than $700 billion to pay for government relief programs in proportion to the recession's severity. (In economic recessions, government revenues decline because people earn less and pay less taxes, and government spending increases on programs like unemployment insurance. In short, recessions become more costly as they become more severe.)

This isn't the first time the US government bailed out "too big to fail" companies. The Federal Deposit Insurance Corporation was created in the 1930s, following a torrent of bank failures, in order to monitor banks and protect consumer deposits. In 1979, the government bailed out Chrysler Corporation. It was a smaller bailout—only $1.5 billion—but the justifications were similar. National security was invoked; the company was building the M1 Abrams tank during the height of the Cold War. The economy was invoked; it was necessary to save 700,000 jobs in Detroit and beyond. And the US was in the middle of an automotive trade war with Japan. The bailout was successful; Chrysler paid the loan back early and with interest.

The "too big to fail" hack essentially results from a change in the threat model. When the mechanisms of the market economy were invented, no business could ever be so critical to the entire economy that its failure would necessitate government intervention. This was partly due to size, but also because critical social functions were not privatized in the same way. Sure, companies could grow, but none would grow at such a scale. That level of growth requires modern technologies.

Attempts to regulate super-sized enterprises have been lukewarm at best, primarily because of the lobbying power of those enterprises, which generally resist oversight. The 2010 Dodd-Frank banking reforms reduced the threat of "too big to fail" institutions, but those were mostly rendered ineffectual as the bill made its way through Congress, or were neutered in subsequent tax reform legislation.

One way to protect against the "too big to fail" hack is to not bail out the mega-corporations directly. The US government had at least two other courses of action in 2008. It could have conditioned any bailouts on restructuring mortgages to eliminate what was a wave of defaults. And it could have bailed out the big banks only if they passed the money on to the borrowers. Both were rejected by then National Economic Council director Larry Summers. The 2008 bank bailouts provide another example of how wealth protects hacks used by the wealthy.

The most effective way to secure an economic system against companies that are too big to fail would be to ensure that there aren't any in the first place. In 2009, sociologist Duncan Watts wrote an essay: "Too Big to Fail? How About Too Big to Exist?" He argued that some companies are so large and powerful that they can effectively use the government as insurance against their risky business decisions, with taxpayers left holding the bag.

Hacks like these exemplify three attributes that we'll revisit later on in the book. First, "too big to fail" is generalizable. As big banks, real estate, and other "essential" sectors of the economy recognize that they are able to employ the "too big to fail" hack, the market economy as a whole becomes vulnerable to enterprises that expand unsustainably. Second, hacks can be systematized and reshape decision-making: the bailouts in 2008 codified "too big to fail" into law. By demonstrating that the federal government was willing to bail out the banking, real estate, and automotive sectors, Congress normalized the hack as just another part of the high-finance game. And third, the very concept of "too big to fail" changes the incentives of those regulating the massive organizations, and consequently the organizations themselves.

Today, I'm certain that companies view a "too big to fail" bailout as

their ultimate insurance policy. Certainly, the few organizations that
were explicitly guaranteed bailouts through Dodd-Frank—Citigroup,
JPMorgan Chase, Bank of America, and Goldman Sachs—know that
the government will bail them out again if needed. It's a hack that has
been normalized, even though it's incredibly damaging to our market economy.

24

Venture Capital and Private Equity

ood delivery apps rely on an unsustainable business model. In 2020, a
pandemic year when most of us stayed home, DoorDash lost $139 mil-
lion and Grubhub lost $156 million. It's hard to find numbers for Uber
Eats, but Uber itself lost $6.8 billion—and that's better than its $8.5 billion loss in 2019. And it's unsustainable for individual investors, too; food
delivery doesn't work for anybody. The drivers—gig workers with no
benefits or job security—are poorly paid. The services hurt restaurants:
they're not profitable for a whole bunch of reasons, they don't bring in
incremental sales, and a restaurant's reputation suffers when the delivery
service screws up. Even the customers don't fare well: they're hit with service fees and higher prices and suffer all sorts of delivery problems. The
only reason that this market even exists is that venture capital firms like
SoftBank are willing to pour tens of billions of dollars into it, hoping that
someday they might capture enough restaurant industry profits to turn
a profit of their own. This investment strategy is a hack: market capitalism is supposed to use the uncoordinated collective wisdom of buyers to
influence sellers. Venture capital funding prevents that from happening;
it inhibits buyers' agency.

Venture capital (VC) as a funding model traces its origins back hundreds of years but didn't really take off until the 1980s. It was a key player
in the rise of early tech companies and in the inflation and burst of the

dot-com bubble in 2001. And it's grown steadily since then: in 2010, the global venture capital market was $50 billion; in 2019, it was $295 billion. I have personally benefited from venture capital; I sold my first VC-backed company to BT in 2006, and my second to IBM in 2016.

Venture capital itself is not a hack. The hack is when unprofitable companies use VC funding to ignore the dynamics of the market economy. We don't want some central planner to decide which businesses should remain operational and which should close down. But this is exactly what happens when venture capital firms become involved. The injection of VC money means that companies don't need to compete with each other in the traditional manner, or worry about the normal laws of supply and demand. They can do what would normally be crazy things—give away their products, pay extravagant salaries, sustain enormous financial losses, provide a service that actually harms people—because of that external funding source. It's basically central planning by elite investors, something that would be called communism if the government did it.

Uber has received $25.5 billion in VC funding since it was founded in 2009. The company hasn't had a single profitable year. In 2019, the company lost $8.5 billion worldwide, or 58 cents per dollar on each of its 5.2 billion rides. The only reason Uber exists at all is that there are still investors willing to pour capital into this sinkhole, probably waiting for the time when driverless car technology allows the company to fire all of its drivers and operate a fully autonomous fleet.

WeWork has also never turned a profit, losing over $10 billion in the past three years. That particular VC-fueled bubble burst when the company tried and failed to go public in 2019. The COVID-19 work-from-home rules further hurt WeWork's chances of success, and the company's co-founder was ousted as CEO and chairman of the board. The only reason that WeWork ever grew so big is because it raised $12.8 billion of VC funding between its 2010 founding and the summer of 2019, and billions more since as debt relief.

These examples are not the same as bad investments or even fraudulent bad investments. Quibi was a venture-backed company that secured over $1.75 billion in funding pre-launch, touting the concept of ten-minute-or-less episodes of content, but shut down just six months after launch after minimal adoption. Elizabeth Holmes founded and ran Theranos on venture capital without ever creating a successful product, and eventually fleeced investors to the tune of $1 billion over several years. Those are both examples of the market working normally, albeit with buyers—in this case, investors—making bad buying decisions and in the Theranos case out-and-out fraud.

As a whole, the VC system subverts market capitalism in many ways. It warps markets, allowing companies to charge prices that don't reflect the true cost or value of what they're selling. It permits unprofitable enterprises and unsustainable business models to thrive and proliferate. It also warps the market for talent—employees—especially in the tech sector. And finally, it warps entire market categories, like transportation, housing, and the media. Uber and Lyft, for example, have created an unsustainable market for hired-car rides by charging artificially low prices that do not accurately reflect the value of drivers' labor.

VC funding is also a hack on innovation. By favoring financial returns over substantive product improvements, it prioritizes certain kinds of innovation and ignores others. To a VC-funded company, all that matters is return on investment. So if one of the goals of a market economy is to incentivize innovation, VC funding subverts that goal. VC investors expect to recover their investment in ten years or less, and that's how they steer their companies.

Similarly, VC culture only rewards endeavors that realize a very high rate of return. Investors bankroll hundreds of companies with different ideas and business models, knowing that almost all of them will fail—and that the few wild successes will more than pay for the rest. So VC-funded managers are motivated to "swing for the fences" rather than grow sustainable, long-term businesses. This is why VC-funded companies can lose so much money, doing all sorts of societal damage along the way. Those losses are paid for by the successes: "unicorns," in VC-speak.

Private equity allows for another hack, and that's debt financing. When private equity firms take on a majority stake to acquire companies, they can use less of their equity and rely on debt. They can use this to saddle the firms they acquire with debt, extract money from them, leave them with more debt, then sell them for even more profit—with all the debtors left holding the (empty) bag. Consider the case of Greensill Capital, which collapsed spectacularly in 2021. Its unsustainable expansion over the course of ten years—from supply-chain finance startup, to multinational middleman with a $4.6 million debt load, to insolvency—was accelerated by investments and loans from SoftBank, who made millions in funds available in spite of the company's increasingly fishy accounting.

There's nothing illegal about any of this. VC funding and private equity are such a normal part of our economy that it might seem odd to call them hacks. But they are; they're hacks of pretty much everything the market is supposed to do. No one calls it a hack; everyone just calls it "disruptive" and "innovative." That it's both legal and accepted doesn't change the fact that money and power decide what behavior is accepted and who gets a seat at the gaming table.

25

Hacking and Wealth

In professional sports, salary caps keep leagues competitive by reducing the unfair advantage of teams with more capital. Basically, all of the teams agree to a maximum total amount they will pay their players. Of course, the agreements are hacked. Depending on the sport and the specifics of the rules, teams can hide payments in signing bonuses, by spreading payments over multiple years, by having team sponsors and affiliated companies also hire players, by hiring a player's spouse, or by hiding players' salaries in an associated minor-league team's budget. There's a lot of money involved in professional sports. The teams do everything they can to subvert the rules.

The hacks we've seen so far in banking and financial systems are largely perpetrated by the wealthy in their attempts to amass even more wealth. This flips our traditional notion of computer hacking on its head. We conventionally think of hacking as something countercultural that the disempowered do to powerful systems standing in their way. The hacker group Anonymous stands as a good example of this sort of hacking. But it's more common for the wealthy to hack systems to their own advantage, whether for profit or power.

The wealthy enjoy several advantages that make them better at discovering and exploiting hacks. The first is that they don't actually have to be superior hackers themselves. The wealthy have more resources to hire the expertise required to succeed at hacking: finding vulnerabilities, creating exploits, executing hacks. Additionally, because money is so important in politics, the wealthy are better normalizers of hacks. That is, they can use their power to ensure that their hacks become legally permissible.

When General Motors declared bankruptcy in 2009, it declared its stock worthless, then created a completely new stock that it then sold to raise capital. Executives and wealthy investors profited, while common shareholders—many of them employees and retirees—were screwed. It was a very profitable hack, but only for those who were already rich.

What we see here is—again—that the rich are better at hacking. People and organizations with concentrated resources are better at finding and implementing hacks. And they're better at ensuring those hacks are legalized and normalized.

In 2020, we began to hear about a new hack of the tax system involving stock trading—*cum-ex* trading, which is Latin for "with-without." Here's how the *New York Times* described it: "Through careful timing, and the coordination of a dozen different transactions, *cum-ex* trades produced two refunds for dividend tax paid on one basket of stocks." That first refund was legitimate, the second was not.

That it's a hack is obvious; it was neither anticipated nor intended that one individual or entity receive two tax refunds for one payment. But the system allowed it, and from 2006 to 2011, bankers, lawyers, and investors who used this hack made off with $60 billion from EU countries.

Germany recently sentenced a banker known as Christian S. to ten years in prison over the scandal. This isn't the final word, though. Christian S.'s case awaits appeal. Two London bankers were handed a suspended sentence and £14 million fine in 2020 for *cum-ex* trading. A German private bank was ordered to pay €176.6 million to German tax authorities. A former senior German tax inspector, who absconded to Switzerland in 2012 when news of the *cum-ex* scandal began to emerge but was eventually extradited, has been charged for providing advice and collecting fees from the bankers involved in the scheme. The Frankfurt offices of Morgan Stanley bank were recently raided as part of the *cum-ex* investigation. More prosecutions are pending. Germany alone is investigating over 1,000 lawyers and bankers for their involvement in *cum-ex* trades.

Here we can clearly see the interplay of hacking, legality, and morality. When asked about his own tax avoidance, then candidate Donald Trump famously said, "That makes me smart"—but it doesn't necessarily make him moral. It might, if he only exploited legal loopholes to do so, but it doesn't mean those tax loopholes shouldn't be closed.

Cum-ex trading has cost European nations and their citizens at least $60 billion, and most of that won't ever be recovered. Hacking is parasitical, mostly performed by the rich and powerful, and it comes at the expense of everyone else.

PART 4

HACKING LEGAL SYSTEMS

26

Hacking Laws

Tax hacks show up in architecture and construction surprisingly often. The mansard roof became popular in Napoleonic France. It allowed for an extra story of living space without the building being taxed for it, because that story was technically part of the roof. The gambrel roof also hid a story and evaded the US 1798 Federal Direct Tax law. Buildings in Peru and elsewhere frequently have bits of rebar sticking out of their sides and roofs and a pile of rubble nearby, because unfinished buildings have less property tax.

This is probably a good place to remind readers what counts as a hack and what doesn't. A British tax on home windows from 1696 to 1851 led tax-averse homeowners to block up their windows. That's a hack because the number of windows was being used as a proxy for home size, and blocking up windows subverted that measure. If the tax had measured home size directly, and if homeowners had demolished their buildings as a result, that wouldn't be a hack. Opting out of or destroying part of a system in order to avoid its costs isn't hacking. Hacking means finding and exploiting the rules of the system, turning them to your advantage as you continue to participate in that system.

Governments take action through words—and those words can change the state of the world. Congress passes laws. Presidents sign executive orders. Agencies make rules. These are all just words associated with enforcement power. These words are in a sense code. And like computer code, they will have bugs and vulnerabilities. The authors of any legal text are imperfect and fallible, and also influenceable. As such, laws can be hacked. Their authors can—accidentally or deliberately—leave vulnerabilities in laws that will inevitably be discovered by hackers. And there is always the will to hack laws.

Sumptuary laws regulated extravagance and luxury. (Think "sumptuous.") Historically, they've mostly been passed to prevent expensive competition among nobility to outdo each other in parties, banquets, feasts, and pageantry. Sometimes, they've been passed to prevent people of a lower class from mimicking the aristocrats too closely. In both cases, those annoyed by the laws have tried to hack them.

Banquets, for example, have regularly been limited with respect to the number of courses or the varieties of meat that can be served. For example, a 1356 Florentine law limited the number of courses at a wedding to three. But the definition of "course" excluded fruit, vegetables, and cheese, and hosts used that loophole to add additional courses. And a single "roast" could consist of one meat stuffed with one or more other meats, which means that—yes—the turducken was originally a hack of sumptuary laws. This demonstrates yet again how the rich can comply with the letter of the law while completely subverting its spirit.

Systems of laws are just another system of rules, and are vulnerable to hacking. In a sense, they're designed to be hacked. The letter of the law is mostly what's enforced, the spirit rarely. If you find a hack—a way of following the letter of the law that seems to violate the spirit—it's not your fault that the law wasn't well written. This is the sort of argument that you hear from tax avoidance proponents everywhere.

And laws are hacked everywhere. In 2020, the Federal Reserve implemented an emergency loan program for companies affected by the coronavirus pandemic. Even though only US companies were officially allowed to participate, foreign companies figured out how to turn themselves into US companies and hack the regulation. The Pacific Investment Management Company, based in Newport Beach, California, runs a hedge fund registered in the Cayman Islands to avoid paying US taxes. But by investing in a Delaware corporation and tying it to the parent California corporation, the hedge fund was able to borrow money commercially to buy securities, then borrow $13.1 million from the government relief program, and finally use that loan to pay back the original and more expensive securities loan. Instant profit, perfectly legal, at the expense of everyone in the US. Sociopathic, perhaps, yet I admire the creativity.

My notion of hacking laws isn't just about legislation. Any rule can be hacked. Historically, the Catholic Church's rules about abstinence varied greatly, and generally involved not eating meat at certain times. This was called a fast, albeit only a partial one, compared to Yom Kippur or Ramadan. But, people being as they are, a great deal of medieval thought went into exactly what counted as "meat" and "not-meat," especially during the month-long fasting seasons of Lent and Advent. Fish didn't count as meat. Barnacle goose was also considered not meat, because it had scaly webbed feet and (supposedly) gave birth in the water. A similar argument applied to beavers: also not meat. (This isn't just a historic curiosity. Even today, Detroit Catholics are permitted to eat muskrat during fast days on the basis of a missionary's ruling from the 1700s.) Some French monasteries served rabbit fetuses, not deemed meat because they were swimming in amniotic fluid. (Really: I'm not making any of this up.) St. Thomas Aquinas declared chicken to be of aquatic origin—whatever that means—and not meat. Some bishops went further, declaring that, because they are not quadrupeds, all fowl is fair game (so to speak).

A more modern hack of fasting rules is the practice among some wealthy Saudi families of treating Ramadan as a month-long party, staying up most of the night and sleeping through most of the day.

Any law is fair game for hacking. And as long as there are people who want to subvert the intent of a law, there will be hacking.

27

Legal Loopholes

The "Zone of Death" is a weird vulnerability in the US Constitution. It arises from contradictory jurisdictional rules between state and local law enforcement. The Venue Clause in Article III, Section 2, of the Constitution states that: "The trial of all crimes, except in cases of impeachment, shall be by jury; *and such trial shall be held in the state where the said crimes shall have been committed . . ."* The Vicinage Clause in the Sixth Amendment says that: *"In all criminal prosecutions, the accused shall enjoy the right to a speedy and public trial, by an impartial jury of the State and district wherein the crime shall have been committed . . ."*

The US District Court for the District of Wyoming has jurisdiction over all of Yellowstone National Park, which extends slightly into Montana and Idaho. Let's say you commit murder in the Idaho portion of Yellowstone National Park. You can't be tried in Wyoming—the jurisdiction in which you were arrested—because Article III requires you to be tried in Idaho. But the Sixth Amendment requires that your jury reside in both the state (that's Idaho) and the district (that's Wyoming) in which the crime was committed. That means your jury must consist of residents of the Idaho portion of Yellowstone National Park . . . which has no residents. Basically, there is no constitutional way to convict you of murder.

No one has yet used this particular hack to get away with murder, but it has been used as a poaching defense. In 2007, a man illegally shot an elk in Yellowstone while standing in the Montana portion. After being indicted, his lawyers used this hack as part of their defense. The court dismissed the argument, supposedly because it would solidify the "Zone of Death" loophole. By doing so, they disabled the hack by means of adjudication.

A more sinister version of this hack occurs all too often on Native lands. Tribal courts cannot try non-Native individuals who commit crimes on Native lands; only federal authorities can do so, and in disturbing numbers of cases they do not. This means non-Native Americans have free rein to assault Native women on tribal lands and suffer virtually no repercussions. It has been reported that a full 80% of Native American women who are sexually assaulted are victimized by non-Native American men.

One last hack. Federal enclaves are parcels of land within a state that are owned by the federal government, and have long represented a vulnerability of the US legal system. Federal enclaves include military bases, federal courthouses, federal prisons and other federal buildings, and national forests and national parks. These have special legal designation because their home states essentially relinquish ownership of them to the federal government, meaning that state and local laws don't apply to them.

Over time, the legal system has sought to patch this vulnerability. In 1937, a US Supreme Court ruling led to state taxes being applied to federal enclaves. In 1970, in *Evans v. Cornman*, the Supreme Court ruled that residents of federal enclaves (such as residents of private homes situated within the territory of a national park) could vote in state elections. Other smaller patches have been made through the courts, but federal enclaves remain exempt from numerous state laws, including criminal laws, anti-discrimination laws, and labor protections.

Residents of federal enclaves can also escape foie gras bans. Foie gras is the liver of a duck or goose that has been subject to a process called *gavage*, in which animals are force-fed twice a day for a couple of weeks until their livers are engorged to ten times their usual volume and are ready to cook. Animal rights activists regularly agitate against the process, and in 2004 California banned the sale and production of foie gras. In the following years, the ban was repeatedly challenged in court. In 2014, the owners of a San Francisco restaurant called the Presidio Social Club pointed out that since the club was located on a federal enclave, California's state ban didn't apply to them. Before a court could rule, however, the club's owners succumbed to the hecklers' veto and pulled foie gras from the menu after animal rights protesters picketed the restaurant. So we don't have a final ruling on this particular hack.

In all of these anecdotes, the real patch is for the legislature to return to the law and fix the loopholes. Congress needs to designate the Zone of Death within the US District Court for the District of Idaho. Congress needs to give Indian nations the jurisdiction and infrastructure to provide safety and recourse to Native women and girls within their territories. Although the 2013 Violence Against Women Act partially closed this vulnerability, a 2019 reauthorization was derailed by the gun lobby for reasons having nothing to do with this particular provision.

28

Hacking Bureaucracy

When you design a set of rules, it's common for those who must comply with them to optimize their actions to fit within the rules—even if what they end up doing goes against the expressly stated goal of those rules. Examples include an exterminator who releases an insect swarm to drum up business or a teacher who teaches strictly to the test to increase student test scores. Economists refer to this as Goodhart's law: when a measure becomes a target, it stops being a good measure. In this manner, bureaucratic rules are hacked all the time by people who don't want to abide by them.

Bureaucracies are hacked from below, by those who are constrained by them, in order to get things done in spite of them. In the 1980s, Administrator Daniel Goldin hacked the normally moribund NASA bureaucracy and found loopholes in the regulations that applied to NASA in order to launch more, and cheaper, space probes like the *Mars Pathfinder* mission. Newly formed public innovation agencies like 18F and the US Digital Service hacked a variety of slow and complicated government hiring, contracting, and procurement processes in order to implement technological upgrades at Internet speeds. Government technologists in the UK and Canada have done the same thing in their countries.

Bureaucracies are also hacked by those who oppose them. Work-to-rule is a labor tactic that is short of going on strike. It's malicious compliance, and basically means following the rules exactly, which—of course—quickly brings things to a standstill. Some of it is obvious: taking all allowed breaks, stopping work exactly at quitting time. A nurse might refuse to answer the telephone, because that's not part of a nurse's job description. The tactic has been tried-and-true for decades, and inspired the plot of Jaroslav Hašek's unfinished satirical novel, *The Fate of the Good Soldier Švejk during the World War,* in the 1920s.

Some are definitely hacks: insist on doing everything through formal channels, multiply paperwork in plausible ways, apply all regulations to the letter. The idea, of course, is to turn the system of rules against itself.

In the 1980s, Malaysia had a system of sharecropping rents, called *sewa padi*. Basically, rents were collected after the harvest and depended on the quality of the harvest. So, of course, farmers would secretly harvest at night before the official harvest began, remove some of the grain at the actual harvest if supervision was lax, or do a shoddy job at threshing so that rice on the stalks could be later gleaned and retained, and then spread spurious claims of crop damage to cover up their behavior. Much of this was just cheating, but some tactics could be considered hacking. The government closed this vulnerability by instituting a new system, called *sewa tunai*, with fixed rents paid before planting.

This particular style of hack is common. In 1902, the Hanoi government tried to eradicate the rat population by paying for rat tails. People quickly realized that the smart thing to do was to trap a rat, cut off its tail, and then release it back into the wild so it could breed more rats to catch. In 1989, Mexico City introduced a pollution-control scheme whereby cars with even and odd license plates could drive on alternate days. People responded by buying a second car, often an old and highly polluting one.

More recently, Uber drivers in Nairobi created a hack to cut the company out of its share of the ride fee. Passengers hail drivers through the Uber app, which also sets the ride charge. At pickup, the driver and passenger agree to "go *karura*," which means that the passenger cancels the ride and pays the driver the entire amount in cash.

The Boeing 737 MAX debacle provides a particularly high-profile example of the regulatory negligence that results from overly close relationships between regulators and regulated industries. In this case, FAA regulators applied insufficient scrutiny to the 737 MAX's Maneuvering Characteristics Augmentation System (MCAS), which the company had modified. As a result of this failure of oversight, two 737 MAX airplanes crashed in Indonesia (2018) and Ethiopia (2019), killing 346 people.

Let's be explicit about the hack here. Regulatory agencies are supposed to be the expert proxy for the average person's interest. I am not an expert in airplane safety (or automobile safety, food safety, drug efficacy, or how banks should organize their balance sheets to keep the economy stable). Government provides that expertise in the form of regulatory agencies, which make rules on my behalf to protect me. This oversight mechanism is what's being subverted.

Analysis of the failure pointed to regulatory failures. The FAA never independently scrutinized the MCAS; it relied on Boeing's own assessments of the system. The FAA didn't have the expertise, and its Aviation Safety Oversight Office delegated much of the work to Boeing. The engineers who worked on the planes were allowed to certify their own work. And there were instances where FAA managers took Boeing's side when its engineers wanted safety changes. The FAA even waived several regulations to permit Boeing an abbreviated certification process that allowed it to sell the planes more quickly. Taken together, the incident paints a picture of an FAA regulatory process hacked by the airline industry, which created an environment rife with regulatory capture, perverse incentives, ethical dilemmas, and dangerous safety lapses.

In 2021, the Justice Department reached a settlement with Boeing over criminal charges related to those crashes: $2.5 billion. That might seem like a lot of money, but the company got off easy. Only $243.3 million went to FAA fines—a low number, according to market analysts—with no binding criminal charges or admissions of guilt required from Boeing, despite credible reports of systemic negligence on safety issues.

The cozy relationship between Boeing and regulators shows the need to reconsider the proper compartmentalization of duties between regulators and regulated industries. Ultimately, the onus for ensuring responsible conduct and products in regulated industries lies with regulatory agencies, and relying too heavily on industry self-certification creates long-term conflicts of interest and atrophies government's capacity for

oversight. More importantly, there is a need to further compartmental-
ize the *individuals* who serve as regulators by requiring lengthy "cooling
off" periods before they take industry employment. Once regulators see
themselves not as public servants, but as future employees in the companies they regulate, there is a perverse incentive for self-serving regulation
that is not necessarily in the public interest.

29

Hacking and Power

Hacking is a way of exerting power. A hack affords more power to the hacker at the expense of someone else—and often everyone else—in a system. It's driven by a desire to forward the hacker's own agenda, rules be damned. (This is true even for the quintessential teenage computer hacker, trying to satisfy her own curiosity. Yes, curiosity is largely benign, but privacy has a purpose.)

The disempowered hack to subvert existing power structures. They do it to bypass bureaucracy or for personal gain. Much of the world has no say in the global systems that affect their lives; they often have no choice but to hack them—as people everywhere hack systems that are causing them problems. Such hacking can be a reasonable response to elite or state hacks like administrative burdens.

But while we might think of hacking as something an underdog does to gain an advantage over some traditional power, it is more often used by the powerful to further increase their own advantage.

As I discussed previously, the largest US banks deployed specialized legal teams to identify and exploit loopholes in the Dodd-Frank Act, and executed a three-year, multimillion-dollar lobbying campaign to get them normalized. Thanks to the size and wealth of the banks, they were able to find and exploit those vulnerabilities; thanks to the power that wealth purchased, those loopholes remain legal.

There are differences in how the disempowered and the powerful hack, though. Criminals, dissidents, unorganized citizens—all outliers— are more agile. They can hack new systems faster, and can magnify their collective power because of it. But when the established institutions finally figure out how to hack the systems that constrain them, they can do it more effectively. And because they have more raw power to magnify, they benefit more from those hacks. This is true for both governments and large corporations.

Just as there's a power dynamic to hacking, there's a power dynamic to getting hacks normalized. The powerful (by which I generally mean the wealthy) are better equipped to ensure that their hacks are long lasting, and that you no longer think of them as sneaky, but as part of the normal way of doing things. That's the way you probably think about hedge funds, venture capital funding, and all sorts of tax avoidance strategies.

The reasons are structural. One, tax loopholes often require the assistance of well-paid lawyers and accountants to exploit effectively. Two, wealthy people and organizations have more money to hide and are therefore more motivated to find and exploit loopholes. Three, tax loopholes often operate in a legal grey area; those who are less well-off don't have the financial resources to fight the tax authorities. And four, lax enforcement means that wealthy tax cheats are less likely to be held accountable.

This generalizes. Successful hacks often require specialized expertise, or the resources to hire people with that expertise, or the resources to shape a system to make it hackable by people with that expertise. On all three counts, wealthy and powerful people and organizations have the upper hand and are far better equipped to perform and entrench hacks at a large scale.

There's also a social power dynamic at play here. The less mainstream and more marginalized, as well as people of classes and races and genders and ethnicities with less power, are both less likely to hack and less likely to get away with it when they try. They might commit crimes, but that's not the same. Women are taught to follow the rules, while white men are taught to break them if they can. This is an important consideration to keep in mind when thinking about hacking and power.

The powerful are also better at stopping hacks by the less powerful. Union tactics like work-to-rule are much less prevalent today, primarily because the powerful have steadily eroded the power of unions. Management in general is increasingly hostile towards union organizing and has pushed for anti-union laws and court decisions. As a result, many employees can be fired without cause. Because work-to-rule methods require union membership or just-cause termination protections, these tactics have become less prevalent over time.

Georgetown law professor Julie Cohen wrote that "power interprets regulation as damage and routes around it." By this she meant that the powerful have the wherewithal to circumvent rules. Once the powerful understood that they had to hack systems—primarily the regulatory processes that prevented them from doing as they pleased—they developed competence to do just that. We have seen that with the banking industry, with financial markets, and with luxury real estate.

Think about the 2016 US Senate refusal to even consider Merrick Garland as a US Supreme Court nominee. This is a hack, a subversion of the Senate confirmation process. What's interesting to me is that we don't know if this hack has been normalized. We know that the Republicans weren't punished for their hypocrisy when Amy Coney Barrett was nominated four years later. We'll learn the new normal the next time a Supreme Court seat opens up when one party controls the presidency and the other party controls the Senate. Will a Republican-dominated Senate do the same thing again? Will Democrats take the opportunity when it arises? If the answer to either one of those questions is yes, then it's likely that Supreme Court justices will forevermore be appointed only when the same party controls both the presidency and the Senate—because the Senate has the power to hack the Supreme Court confirmation system in this particular way.

This is why stories of hacking by the less powerful—by the poor, by the disadvantaged, by political dissidents in authoritarian countries—are harder to come by. They're declared illegal, so the hacks become cheats. Tax loopholes used by the poor are closed by the IRS. Sit-in and slowdown strikes, once common in the 1930s, are no longer protected by US federal law. We don't even think of these as hacks. This doesn't mean that the less powerful aren't as good at hacking, only that they're less effective at normalizing their hacks.

When examining a system, pay attention to who it serves and who it doesn't. Those who are ill served in some way are those who will hack it. That's both the powerful and the disempowered. And while both will hack away at their constraints, the powerful are more likely to excel at it—and avoid any consequences.

30

Undermining Regulations

As far as users are concerned, Uber is a taxi service. It looks like a taxi service. It acts like a taxi service. But if you ask Uber—and any of its competitors—it is not a taxi or a livery company. It is an Internet services company that connects people who are driving cars with people who want to be driven somewhere. Those drivers are supposedly independent contractors, not employees; Uber claims to have no control over them. Uber schedules the drivers and handles their billing, but that's nothing more than a courtesy. To hear Uber tell it, the company really doesn't have anything to do with cars at all, at least as far as any government regulations are concerned.

Ride-sharing apps are a hack of the taxi industry, or—more generally—society's attempt to manage its short-term transport needs. Their business model allows them to ignore dozens of laws regulating licensed taxis and limos, including worker protection laws, safety laws, consumer protection laws, permit and fee requirements, and public-good laws. Taxi drivers are required to have background checks. Uber and Lyft drivers are not (although they now grudgingly do so). Taxi companies must pay minimum wage and are subject to citywide caps on the number of vehicles they operate at any given time. Not Uber and Lyft. The list goes on and on.

This all started around 2012, and Uber has since leveraged its competitive advantage over traditional taxis and limos to dominate the market. As of 2021, it operates in over 10,000 cities in 72 countries, completing 19 million trips each day. It has 3.5 million drivers and services 93 million monthly active customers. And it still can't turn a profit.

Municipalities around the world have tried to close the vulnerabilities Uber has used to hack the taxi market with mixed success. In 2017, the European Union's top court ruled that Uber is a transportation service, not the technology company it claimed to be in the hope of evading transportation regulations. In 2018, the UK Court of Appeal ruled that Uber drivers are employees, contrary to Uber's contention that they are independent contractors; the French *Cour de Cassation* made a similar decision in 2020. In the US, California passed legislation in 2019 requiring companies like Uber to treat their workers as employees; litigation ensued, and continues. Other cities and states are trying to do the same, although most states have preempted local rulings on this issue.

Airbnb is a similar hack of the hotel industry. Airbnb lodgings are not the same as hotels, although they serve the same purpose of short-term lodging. But Airbnb maintains that because it is not actually a hotel company, Airbnb accommodations should not be subject to any of the laws and regulations—or occupancy taxes—imposed on conventional hotels. Because Airbnb doesn't own any properties, it maintains that it is just a technology company. The people who own the accommodations are independent contractors, and are responsible for paying taxes and complying with local regulations. Of course, most fail to do so.

Municipalities either let Airbnb slide without paying its share of occupancy fees or try to fight back. Some sought to limit its expansion through regulation, and Airbnb sued them (while still operating), resulting in lengthy court battles. In addition, Airbnb often deployed property owners as grassroots lobbyists. Airbnb would send a message out to owners saying the city was threatening their ability to make money, even sending information about specific meetings the hosts should attend.

These companies are just two examples of the "gig economy," which is characterized by attempts to hack labor law, consumer protection law, and other laws and regulations. TaskRabbit, Handy, and DoorDash all employ the same hacks. Amazon does it too, running what's basically a private Uber-like system for its delivery vehicles. Because those drivers are independent contractors, the company can ignore all sorts of laws that conventional delivery drivers must follow.

That companies hack regulations is a surprise to no one. What's important here, especially when talking about ride sharing, short-term rental, and short-term loan companies, is that regulatory evasion is central to their business model. Many "disruptive" gig economy services would be completely unviable if forced to comply with the same regulations as the "normal" businesses they compete with. As a result, they—and their venture capital backers—are willing to spend unbelievable sums of money to combat these regulations. This has two implications. The first is obvious: their regulation-compliant competitors are put at a disadvantage. And two, the long-term profitability of these companies assumes either the continued avoidance of regulation (and, by extension, the exploitation of the poorly paid gig workers they employ) or the wholesale replacement of their gig workers by machines.

The response by these companies to state and local governments' attempts to patch the vulnerabilities upon which they rely demonstrates how far they will go. Following a 2018 California State Supreme Court ruling and the 2019 state law mentioned above, several gig economy companies banded together to push a referendum (Proposition 22) that would remove many employee protections from their gig workers: employee classification, wage floors, unemployment insurance, healthcare insurance, and so on. Led by Uber, Lyft, and DoorDash, gig economy companies spent $200 million to support this referendum and convince workers that it was in their interests to endorse it. The measure passed in 2020, rolling back California's efforts to protect workers. The battle is not over, and undoubtedly there will be developments after this book goes to press.

I could probably write an entire book about how companies and industries hack regulations that limit their profits, but I'll just offer a couple more examples. Payday loans are short-term loans targeted at poor people, generally made in small amounts at astronomically high interest rates. Four-fifths of borrowers renew or roll over the loans, trapping themselves in a vicious cycle of debt, interest, and fees, and resulting in an average interest rate of 400% per year, plus fees. States have worked to regulate the payday loan industry and reduce the interest rates it can charge, but the payday loan companies have consistently found ways around the rules. They branched out into issuing installment loans instead of loans where the full repayment is due the next payday—thus technically skirting the definition of payday loans. They also operate as loan brokers: middlemen that can charge unregulated fees. In Montana, payday loan providers moved to Indian reservations to avoid state and federal regulation. In 2020, the Trump administration's Consumer Financial Protection Bureau (CFPB) rolled back a whole list of new regulations that would have restricted the most predatory practices of this industry.

One final story: During the COVID-19 pandemic, the US and Canada closed their land border to nonessential travel. You could fly between the countries, but there were all sorts of restrictions on driving. This was a problem for the Canadian "snowbirds" who winter in the US, but there was a loophole: cargo was still permitted. Availing itself of the cargo loophole, a shipping company in Hamilton, Ontario, offered a service that would truck a customer's car into the US and to the Buffalo Airport, and a helicopter company would fly the customers there to meet it. Those who could afford the service were able to completely evade the land border closure.

Wherever there is a regulation, there are people who are constrained by it. Regulations generally serve a useful purpose, but they can also benefit incumbents, stifle innovation, and reflect an outdated mode of thought. New companies have an incentive to look for vulnerabilities in those regulations and construct hacks that meet the letter of a regulation while completely violating its spirit. And since all regulations will either be incomplete or inconsistent, they're all vulnerable to these hacks.

This all leads to an important question: How do we prevent hacks from deep-pocketed, technically sophisticated, politically savvy corporations whose very existence depends on hacking regulations? What does a clever, resilient solution look like in this instance?

One security measure is red-teaming new regulations before they're enacted. According to Jeremy Rosenblum, a Philadelphia attorney who advises payday lenders, the industry needs to constantly work to develop new financial products in advance of regulatory interference: "If you're serving this market, you have to be considering alternative strategies if the CFPB does come up with regulations." This is the same philosophy that every company discussed in this part follows. To counter that, regulators need to be proactive in their regulatory efforts and consider possible vulnerabilities and industry responses in advance. By doing so, regulators can better anticipate and prevent socially deleterious industry action and financial innovation.

Another is iteration and agility. While it's nice to hope—or even believe—that effective regulations are put in place in advance to prevent these kinds of hacks, regulators need to be prepared for unexpected and socially deleterious innovation. To combat this, they need to monitor regulated parties and be ready to act quickly to police new products that emerge post-regulation, knowing that they won't necessarily get it right the first time around—and patch all vulnerabilities as soon as they emerge.

31

Jurisdictional Interactions

The Double Irish with a Dutch Sandwich tax loophole that companies like Cisco, Pfizer, Merck, Coca-Cola, and Facebook used to avoid paying US taxes stemmed from the limitation of laws by national borders. By making clever use of foreign subsidiary companies and transferring both rights and incomes between them, large US corporations are able to avoid paying taxes on much of their global income. (Note that individual US citizens are taxed on their entire income, regardless of the country in which it was earned, so this trick only works for corporations.)

This is just one of many hacks involving tax havens around the world. Global tax avoidance costs the US just under $200 billion a year, 1.1% of GDP. Total cost to global tax revenue is between $500 and $600 billion, depending on the estimate. What's interesting about these hacks is that they leverage the interactions amongst a series of vulnerabilities in the laws of multiple countries.

The solution is both simplicity and transparency. In the US, twenty-eight states and the District of Columbia have adopted Combined Reporting Systems for State Corporate Income Tax, which helps to prevent domestic multi-jurisdictional profit shifting. Under combined reporting systems, companies and their subsidiaries must report their total profits (in this case, their total "domestic" profits) and the percentage of their overall business that takes place within a given jurisdiction (that is, a state). The jurisdiction is then entitled to tax a share of that profit proportionate to the percentage of a company's business that takes place in it, thus preventing companies from dodging their tax obligations through jurisdictional interactions and profit shifting. This approach has already helped states recover billions of dollars in tax revenue that had previously been hidden through domestic tax havens.

However, this innovation hasn't resolved the broader issue of multinational profit shifting and tax avoidance. First, almost all US states that use a combined reporting system for taxation (Montana being a notable exception) do not require companies to disclose their offshore profits, allowing companies to avoid paying taxes on domestically earned profits that they have shifted abroad. Second, as I noted previously, US corporate income taxes are not assessed on profits earned abroad, which facilitates tax avoidance and overseas profit shifting at the federal level.

The Tax Cuts and Jobs Act of 2017 made a half-hearted attempt to address this issue through the Global Intangible Low Tax Income provision, which required companies to pay a nominal tax (10.5%) on untaxed profits in an overseas tax haven, but it has largely failed to stem international profit shifting.

The best idea I've seen for solving this problem again combines simplicity and transparency. It's called Mandatory Worldwide Combined Reporting (MWCR), a remarkably simple method for resolving notoriously complex jurisdictional taxation issues. Similar to a combined reporting system, this would require that a company and its subsidiaries report their total worldwide profits, as well as the percentage of their overall business (typically expressed through revenue) that comes from a given jurisdiction. The jurisdiction would then be entitled to tax a share of that profit proportionate to the percentage of a company's business that takes place in it.

At this book's time of writing, the Biden administration and the Organization for Economic Co-operation and Development (OECD; a club of rich and developed nations) were both working to make something like MWCR a reality. In 2021, the OECD announced that 130 countries and jurisdictions had agreed to each tax the largest multinational corporations at a minimum rate of 15% of profits earned from their respective territories, as opposed to today's system, where companies are only taxed by their "home country." Biden's proposal is similar, but with key differences, such as requiring compliance by a wider range of for-profit entities. Time will tell how these proposals evolve and how corporations will try to hack them, just as they have for previous fixes.

Countries sometimes invite this kind of jurisdictional arbitrage by deliberately subverting their own laws to attract a global clientele. For example, a system of ship registration called "flags of convenience" has made it easy for shipowners to avoid rules about ship maintenance, ignore labor laws, and evade prosecution for environmental damage like oil spills. Historically, ships would fly the flag of their own country, giving them government protection but also subjecting them to its laws. In the early twentieth century, Panama allowed anyone to fly its flag for a fee. This was quickly popularized by other countries like Liberia and Singapore, and became an opportunity for smaller countries with few natural resources, like the Republic of Vanuatu. Shipowners loved this hack, because those countries had few and lax laws. Between the 1950s and 2010s, these "open registries" ballooned from 4% to 60% of ships. The 1994 United Nations Convention on the Law of the Sea specifies that there should be a "genuine link" between the ship and its flag; however, twenty-five years later the interpretation of that phrase is still a subject of debate.

The same sort of reasoning is why corporations like to incorporate in Delaware. The state first began to adapt its tax laws in the late nineteenth century, making changes to attract businesses from larger, more prosperous states like New York. Delaware became an "onshore" tax haven for US companies, not only because of the ease of doing business, but also because of the "Delaware Loophole": the state collects zero tax on income relating to intangible assets held by a Delaware holding company. This allows companies to shift royalties and similar revenues from where they actually do business to holding companies in Delaware, where they are not taxed. But this means a loss of millions of dollars for states in which corporations are actually operating. This loophole costs the other forty-nine states approximately $1 billion a year.

The hack here isn't that companies register their ships in Panama or incorporate in Delaware. The hack lies in those jurisdictions' deliberate exploitation of the rules governing jurisdiction in order to make their own more attractive. By pitting itself against other states, Delaware subverts the intent of federal interstate commerce rules and state tax authorities. Similarly, flags of convenience subvert the intent of the UN Convention on the Law of the Sea.

These are all examples of the hacks made possible by an organization that is larger than the body that is regulating it. Corporations generally do business both in and out of Delaware. Maritime shipping companies are global—much larger than Panama. We're seeing this now with the big tech companies. No public institutions possess a regulatory footprint that can match them. Companies like Facebook are global, yet regulations affecting them are national. Regulatory structures suitable for the information age just don't exist yet, and that enables companies to profit from jurisdictional arbitrage.

32

Administrative Burdens

Sometimes a hack is the product of necessity, born of adversity and the need to adapt. If one tactic doesn't work, try another. That's the story of administrative burdens. They're a way of hacking policy. In particular, of hacking social benefits systems like unemployment insurance or Medicaid, which—in America—are often politically divisive. Opponents of these policies will first try to simply ban them outright. But sometimes that's not possible: the votes simply aren't there, or there's a pesky constitutional provision in your way.

That's when people get creative. If you're in charge of implementation, you can make the law very, very difficult to follow. In other words, you can drown the policy, and those trying to access it, in bureaucratic hurdles. The tactics vary—from long waiting times and excessive paperwork, to cumbersome filing systems and repeated in-person interviews, to lousy websites—but the goal remains the same: to impose a burden so onerous that people otherwise eligible for the benefit, many of whom are already weighed down by poverty, poor health, limited education, and unstable housing, simply cannot overcome. Public-policy scholars Pamela Herd and Donald Moynihan have named this phenomenon "administrative burdens," and it's a policy hack.

Florida's unemployment insurance scheme provides a good example. According to one advisor to Governor DeSantis, its system was purposefully designed "to make it harder to get and keep benefits." The entire application process was moved online to a system that barely functions. A 2019 audit noted that the system "frequently gave incorrect error messages" and would often entirely prevent the submission of applications. The form itself is spread across multiple pages, so that after entering some details, such as name and date of birth, you need to proceed to the next page. But often this causes the website to crash, sending the applicant back to square one. On top of this, the website is only accessible at specific hours of the day, and requires applicants to revisit the site every two weeks to "verify their claims."

This system caused particular pain for 4.5 million COVID-19–unemployed Floridians. In 2020, many people spent hours or even days trying to submit their claims. According to the website, 2.4 million people were ultimately deemed ineligible by the opaque state system, which had the follow-on effect of restricting their eligibility for the CARES Act Federal Pandemic Unemployment Compensation.

Some administrative burden stems from legitimate differences in how to implement a policy. When you design any system that awards a benefit, you have to worry about two types of error. The first is that someone deserving will not receive the benefit. The second is that someone undeserving will receive it. Minimizing one necessarily results in increasing the other. If you make it easy for people to apply for and obtain benefits, you'll also inevitably make it easier for a share of those who do not deserve them to slip through. And if you increase the vetting process to prevent the undeserving from applying for and receiving the benefit, you'll also inevitably deny some of the deserving. Depending on your politics, you'll prefer one outcome over the other.

Deliberate creation of administrative burden takes this to an extreme. Instead of weeding out the unqualified, the burden associated with receiving the benefit is increased to the point where many people who should qualify simply give up. It's passive-aggressive benefit denial.

We could see this tactic used in the US around abortion, during the fifty years it was constitutionally legal. When states were unable to pass laws banning abortion outright, advocates shifted to using administrative burden to make abortion significantly more difficult to access, even

as abortion remained technically legal. Tactics included requiring waiting periods, mandatory counseling, multiple clinic visits, parental con-
sent, and ultrasounds. The biggest offender was Louisiana, which enacted
eighty-nine abortion regulations since 1973, including onerous licensing
requirements for clinics, and rules that can force their immediate closure
for even the most minor paperwork violations. When the US Supreme
Court ruled in 1992 that states may not "place a substantial obstacle in
the path of a woman seeking an abortion," the battles over the subsequent
thirty years shifted to defining what is or is not regarded as substantial.

There are many other examples. The Women, Infants, and Children
(WIC) program is a government nutrition program that places lengthy,
detailed, and almost comically complicated restrictions on exactly what
foods can be purchased. For example, you're not allowed to mix brands
of baby food. The administrative burdens are effective; less than half of
families who are eligible for WIC benefits receive them. The processes
for applying for and receiving food stamps and Medicaid can be similarly
hacked. Arkansas, for example, succeeded in kicking many people off its
Medicaid rolls when it enacted a work requirement—not because those
people didn't meet the work requirement, but because they couldn't deal
with the associated paperwork.

All of these are examples of the rich and powerful hacking systems
to the detriment of the average citizen. And the effects disproportionately
hurt those who lack the skills, resources, and time to overcome them.

Outside of judicial intervention, it's difficult to find a satisfactory
solution because political authorities are the ones creating these administrative burdens. Nonetheless, one partial solution could be the use of
independent benchmarks or system audits by outside organizations to
determine the scale and impact of administrative burden. While this
would not directly address the problems created by administrative burden, by quantifying its impact on affected groups (particularly legally
protected classes) with high-quality data collection, analysis, and visual-
ization, independent audits may be able to convince legislators to act or
create grassroots pressure for action. Other than that: I don't know what
to do.

33

Hacking Common Law

The complex systems we're discussing here tend to be overspecified or underspecified—they're what are known as "wicked problems." What this means is they are too complex for traditional analysis techniques. The only solutions tend to be iterative. But an iterative solution can be hacked, and can use hacks to improve itself.

Hacks involve contradicting a system's rules. But those rules are often subject to interpretation, and those interpretations can change. To explore this, let's look at a legal system that's designed to evolve in just this way: common law. Common law is the best example—and model for the future—we have of a large system that is able to adapt through iterative hacking. It's built into the system by design. And it's effective.

In 1762, author and schoolmaster John Entick was suspected of writing libelous pamphlets against the English government. Under the direction of the secretary of state, the king's chief messenger and others broke into Entick's home, confiscating hundreds of charts and pamphlets as evidence. In an unprecedented move, Entick sued the messengers for trespassing on his land, despite their law enforcement status.

This doesn't seem like a hack now, but in 1765 it was an unintended and unanticipated use of trespass law. Before this case, trespass law was only used to prevent citizens from invading each other's property—it did not constrain the government. The police had a presumptive right to search an individual's property within their law enforcement purview. Entick maintained that his individual right to be secure on his property superseded that. He subverted the existing norms of how the law applied. It was a progressive—even radical—interpretation of that law.

The English courts decided that Entick's interpretation of the law was valid and superior. "By the laws of England, every invasion of private property, be it ever so minute, is a trespass." The ruling in Entick's case extended the concept of liability for trespass to the secretary of state and his deputies. It would become part of English common law from that date forward. Entick hacked trespass law. He advanced an interpretation that logically followed from the words of the law but was unintended and unanticipated. The court allowed the hack and enshrined it in law. *Entick* became a landmark case in establishing the civil liberties of individuals and limiting the scope of state power. In the United States, the ideals of the *Entick* ruling are enshrined in the Fourth Amendment.

Sometimes a hack is beneficial. It might violate the intent of an existing rule or norm. But it doesn't necessarily violate the greater social contract. In the above example, the court decided that the social contract was enhanced by enabling citizens to be secure on their own property, and by not enabling the privacy of their homes to be violated by anyone for any reason. While a hack benefits the hacker at the expense of another part of the system, sometimes that expense is minimal. If a hack falls within the spirit of the social contract, then it becomes an innovation that the system would benefit from absorbing.

In these cases, no singular governing body makes that decision— just many courts trying to reconcile many interpretations of many precedents to apply to new hacks as they emerge. The rules are a complicated, incomplete, and sometimes contradictory mess. They're not designed for a purpose in the same way that ordinary legislation is. They're iterative, and they evolve. They're added to by many different people, each with their own goals for the overall system. In systems governed by multitudes, we need a different sort of mechanism for adjudicating challenges and subversions of the status quo. This is basically how common law works.

A quick definition: common law is law derived from judicial decisions in the form of legal precedents. It's different from statutory law, which is passed by legislatures, and regulatory law, which is established by government agencies. Common law is more flexible than statutory law. It allows for consistency across time, but can also evolve as judges reapply, analogize, and transform past precedents to fit new circumstances. That evolution is basically a series of adjudicated hacks that are either declared illegal or that become future precedent.

Take patent law. It's based on statutory law, but the details are largely provided by judge-made rules. And it's complicated. Patents can be worth billions, and lawsuits are common. Because there's so much money at stake, hacks of the system abound. I'll just give one example: patent injunctions. The idea with patent injunctions is that someone whose patent is being infringed on can obtain a quick injunction preventing that infringement until the court issues a final ruling. Until 2006, they were easy to get. As a result, they became a go-to anticompetition hack for large companies, particularly tech companies. Patent injunctions were used to compel smaller competitors to either stop selling their products or to pay exorbitant fees to the patent holder (a practice that many likened to extortion).

The patent injunction hack was adjudicated when MercExchange, a technology and online auction company, sued eBay, claiming that eBay was violating MercExchange patents in its online auction system. The US Supreme Court took up the case in 2006, rewriting the rules on patent injunction, patching the vulnerability by ordering courts to apply a more rigorous, four-factor check when deciding when an injunction is merited.

Laws are never complete. Grey areas, blind spots, or null spaces become evident with time and social change. Just as with legislation, loopholes, omissions, or mistakes can occur in either statutory law or common law. Someone twists the existing set of laws to fit into those spaces, in ways that were unintended and unanticipated by the law's creators, in order to gain some advantage. Then, someone else—generally someone who is put at a corresponding disadvantage because of the hack—challenges the hack in court. A judge is called upon to act as a neutral arbiter and to decide whether the hack is legitimate or illegitimate. If it is illegitimate, it's declared illegal—and that effectively patches the system. If it's legitimate, it becomes part of common law and is henceforth legal. Common law is inherently a hack of the adjudication system. And its decisions, relying on creative applications and reinterpretations of broad precedents and principles, are themselves a kind of social hack to resolve the otherwise unresolvable.

Hacking is how law adapts to new circumstances, new developments, and new technologies. No one in the legal profession calls it hacking, but that's basically what it is. Common law is nothing but a series of hacks and adjudications. It's the best system we have of harnessing the power of hacking to continually improve the law. Hacking is how the law adapts over time.

Here's another example. During the Middle Ages, when landowners in England left to fight in the Crusades, often a landowner would transfer the title of his real property to someone he trusted. The idea was that while he was away, his deputy could care for his property and ensure that any continuing obligations, like feudal payments, were met. It didn't always end well. Sometimes when the crusader returned, his former friend would refuse to transfer the title back to him. This was a hack of the law: selling the property was not the crusader's intent.

To resolve the matter, aggrieved crusaders petitioned the lord chancellor and his Court of Chancery. His solution—which patched the vulnerability—was to create a new right. In his conception, there could be two owners of a given property: the *legal* owner—the person on the title—and the *equitable* owner—the person who, in all fairness (that is, equity), owned the land. The equitable owner enjoyed the benefits of the property, like using the land. In this case, the legal owner was the crusader and the equitable owner was the caretaker. It was an easy patch: the incentives of the key stakeholders were aligned. Nobility wanted to preserve their property rights, and returning crusaders were a powerful and sympathetic petitioning group.

Today, this same division of rights persists in many common law countries. In the US, a division still exists between matters of law and matters of equity. This division allows for trusts as a financial structure. Basically, someone else owns the trust (and the assets it holds), while you, the "real" owner and beneficiary, are entitled to the fruits of those assets (for example, monetary distributions).

34

Hacking as Evolution

Orthodox Jews are masters at hacking their religious rules. Work is prohibited on Shabbat, the Jewish Sabbath that runs from Friday evening to Saturday evening. Work includes lighting a fire, which has been extended to include creating a light of any kind, or doing anything that requires electricity. Growing up, my cousins had a timer attached to the television's power cord. The timer would turn the television on and off automatically—no human action required—so the only debate was what single channel to set the TV to before sundown on Friday. Carrying things in public is prohibited, which means you can't carry a house key with you when you go out. But if that key is integrated into a wearable piece of jewelry, then you can take it with you.

Since carrying things in your own home is permitted, some communities will run an unbroken piece of wire called an *eruv* around an entire neighborhood, which hacks ancient definitions of semiprivate common areas and redefines "home" to include everything inside that wire boundary line.

Non-Jews are not subject to the same rules. In my synagogue growing up, a Gentile custodian was deliberately hired so he could do things on Shabbat that the Jews could not. It's forbidden to ask for help directly, though. While you can't ask "Can you turn up the thermostat?" you can

say "It's a little cold in here." Similarly, an observant Jew can't walk into
an elevator and ask "Can you push five for me?" but he can wonder aloud,
"Is five pushed?" Many elevators in the religious parts of Israel just automatically stop on every floor on Shabbat.

When I was a kid, these sorts of ways of precisely following the letter of the rules to avoid their spirit felt contrived. But they're really the
method by which the 2,000-year-old Jewish law has adapted over the
centuries to modern times. It's hacking and—more importantly—the
integration of those hacks into our ever-evolving society.

Hacking is about finding novel failure modes that have not yet been
exploited. When they actually work, they have unexpected outcomes.

This is important. Hacking isn't just malicious manipulation inflicted
upon a system. A successful hack changes the hacked system, even more
so as it is repeatedly used and becomes popular. It changes how the system
works, either because the system gets patched to prevent it or expands
to encompass it. Hacking is a process by which those who use a system
change it for the better, in response to new technology, new ideas, and
new ways of looking at the world. This is hacking as evolution. We saw
that with modern banking, high-frequency trading, luxury real estate,
and—probably—much of what the gig economy companies are doing.
And it continues. Today, there's a Bluetooth device that makes a smartphone usable on Shabbat. The hack is that the buttons constantly have a
small current running through them, so pressing them does not close a
circuit—which makes it permissible under Jewish law.

Harnessed well, hacking is a way of accelerating system evolution by
incorporating an adversary in the process. Harnessed for ill, hacking can
be a way of accelerating system destruction by exposing and exploiting
its flaws for selfish gain in a way that tears it apart.

Innovation is essential if systems are to survive. An ossified system
can't respond to hacks, and therefore has trouble evolving. Political scientist Francis Fukuyama makes this argument when he theorizes that both
states and institutions are developed to respond to particular environmental conditions, and fail or are conquered by others because they can't
evolve when the environment changes. (He used the Ottoman Empire as
an example.) Contemporary political science research suggests that when

conservative groups representing the rich and powerful refuse to allow their societies to evolve, they can break their political systems as a whole.

This disruptive power can also be harnessed by those at the bottom of our power structure and serve as an engine for social change. It's how revolutions happen. Hacking is one of the weapons of the weak, and an important one at that.

Here's one example: people are hacking the notion of corporate personhood in attempts to win rights for nature, or great apes, or rivers. The very concept of corporate personhood is a hack of the Fourteenth Amendment, which lays out the rules of citizenship and the rights of citizens.

In Darwinian evolution, Mother Nature decides which hacks stay and which hacks go. She can be cold and brutal, but she doesn't play favorites. In social system evolution, the powerful are the favorites, and often get to decide which hacks stay and go. If this isn't fixed, then allowing hacks to drive evolution of systems will perpetuate status quo injustices. The future of social hacking has to combine the push to evolve with a focus on the greater good—or we'll see our social systems begin to break down. And then it's hacking as revolution.

Maybe a better metaphor for hacking is that of an invasive species. Different species evolve in specific environments, balanced with respect to predators, prey, environment, and other factors. When a species is transported from one environment to another, it can often take advantage of differences in novel and surprising ways. Maybe the predator that used to keep it in check is not in the new environment, and nothing else takes its place (such as the Burmese python in Florida). Or maybe an environmental factor that limited its growth is not there (such as cold weather for kudzu, the Scourge of the South). Or maybe a new food source is unnaturally—for that species—abundant (as is the case for the ravenous Asian carp). The result is that the invasive species is able to multiply at a heretofore unseen rate. Hacks are like that. They're discontinuous jumps in capability, introduced into an ecosystem that isn't prepared for it. The invasive species could die out, if the ecosystem happens to deploy the right defenses. But it could also overwhelm the system. The catastrophic end-state is called "ecosystem collapse," when a hack is so devastating that it destroys the entire ecosystem.

PART 5

HACKING
POLITICAL SYSTEMS

35

Hidden Provisions in Legislation

When the Russian SVR hacked into the SolarWinds company and slipped a backdoor into an Orion software update, 17,000 or so Orion users installed that corrupted update and inadvertently gave the SVR access to their networks. That's a lot of vulnerable networks, and it's inconceivable that the SVR would try to penetrate them all. Instead, it chose carefully from its cornucopia of vulnerable victims to find the most valuable prospects.

This is known as a "supply chain attack," because the SVR didn't attack any of those networks directly. Instead, it attacked a software system that all of those networks used. Supply chain attacks are a clever way to attack systems, because they can affect thousands at once. Other examples of this kind of attack include hacking the Google Play store to include a fake app, or intercepting network equipment in the mail to install eavesdropping capabilities (the NSA has done that one).

We can think of hacking the legislative process in the same way. In the previous chapters, we've considered how hackers find and exploit vulnerabilities in laws after they're passed. Hackers can also target the legislative process itself. And like the hacked update to the Orion network management software, hackers can deliberately insert vulnerabilities into pending legislation and take advantage of them if the legislation is passed into law.

In a way, we're taking the hacks we've been discussing and moving them up a level. Instead of finding vulnerabilities in laws and regulations, these hacks are against the very process of creating those laws and regulations. Powerful hackers can do this.

This isn't just hacking a system, it's hacking the means to patch the system.

Loopholes are common in law, but most of them don't qualify as hacks. They're deliberate exceptions to a more general rule, created to support a particular policy goal, to appease particular constituents, or as a compromise to appease other legislators. Examples include a 2004 law, lobbied for by Starbucks, that counts roasting coffee beans as domestic manufacturing or, on a more general level, antitrust exemptions for "natural monopolies" for industries that require coordination between different companies, like sports leagues. These are not unintended and unanticipated. They're not based on ways to outsmart the system of creating, debating, and passing legislation. As such, they are not hacks.

This doesn't mean that the legislative process that creates these loopholes isn't hacked all the time. All it takes is for someone to add a strategically worded sentence to a bill. That sentence might refer to several other laws, and the interplay of those laws might result in a specific outcome, unknown to and unanticipated by everyone else.

An entire industry of lobbyists is dedicated to engineering such unanticipated outcomes on behalf of their moneyed sponsors. In 2017, during the drafting process for the Tax Cuts and Jobs Act, over half of the lobbyists in Washington, DC, disclosed that they worked solely on tax issues. That was over 6,000 lobbyists, more than 11 for every member of Congress.

For example, a 2013 debt deal passed by Congress included the following sentence: "SEC. 145. Subsection (b) of section 163 of Public 5 Law 111-242, as amended, is further amended by striking "2013–2014" and inserting "2015–2016." That seemingly innocuous provision, inserted by Senator Tom Harkin, functioned as a hidden gift for Teach For America. Basically, that sentence extended by two years another piece of legislation that benefited students still in teacher training programs, including Teach For America recruits.

In 2020, Congress passed the $2 trillion CARES Act, a COVID-19 stimulus bill. On page 203 of the 880-page bill, there was a change in how real estate investors could offset their losses. This tax break profited real estate moguls, such as then president Donald Trump, $17 billion annually—$17 billion in potential tax revenue. It didn't matter that the provision had nothing to do with COVID-19, or that the retroactive tax break covered a period long before COVID-19 arrived. Speed and stealth aided in sneaking this passage through. The text of that bill was finalized less than an hour before the vote, and Republican staffers added the provision at the last second to the final text of the bill.

The vulnerability lies in the fact that bills are so long and so complicated, and contain so many provisions without clear and obvious effects. The exploit lies in the act of slipping a provision into the bill in such a way that legislators don't notice. We like to think that this sort of chicanery requires the complicity of a member of Congress who might or might not anticipate the effects of his or her contribution to the bill, but it's also possible for a staffer to do it without anyone else realizing it—or even for a lobbyist to craft wording that ends up being used.

This kind of thing is so common it hardly qualifies as a hack anymore. Over the past several decades, power has been increasingly centralized in the hands of political party leaders in each chamber and away from legislative committees, which has facilitated this cloistered and opaque legislative process. This state of affairs, combined with Congress passing a smaller number of larger bills when compared with past congressional sessions, provides ample opportunity for the enactment of hidden provisions that benefit favored individuals and industries. It was even the plot of a *Simpsons* episode, where Krusty the Clown gets elected to Congress and sneaks a change to the air traffic control law into a bill giving flags to orphans.

Fixing all of this isn't easy. Even though legal language is analogous to computer code, the processes by which the two are created and used are very different. Computer code is written by a group of people following an overall plan, generally under the direction of a single company or individual. These programmers know what their code is supposed to do, when it doesn't do that, and when it can't do that. And they alone have the authority to fix bugs in their code.

Law isn't like that. It's decentralized at every level. In a democracy, law is written by many different competitors. They have different goals and different opinions about what the law is supposed to do. A bug to one is a feature to another, even if everyone knew exactly what they were voting for throughout the entire process.

Hidden provisions, and the vulnerabilities that they represent, would be less of an issue if House and Senate rules mandated a certain amount of review time for bills once the text was finalized and published, perhaps proportionate to the length of the bill. Hidden provisions are no longer "hidden" if they're discovered and scrutinized by a robust media, and then publicized in enough time to spur change or extract a political cost. By providing representatives with some reasonable minimum amount of time to review and demand amendments to high-profile bills, there's at least some chance to uncover hidden provisions that wouldn't pass muster otherwise.

As part of its ninety-seven recommendations for streamlining the US House, the 2019 Select Committee on the Modernization of Congress proposed that it "finalize a new system that allows the American people to easily track how amendments change legislation and the impact of proposed legislation to current law." Basically, it's proposing a Track Changes system for legislation, one that expands upon an earlier "Comparative Print Project."

The goal would be to make it easier to see and understand legislative changes, which could make it easier to detect hidden provisions. This certainly won't fix the problem, especially because the committee is only proposing expansion of access to "all House offices," but it would be a step in the right direction. If made available to the public and combined with measures that ensured adequate legislative review time, this could be even more potent.

Sufficient time isn't enough; we need to also offer incentives for people to discover hidden provisions. Taking a page from software vulnerabilities, we could all benefit from the legislative equivalent of a bug bounty system, whereby citizens could be rewarded for discovering vulnerabilities in pending legislation. The most obvious place for this kind of thing would be laws with tax implications; the bounty could be a very small percentage of the expected tax revenue.

Alternatively, bills could benefit from red-teaming exercises, in which specialized teams (playing the role of private companies or wealthy elites) attempt to "hack" the pending legislation and discover previously unknown vulnerabilities.

While both of these exercises could be valuable, they run into a core issue with modern legislation: namely, that bills are often put together in secret by a relatively small number of legislators and lobbyists, and many of the loopholes are intentionally crafted. Imagine that a red team finds a vulnerability in a tax bill. Is that a bug or is it a feature? Who gets to decide? And on what basis? Further, many bills are quickly passed by Congress once unveiled, making it impossible for anyone to read and understand every line; red-teaming would only be feasible if sufficient time were afforded to engage in it and act upon the findings.

For example, the 2017 Tax Cuts and Jobs Act was voted on only hours after the final language was made available to legislators. This was deliberate; the authors didn't want professional staff to have adequate time to review the bill with any thoroughness. Similarly, the CARES Act was released at 2:00 pm on December 21, 2020. Even though the bill ran 5,593 pages, it was passed in the House around 9:00 pm and in the Senate by midnight. The measure contained $110 billion in lightly scrutinized "tax extenders," and a permanent cut in excise taxes for "producers of beer, wine, and distilled spirits." Many lawmakers were unaware of the many tax loopholes it contained.

We may have to wait for AIs, which operate at computer speed, to read, understand, and identify hacks before the laws are enacted. That would certainly help solve the problem—although it would equally certainly create new ones.

36

Must-Pass Legislation

Some bills are simply more important than others. Appropriation bills or bills that respond to external forces, like natural disasters, pandemics, or security threats, are often considered must-pass legislation. These bills provide an opportunity for legislators to attach policy changes, known as riders, that would never float on their own. Maybe they are unpopular, against the public interest, skewed to benefit special interests, or are the result of political wheeling and dealing.

Placing non-germane riders on these must-pass pieces of legislation enables lawmakers to avoid the scrutiny or backlash that would accompany a vote for a politically difficult provision, credibly claiming that they were merely voting for the measure as a whole. This now-common hack subverts the way legislation is supposed to work: a discrete proposal is made for a new law, and then that proposal is voted on.

Three examples:

- Between 1982 and 1984, a series of riders—called the Boland amendment—were added to several must-pass appropriations bills; the amendment limited US assistance to the Contras in Nicaragua.
- In 2016, an agriculture and food spending bill included a rider that prohibited the FDA from regulating "large and premium cigars."
- In 2021, lawmakers attached three intellectual property copyright

bills to the completely unrelated Consolidated Appropriations Act. These measures had languished on their own in the face of widespread protests from tech enthusiasts and technology companies but were enacted when attached to a far larger, more complex, must-pass bill.

This sort of hack exploits the fact that the president can't veto individual line items in a bill. He eithers vetoes the entire bill or accepts it in full, with any and all riders included. It also exploits the congressional committee process. The full legislature cannot vote on a bill unless it's been approved by the relevant committees. This means committee members can simply tack riders onto legislation, either openly or in secret.

Attempts to curtail the practice have largely been ineffective. Congress attempted to give President Clinton a line-item veto power in 1996, but it was declared unconstitutional in 1998. It was utilized eighty-two times in its one-year run, and the suit against it was brought, in part, by a group of potato growers who objected to Clinton vetoing a rider that benefited them.

In the case of modular computer code, each independent segment performs a single function, a structure that can make programs more resilient, maintainable, and diagnosable. Legislation that similarly deals with fewer discrete issues would be less susceptible to the sort of hacking I've just described. This is the logic behind single-subject laws and constitutional provisions, which mandate that laws must deal with only one primary issue. Such a bill, called the One Subject at a Time Act in 2021, has been regularly proposed in Congress but never passed into law.

At the state level, efforts to limit non-germane riders have been somewhat more effective. Forty-three state constitutions require each individual piece of legislation to be limited to a single subject. Minnesota's constitution states: "Laws to embrace only one subject. No law shall embrace more than one subject, which shall be expressed in its title." However, even these restrictions can prove remarkably hackable. As Columbia University law professor Richard Briffault wrote, "Whether a measure consists of one subject or many will frequently be 'in the eye of the beholder.'" On the one hand, as the Michigan Supreme Court explained, "There is virtually no statute that could not be subdivided and enacted as several bills." On the other hand, as an older Pennsylvania Supreme Court case put it, "No two subjects are so wide apart that they may not be brought into a common focus, if the point of view be carried back far enough."

Another defense is system resilience. Must-pass legislation is particularly vulnerable to riders because of the extreme negative consequences associated with non-passage of the parent legislation. However, some of these consequences, such as a government shutdown from non-passage of appropriations bills, are totally artificial and could be ameliorated with good policy. For instance, several organizations have proposed that Congress increase the resilience of government operations by creating a process for automatic continuing resolutions. Under an automatic continuing resolution, government funding would continue at comparable levels if Congress failed to pass a regular appropriations bill. By reducing the consequences of delayed action on must-pass legislation, this reform would make it easier for rider opponents to vote down the budget bill until the rider is removed.

37

Delegating and Delaying Legislation

In the years after the Cold War ended, Congress was faced with the unwelcome prospect of closing military bases around the country—not an easy task. Those bases represented hundreds, even thousands of jobs, and no legislator would ever agree to closing a base in their home district. Instead of making the hard decisions, Congress came up with a hack to depoliticize the process. It delegated its lawmaking power to a separate, external body by establishing a Base Realignment and Closure Commission. That commission was empowered to decide which bases to close or scale back, and its recommendations would automatically take effect unless Congress did something to overrule it. It worked; there have been five such commissions since 1988, resulting in the closure of more than 350 military installations.

This hack enables Congress to resolve difficult or politically controversial issues without actually having to decide anything itself. It reduces the extent to which partisanship skews decisions regarding base closures. It also allows Congress to circumvent burdensome rules and processes that might otherwise slow the decision down.

It's not used often. In 2010, Congress formed the Independent Payment Advisory Board (IPAB), which was supposed to cut Medicare spending. Normally, changes in Medicare require an act of Congress to take effect. Congress authorized this board to make changes that could only be overruled by a congressional supermajority. Again, avoiding the responsibility to craft and pass an actual Medicare cost-cutting vote was the intent. Unlike the base-closing commission, this one never completed its work. Thanks to medical service providers' opposition to the law, and the smearing of IPAB by politicians such as former vice presidential candidate Sarah Palin, Congress never appointed any members, instead repealing IPAB in 2018 after five unstaffed years.

A similar hack is a "title-only bill," which is basically an empty shell. It has no substantive content, but lawmakers in the state of Washington introduce a bunch of them each session. They're placeholders, just in case lawmakers want to circumvent legislative rules and deadlines later in the year. In the final days of the 2019 legislative session, Democrats used a title-only bill to pass a bank tax with minimal public oversight and debate.

More generally, this hack is part of a larger class of legislative delegations to the executive branch. For many, the "administrative state" and the extensive rule-making authority granted to the executive branch by the legislative branch represent an unbalanced hack of the legislative system. And this is a hack that's used regularly. In the US, between 3,000 and 4,000 new administrative rules are finalized each year, dwarfing congressional output. And while much of this is simply the effect of an increasingly dysfunctional Congress ceding power to relatively efficient federal agencies, some of it is a result of members of Congress not wanting to be on the record as supporting or opposing various laws.

Fixes aren't apparent or easy. If the legislative branch feels, at any time, that the executive branch has overstepped its regulatory authority or pursued imprudent goals, it could pass a law adjusting the scope of its delegated authorities or countermanding the action. Some legal scholars think Congress should do just that. Others think the US Supreme Court should put a stop to the practice.

Aside from abrogating their legislative responsibility, legislators can also refuse to hold votes. The filibuster is an obstructionist tactic in which a legislator delivers a lengthy speech in order to prevent a timely vote on a proposal or bill and thereby block its passage. It is perhaps most famously practiced in the US Senate, but has also been used as a tactic in legislatures around the world, from the UK and Canada, to Austria and the Philippines.

To be fair, filibustering isn't a new hack. It dates back to 60 BCE, when Roman senator Cato the Younger deliberately gave interminable speeches in order to delay voting. Since the Roman Senate had to conclude all business by dusk, the body couldn't vote if he refused to be silent. Cato managed to do this for six months, which is a *lot* of talking.

The filibuster is only possible in the US because of a vulnerability in the rules that was an accidental side effect of another legislative rule change. Back in 1805, Vice President Aaron Burr declared that the US Senate should not have too many procedural rules. One of the rules dropped on his recommendation—in 1806, after he left office—was the "motion to previous question," which ended debate on legislation. It took until 1837 for someone to notice and exploit the vulnerability. This was patched in 1917 with the cloture rule ending debate, which meant that a filibuster required nonstop talking to sustain. The current three-fifths majority—or sixty senators—requirement was only added in 1975, and the talking requirement was eliminated. It's a hack on top of a patch on top of a hack, and it can only be changed by another hack.

The filibuster subverts the legislative system. A legislative body is supposed to preserve the minority's right to be heard, while still respecting majority rule. However, the modern filibuster flips that on its head, because now the minority party can use the filibuster to halt the legislative process for any bill without a sixty-vote majority, which actually prevents meaningful consideration or debate of an issue. It's also bad for the rights of minorities in society, not just the minority party in the Senate. Historically, the filibuster was most often used to block legislation advancing racial equality.

In the US, this is now normal. The Senate has such relaxed rules that a senator doesn't have to actually speak for days or months to filibuster; he or she can simply state a theoretical intention to do so in order to delay a vote. But back in 60 BCE, it was certainly unanticipated and unintended by whoever created the rules of the Roman Senate. Obstructive speechifying was a subversion of those rules, designed to prevent the very thing that the Senate was there to do: vote on legislation.

The filibuster isn't the only legislative delaying tactic. In the UK, House of Commons members can move that the House of Commons meet in secret. It's intended for matters of national security, but has been misused as a delaying tactic—most recently in 2001. In the Japanese Diet, the tactic of "ox walking" means walking through the voting lobbies extremely slowly—enough to delay the entire voting process. Deployed strategically, it can result in a bill being shelved until the next legislative session. In Italy, a 2016 constitutional reform bill in parliament had 84 million—not a typo—amendments inserted in an attempt to delay voting on it.

Whether these sorts of hacks are good or bad depends on whether you think the main purpose of the governance system is providing political accountability or delivering impartial, efficient policy decisions. If you think government should only act when it has clear supermajority support or extensive deliberation, then these delaying tactics might be good if minority parties can use them to get a seat at the negotiating table. If you think government should be more active and respond to pressing policy challenges quickly while facing the voters' judgment later, then adding ways for minority parties to effectively veto legislation is very bad indeed.

Solutions range from patching the underlying system so that the hack is no longer possible—eliminating the filibuster in the US case—to making it a more costly hack to implement, and therefore less frequently used. Right now, sustaining a filibuster is easy: no one needs to talk on the Senate floor for hours or days on end, they just need to declare their intent to filibuster a motion. Because it's incumbent on the majority to find sixty votes to break the filibuster, it's far harder to break a filibuster than it is to keep one going. I've heard suggestions for several possible reforms, but the most exciting option comes from Norm Ornstein at the American Enterprise Institute, who argues for flipping the equation. Instead of requiring sixty votes to end a filibuster, the rules would require forty votes to sustain it. The idea here is that the majority could keep the Senate in session around the clock for days or weeks. And the minority needs be present and alert, sleeping near the Senate floor, ready to vote on a moment's notice.

38

The Context of a Hack

What I am developing is a sophisticated notion of hacking. It's not that hacks are necessarily evil. It's not even that they're undesirable and need to be defended against. It's that we need to recognize that hacks subvert underlying systems, and decide whether that subversion is harmful or beneficial.

For example, I've talked a lot about hacking the tax code. Most of the examples involve hackers (accountants and tax attorneys) finding inadvertent vulnerabilities (loopholes) in the tax code.

Loose language in the American Jobs Creation Act of 2004 created several vulnerabilities in the tax code, which well-heeled firms were able to exploit to great effect. Most notable among these was the domestic production activities deduction, which was supposed to help domestic manufacturers compete internationally; it defined manufacturing so broadly—"combining or assembling two or more articles"—that all sorts of companies took the credit. World Wrestling Entertainment claimed it for producing wrestling videos. Grocery stores claimed it because they spray ripening chemicals on their fruit. Pharmacies claimed it because they had photo printing booths. A maker of gift baskets claimed it because it combined wine and chocolate into a single box. The government took that company to court over the deduction, and lost.

It's impossible to know for sure, but this problematic wording seems to have been deliberately inserted into the law by legislators responding to lobbyist pressures and the need to get enough congressional votes to pass it. It was just one of the many tax breaks in that law, albeit the one that seems to have had the most inadvertent effects. It was such a popular tax break that it stayed around until 2017, when it was replaced with the qualified business income deduction.

As we've moved from simpler to more complex examples, it's become harder to determine if any particular hack is good. What, exactly, is the "intent" of the rules of hockey, and are they furthered or impaired by curved sticks? Curved sticks make for a faster puck and a more exciting game. But a faster puck is more dangerous, and results in more injuries. When the National Hockey League established rules specifying just how curved a stick could be, it tried to balance both safety and sportsmanship considerations. And those rules have changed since 1967, as the league tweaked that balance: first a one-and-a-half-inch maximum curvature was allowed, then one inch, then half an inch, and currently three-quarters of an inch.

It's even harder to determine the intent of the legislative staff who crafted that overly broad tax deduction for manufacturing. Did some lobbyist hack the legislative process, giving some member of Congress or that member's underlings deliberately vague language that the lobbyist knew would be abused? Did the member of Congress believe corporate taxes were inherently bad and slip in language that the member knew would be overlooked as the bill moved through committee and into debate? Was the law just poorly written?

Whether or not a hack is an improvement also depends on who sits where. A clever entrepreneur might use a regulatory loophole for their own gain. Their customers may also be happy, but the government may suffer.

We've defined a hack as a technique that adheres to the rules of the system but subverts its intent. This isn't always a bad thing. As we've seen, some hacks are also beneficial innovations. They end up being normalized and improving the overall system. In China, for example, the reformist governments of the 1980s and 1990s maneuvered around opposition to private ownership through hacks such as offering occupants seventy-year renewable leases on their land. They followed the Communist Party's rules, but completely subverted their intent.

Putting any particular hack into one bucket or the other isn't something that the system can do. It has to be done by a more general, overarching governing system, because the definition of hacking depends on context.

An ATM exists within the broader context of a banking system. The rules of hockey exist within the broader context of the players, league, fans, and society. The examples in this book—of banking, the economy, law and legislation, and human psychology itself—exist within the broader context of society: our identities, relationships, desires, values, and goals.

This leads to the obvious question: Who gets to define intent? Who decides whether a hack is beneficial or not, or whether the subverted system is better or not? This can be a very complicated matter, especially in systems with multiple designers, or that have evolved over time. Hacks are often beneficial to some and detrimental to others.

And here are some truths about a system that cannot be understood within it, and that only become clear at a higher level. All computer programs are ultimately a complex code of circuits opening and closing, representing zeroes and ones, but no human cares about that, and no one writes in machine code. What we care about are the tasks and jobs that code represents: the movie you want to watch, the message you want to send, the news and financial statements you want to read. To illustrate this point in the language of biology: the molecular structures and chemical reactions that characterize life look like incredibly complex noise unless you step up to the level of the organism and realize that they all serve the function of keeping the organism alive.

Over the past chapters, we've encountered many different governing bodies whose job it is to accomplish that adjudication. Simpler systems can have a single, and single-purposed, governing body. The Nevada Gaming Commission updates casino rules on the basis of hacks. The Fédération Internationale de l'Automobile does the same for Formula One racing and the Fédération Internationale de Football Association for soccer.

Do hacks subvert the intent of the systems? Or do they actually further it? What is the intent of these systems, anyway? The answer (and there is no one answer) isn't simply a matter of analyzing the hack and the system; your answer will depend on your morals, ethics, and political beliefs. There will be reasonable differences of opinion about whether any of these hacks should be normalized or not. In the end, what matters is who benefits and who loses. That, too, is politically contested. So there's a debate, and maybe a vote. And money and power influence both.

Here's an example. In 2020, President Trump wanted to appoint retired Army Brig. Gen. Anthony Tata to the position of under secretary of defense for policy, which requires US Senate confirmation. When it became clear that the Senate would never confirm him, Trump withdrew his nomination and instead designated him as the official "performing the duties of" the deputy under secretary of defense for policy. He also repeatedly used the term "acting" to circumvent Senate confirmation. These are hacks of the 1998 Vacancies Reform Act. But are they a flagrant disregard of reasonable Senate oversight duties or a reasonable response to the overly broad requirement that the Senate confirm 1,200 different executive positions? It depends on your opinion on how government should work.

39

Hacking Voting Eligibility

There are many ways to cheat in an election. Stuffing ballot boxes, fiddling with the vote tallies: history, both old and recent, has many examples. But often the best way to manipulate election results isn't to cheat directly, it's to hack the process. Like markets and legislative processes, democracy is based on information, choice, and agency. All three can be, and are, hacked. That is, hackers can subvert the intent of democratic elections by tweaking the rules.

If you don't vote, you don't matter. This is why many hacks interfere with voter agency.

Ratified in 1870 after the end of the Civil War, the Fifteenth Amendment made it illegal to deny the vote to men based on race, color, or previous status as a slave. (Women still couldn't vote or hold office.) Soon after, Black men brought their increasing influence to bear in elections, and started being elected to public office. This outraged Southern whites and the formerly slaveholding political elite, who promptly began hacking the election process to limit the voting rights and political power of newly enfranchised African American men. (They also used a lot of tactics that weren't hacks, such as violence and murder, to accomplish this goal.)

In Alabama, for example, a coalition of conservative Democrats calling themselves "Redeemers" seized power in an 1874 election marked by fraud and paramilitary violence. (Not a hack.) Over the next thirty years, they gradually chipped away at African Americans' political influence through carefully targeted voting restrictions. These efforts culminated in the ratification of a new state constitution in 1901, in which the stated goal of its drafters was "to establish white supremacy in this state." The constitution introduced or entrenched poll taxes, property ownership requirements, literacy tests, and various disqualifications that limited the number of African Americans entitled to vote. (*That's* the hack.) It worked; in the early 1870s, over 140,000 African Americans were eligible to vote. In 1903, fewer than 3,000 were able to register.

"Literacy test" is a misnomer. Literacy tests in this context were not tests of reading ability, they were complex tests designed so that people would inevitably fail them. We can argue about their constitutionality, but the hack part was giving local election officials substantial leeway to determine which prospective voters were required to pass this impossible test. This allowed voting officials to selectively deny the franchise at will. The 1964 Louisiana literacy test is an example that can be easily found online. One question—yes, this is real—"Write every other word in this first line and print every third word in same line, [original type smaller, and the first line ended at comma] but capitalize the fifth word that you write."

Fast-forward to today. Alabama still employs a variety of voter-suppression tactics to limit the participation of felons, minorities, immigrants, and rural voters in the election system. Alabama's barriers to voting rights begin with registration. The state doesn't offer electronic voter registration, registration in DMV offices, automatic voter registration, election day registration, or any sort of preregistration for coming-of-age voters. State law requires people to show proof of citizenship in order to register. This law has not been implemented because of an ongoing federal investigation, but if allowed to stand, it will have the effect of denying the vote disproportionately to minority citizens, who often don't have passports or other documentation. Kansas has turned away thousands of new voters from the polls using a similar rule.

Historically, most felons were disqualified from voting in Alabama. This policy, too, served disproportionately to disenfranchise minorities. The hack consisted of the "Black Codes" implemented by many Southern states that categorized relatively trivial offenses (think cattle theft) as felonies. African Americans convicted of these crimes would be forever disenfranchised. In 2017, Alabama's legislature repealed that law, providing almost 60,000 citizens with a pathway to restoring their right to vote. But the secretary of state hasn't gone to the trouble of publicizing the policy, so many felons remain unaware of their rights. And even those felons who are aware of their rights face substantial difficulties actualizing them, because of administrative difficulties and a poor understanding of the law by state and local officials.

People can also be denied the right to vote by removing their names from the voting rolls without their knowledge. The common manner in which this is applied is to remove those who haven't voted in recent elections. This works because inactive voters are unlikely to return to the polls before the voter rolls are purged. Alabama has removed 658,000 infrequent voters from its voter rolls since 2015.

These are all the sorts of administrative burdens first touched on in Chapter 32. They don't generally have much impact on people with money and status. But for citizens with fewer resources or time to spare, who are disabled, or who are new to the political process, rules like these make it much more difficult to exercise the franchise. All too often, people make a sincere attempt to navigate these rules, fail to do so, and are then unable to vote. More often than not, these rules limit election participation by poorer people and minorities, who often lean towards the Democratic Party. As a result of these hacks, only 69% of voting-age Alabamians are registered to vote.

40

Other Election Hacks

Another hack of agency centers on the voting process itself. Basically, the idea is to make voting so difficult for eligible, registered voters who aren't supporting your candidate that they won't bother to come to the polls. Many of these examples can also be classified as administrative burdens.

Immediately after the Fifteenth Amendment was ratified, Southern states enacted voting restrictions that didn't specifically mention race, but that nonetheless predominantly affected Black Americans. These included poll taxes that the poorest couldn't afford to pay; rules that only enfranchised people whose grandfathers were qualified to vote before the Civil War; and—as previously mentioned—devilishly designed, selectively administered, capriciously judged literacy tests. Several of these hacks were only banned after passage of the Twenty-Fourth Amendment (which was ratified in 1964), the 1965 Voting Rights Act, and the 1966 US Supreme Court ruling in *South Carolina v. Katzenbach*. After key parts of the Voting Rights Act were struck down by the Supreme Court in 2015, these tactics returned, most commonly in the form of voter ID laws.

In Alabama, for example, potential voters must present a state-issued photo ID or be turned away from the polls. Seemingly a simple requirement, it doesn't play out so simply in Alabama. Close to 25% of eligible voters live over ten miles from a Department of Motor Vehicles (DMV) office, and many don't own a car. These are poorer citizens in the state, and they disproportionately reside in minority communities. State authorities then tried to close thirty-one DMV offices (which issue both driver's licenses and non-driver identification cards); the offices on the chopping block were all located in the six counties where African Americans composed over 70% of the population. After the US Department of Transportation objected, this plan was eventually rejected. Still, over 100,000 Alabama residents of voting age don't have acceptable IDs for voting—tellingly, while the figure represents a little less than 3% of Alabama's total voting-age population, it represents more than 10% of the African American voting-age population.

There can be a legitimate difference of opinion about the necessity of implementing an administrative hurdle, and the relative balance between allowing everyone authorized to receive a benefit and preventing anyone unauthorized from receiving it. Yes, there is value to ensure that only eligible voters vote. But with the actual incidence of election fraud so low (a matter that has been abundantly established in courts across the country), it's pretty clear that the measures described above are primarily aimed at preventing eligible voters from being able to vote.

Finally, people can be denied the right to vote by the lack of polling places near their homes. Alabama has been closing polling places since 2013, often in African American neighborhoods. For example, the city of Daphne (population 28,000) downsized from five to two polling places in 2016, and the three stations removed were all located in predominantly African American areas of town.

I don't have to pick on Alabama in these chapters. Other states are just as aggressive in voter suppression, and are becoming increasingly so. Georgia, for example, also enforces voter ID and proof of citizenship requirements, voter roll purges, reductions in early voting, and polling place closures concentrated in African American communities. (Don't even ask me about Florida.) And today, new measures are being enacted all over the country to try to suppress young voters, especially idealistic college students who are often assumed to veer towards the Democratic Party.

Gerrymandering isn't a new hack. The word comes from Massa-

chusetts governor—and Declaration of Independence signer—Elbridge
Gerry, who enacted a bill in 1812 that created a state senate district in
Boston that was shaped like a salamander and was engineered to con-
solidate and strengthen the Federalist vote and fracture the Democratic-
Republican vote. The basic idea is that if you can control the proportions
of different voters in voting districts, you can influence who wins and
thereby dominate the overall representation in a multidistrict legislative
body. You engineer the demographics so that your party wins many districts by a small percentage—let's say 10%—and the other party wins as
few districts as possible by a high percentage: say 90%.

There are two ways to gerrymander. The first is to "pack" a district
to include as many of the opposing party's voters as possible. That helps
the governing party win neighboring districts where the opposition's
strength has been diluted. The second is to "crack" a district by splitting
up clusters of opposition voters among several districts, so that they will
be outnumbered in each district.

The basic problem is conflict of interest: the legislators who are
in charge of drawing the districts are the ones who benefit from their
demographics. The solution, obvious to anyone who studies the issue, is
compartmentalization. Districts should be drawn by independent commissions whose members have no stake in their outcome. Michigan, for
example, approved a ballot initiative mandating exactly this in 2018. That
the state's Republicans were still fighting this commission in 2020 illustrates the power of the gerrymandering hack.

Beyond questions of how and in what district citizens vote, there
are countless levers policymakers can use to hack and skew the electoral
process. Public officials often have discretion on scheduling elections,
recording and recounting of votes, and which candidates and proposi-
tions are allowed on the ballot. In territories where they exist, election
commissions can even disqualify candidates for failing to file on time,
having insufficient support, or other technical issues. Using these powers
selectively is the hack.

One final tactic: In 2018, Wisconsin governor Scott Walker simply
refused to call a special election for state legislative seats, fearing that
they would be won by Democrats. He was eventually ordered to conduct

the election by a federal appellate court judge. Governors in Florida and Michigan have also tried this hack. In 2018, Stacey Abrams narrowly lost a Georgia gubernatorial election to Brian Kemp, who oversaw the election at the time as secretary of state, and purged the rolls of half a million registered voters just before the election.

41

Money in Politics

Money can control information and choice. Money can buy agency: the power to make change. These are all political hacks because they subvert the intent of the democratic voting process. This is especially true in the US, where elections are unnaturally expensive.

The reasons are complicated, but I'll list four basic ones. One, US election cycles are long; candidates begin to campaign over a year before the election itself. (Comparatively, Japanese campaigns last twelve days from start to finish, and French campaigns two weeks. UK elections come after an average of two to four weeks of campaigning. No Australian or Canadian campaign season has ever exceeded eleven weeks—and that extreme occurred only in 1910 and 1926.) Two, US party discipline is weaker than in other countries. Where party discipline is strong, it makes less sense to bankroll specific candidates and pit them against each other in primaries. Three, the US is a large country with a large population, expensive television advertising markets, and—as opposed to other countries—no limits on campaign spending. And four, the US has enough loopholes in its contribution disclosure laws to reduce the political accountability of those who accept inappropriate campaign contributions (such as by non-US citizens).

There is enormous incentive to hack the systems that regulate cam-

paign financing, and for candidates to use their campaign coffers to hack
the political process itself.

Many wealthy people like these hacks and have worked to make
them legal, since they proportionally increase their political influence.
After passage of the Federal Election Campaign Act of 1972 and its 1974
amendments that limited contributions and expenditures, a 1976 ruling
excluded money spent to support a party or candidate but not in coordination with the party or candidate. This led to the rise of "soft money"
spent on "party building" activities, which often ended up being political
attack ads against the other party's candidates. Over the years, various
wealthy individuals and groups slowly challenged the limits of campaign
financing rules. This was curtailed in 2002 by the Bipartisan Campaign
Reform Act. But more rules brought more hacks. Then the 2010 *Citizens
United* decision, affirmed by a 2014 US Supreme Court ruling, reopened
the door to allow all sorts of formerly forbidden money in politics, including contributions from corporations.

To be sure, money doesn't guarantee political success, but the lack
of it nearly always guarantees political failure. As Harvard law professor
Lawrence Lessig argues, "To be able to run in the voting election, one
must do extremely well in the money election." Money can keep candidates alive in a lengthy political process like the US presidential primary
system. We saw this in the 2012 Republican primary, where billionaires
Sheldon Adelson, Foster Friess, and Jon Huntsman Sr. had an enormous
influence on the process by singlehandedly funding candidates when few
others would. It's kind of like a venture capital system for politics. You
don't need to be among the best and brightest, you just need to convince
some wealthy investors that your candidacy is a good bet.

Money can also help sow chaos. The US has a de facto two-party system, so one hack is to fund an independent or third-party candidate that
will siphon votes from your opponent. If you're a Republican, you might
fund some unaffiliated liberal upstart to compete against and thereby
undermine the front-running Democrat in that race. If you're a Democrat, you might fund some independent conservative candidate to split
the Republican vote.

In the US, the "independent spoiler" hack is a hard one to pull off, because both parties have an interest in patching this particular vulnerability. Some states enforce very early filing deadlines that penalize candidates who enter the race late, or rules that make it harder to get on the ballot if you're not a Democrat or Republican. Forty-four states have "sore loser" laws that prevent the loser of a primary election from running in the general election as an independent candidate.

This isn't to say it never happens. After seeing how Ralph Nader affected the 2000 election, Republican operatives around the country tried to take advantage of Green Party candidates to siphon Democratic votes. In Seattle, an eighteen-year-old former Nader volunteer named Young Han contemplated running in the 2002 state legislature race. A "Mr. Shore" helped Han organize a campaign announcement and also donated to the campaign. Mr. Shore was actually a Republican strategist based out of Washington, DC. His wife, similarly, was propping up a Green Party candidate in a Seattle county-wide race. Something similar happened in Arizona in 2010, New York in 2014, and Montana in 2018 and 2020. Republicans helped Kanye West's attempt to get on the 2020 presidential ballot, hoping he would pull Democratic votes away from Joe Biden. In the end, all the hacks failed; this is all a lot easier in theory than it is in practice.

It's easier if you also can add confusion. In a 2020 congressional race in Florida, a "former" Republican named Alex Rodriguez ran against Florida Democratic state senator Jose Rodríguez and appropriated the senator's signature issue: climate change. Alex had no political background—and didn't actually run a campaign—but the resulting confusion gave him 3% of the vote, and Republican Ileana Garcia won by thirty-two votes after a manual recount. Alex Rodriguez's campaign was supported by $550,000 from a recently formed company named Proclivity, Inc., and PACs linked to Republican staffers.

The vote-splitting strategy can be taken to extremes. In India, a person with the same name as a political opponent is sometimes asked to run for the same office as their namesake. In a 2014 parliamentary election, for example, five of the thirty-five candidates running for a particular seat were named Lakhan Sahu—and only one of those was an actual politician with a legislative record. The candidate from the major opposing party called it a "mere coincidence" that so many Lakhan Sahus were motivated to jump into the fray at exactly the same time.

In the US, the general vulnerability is the two-party system, but vulnerability also lies in the first-past-the-post winner-take-all system of elections. Because we don't require that candidates get a majority of the vote, but merely a plurality, political candidates are less likely to win if another candidate has a similar policy profile (or even a similar name) and splits the votes of would-be supporters.

One fix is ranked-choice voting, in which voters rank their choices for an office, the lowest-scoring candidate is eliminated, and votes for those bested candidates are redistributed in sequential "runoffs" until one achieves a majority. A ranked-choice system prevents third-party spoilers (a would-be spoiler's votes are just reallocated to a different candidate, most likely one from whom they were intended to siphon support), and helps to ensure that the candidate most acceptable to a true majority of the electorate wins the election. Australia's 2022 parliamentary elections served as a demonstration: many third-party candidates received first votes that weren't subsequently "wasted."

42

Hacking to Destruction

In 1729, Paris had defaulted on its municipal bonds, so the government set up a lottery where each bond owner could buy tickets on the basis of the value of his bonds. Each ticket cost one-thousandth of a bond's value, and every month the government would select a single winner and award that person the bond's face value plus a 500,000-livre bonus.

Voltaire noticed that the payout was greater than the number of tickets in circulation, so—and here's the hack—he formed a syndicate with some wealthy patrons to buy up all the necessary bonds and tickets. They collected their winnings month after month, and in less than two years made about 7.5 million francs: $100 million in today's dollars.

The organizers of the Paris lottery eventually realized that many prizes were being claimed by the same few people. Voltaire, being Voltaire (and knowing that no good thing lasts forever, so why not have some fun), left riddles on the back of each ticket that made it easier for the government to track the hacker. The French finance minister took the syndicate to court, but since they had done nothing illegal, they were allowed to keep their winnings. The Parisian government then canceled the lottery—an effective defense, albeit an extreme one.

More recently, Ohio built a website through which employers could report employees who refused to work during the COVID-19 pandemic, so that they wouldn't receive unemployment benefits. A hacker realized that there was no authentication in the reporting process; anyone could submit a report. So he wrote a program that automatically submitted fake reports—even defeating the CAPTCHA—and posted it online. We don't know how many of these were filed by the online system, and Ohio government officials claimed that they had been able to weed them out, but the state ended up abandoning the plan to use the reports to kick people off the unemployment rolls.

Back in Chapter 10, I said that hacks are parasitical. Like any parasite, a hack must balance the subversion of a system with its destruction. Too much hacking, and the system collapses. Sometimes, as with the Paris lottery, the system is abolished as the result of the hack being just too successful. Other times, as with the Ohio unemployment reporting website, the goal of the hacker is to shut down the system.

Financially motivated hackers tend not to want to destroy the systems they're hacking. If there are too many ATM hacks, the machines will disappear. If a sport is hacked to the point where it's no fun to play or watch, it will wither and die. Those hackers fundamentally want to maintain the system they're hacking, but create better outcomes for themselves. If they destroy the system, it's generally incidental and accidental.

This isn't necessarily true when the hackers are following some moral or ethical precept. They're hacking the system because they don't like the system, not because they want to profit from it. Like the Ohio unemployment website hacker, their goal is to reduce its functionality, undermine its efficacy, or destroy it. We saw another example of this in 2020, when TikTok users coordinated to submit fake ticket requests to a Trump campaign rally in Tulsa, in order to engineer an arena full of no-shows. It was a basic hack, exploiting the fact that all it took to reserve a ticket was an easily obtained dummy email address and a dummy phone number care of Google Voice. The ticketing system wasn't ultimately destroyed, but the low audience turnout embarrassed Trump, and the campaign switched to other, less vulnerable, ticketing systems.

Whatever the motivation, hacking can destroy social systems on a much larger scale than that of Voltaire's lottery, Trump's ticketing system, or Ohio's unemployment benefits. We saw hints of that in the 2008 banking crisis, where repeated hacks of the system almost brought down the entire US financial network. We're seeing hints of it with money in US politics and with political misinformation and social networks. And it happens in political revolutions, when all the mechanisms of society are hacked for a wildly different intent. So while hacking can be a good thing, and necessary for system evolution, there can be too much of it too quickly.

Take another economic example: printing paper money. Paper money is at least as old as the eleventh century Sung Dynasty in China, and it's a hack. Currency is supposed to represent some real amount of economic value, but today, most governments have the power to print as much currency as they want, regardless of how much the economy is actually producing. This means governments can hack public financing systems by creating enough new money to pay off their bills, rather than funding programs through taxes or debt to private investors. In Europe, this hack was first devised by economist John Law to help Louis XV of France pay for his wars.

This is an example of a beneficial, and now normal, hack. The ability to print money can be essential during economic crises. It's how the US government funded the interventions that calmed markets in 2008–2009, and limited the economic fallout from the pandemic and lockdowns in 2020. And it's part of how the US government funded massive military mobilizations that helped to win World Wars I and II.

But when governments become reliant on printing money to service foreign debt, things can go really bad. While hyperinflation is rare, it can cause incredible damage incredibly quickly. When Zimbabwe experienced hyperinflation in 2007, the Zimbabwean dollar lost more than 99.9% of its value over a single year, locals' average wealth fell below 1954 levels, and the amount of money that could once buy twelve cars wasn't enough to pay for a single loaf of bread. In Venezuela, hyperinflation began in 2017 and eventually pushed prices so high that the average family would need more than 100 times the minimum wage to pay for bare essentials, leading more than 10% of the country's population to emigrate.

Other examples of hacking to destruction come from the recent rise of authoritarian governments around the world, in countries like Russia, Syria, Turkey, the Philippines, Hungary, Poland, Brazil, and Egypt. Elections are still held and votes are still counted. Legislatures still pass laws, and courts enforce them. Rights to free speech and association often remain on the books, at least formally. But all of those mechanisms and institutions have been hacked—subverted to serve the needs of the dictatorship.

Conversely, some systems need to be hacked in order to be destroyed. Boycotts, and civil disobedience in general, are hacks: they subvert the rules of markets and politics as usual in order to protest unjust practices. The backlash they provoke makes the implicit violence and cruelty of systems explicit, shifting the political agenda to destroy systems such as overtly discriminatory laws that were long accepted as "normal" and ignored. The challenge we face is making sure our hacks destroy the bad while leaving the good . . . and knowing which is which.

PART 6

HACKING COGNITIVE SYSTEMS

43

Cognitive Hacks

Here's a hack I used regularly to save money on flights back in the 1990s when we were all still using paper tickets. Obtaining a paper boarding pass was a separate action from buying the ticket, you could get it weeks in advance, and you had to talk with an actual human to do that.

I was living in Washington, DC, and flying a lot for work. I had reason to spend weekends in Chicago, but work wouldn't pay for the expensive stopover. But I had a hack. Say I had a ticket from Seattle to DC for Sunday, with a change in Chicago. First I would to go the airline's ticket office and get printed boarding passes, which the agent stapled to my tickets. I would remove and hide those, and on another day return to the ticket office and change both flights to Friday—itinerary changes were inexpensive back then. The agent would make the change in the computer and issue me a new pair of boarding passes, again stapled to that same ticket. I would then fly Seattle-to-Chicago on Friday, as I was supposed to, then spend the weekend in Chicago. Back at the airport on Sunday, I would go to my Chicago-to-DC gate with the original ticket and boarding pass (which I'd saved). Even though I wasn't in the computer with a reservation, I had a properly dated ticket and a proper boarding pass—and the ticket and boarding pass from Sunday's Seattle-to-Chicago flight to show if anyone asked. Confused, the gate agent would override whatever the computer was telling him, issue a new boarding pass, and let me on the plane.

It was a great hack, and it worked until the airlines moved to e-tickets and ditched the separate boarding passes. But what exactly was I hacking? It wasn't the airline reservation system. The computer clearly said that I didn't have a reservation for the flight. What I was really hacking was the gate agent himself. I was a confident white male business traveler with a proper-looking ticket and boarding pass in hand. The problem could be attributed to a computer screwup, or so the gate agent conveniently assumed. It might sound weird to say this, but I hacked the gate agent's mind.

Our brain is a system, evolved over millions of years to keep us alive and—more importantly, from our genes' point of view—to keep us reproducing. It's been optimized through continual interaction with the environment. But it's been optimized for humans who lived in small family groups in the East African highlands 100,000 years ago. It's not as well suited for twenty-first-century New York or Tokyo or Delhi. And the human brain can be manipulated because it engages in many cognitive shortcuts to accommodate our modern social environment.

It's fairly simplistic to talk about how human biological, psychological, and social systems "naturally" work, then claim that a hack subverts their intent. They occur naturally and unplanned. Even so, doing that can provide a useful framework for discussion. We can refer to the "purpose" or "intent" of biological and psychological systems—the purpose of the pancreas, the purpose of our sense of trust—without having to invoke anything other than evolutionary processes. (Kind of like our economic or political systems, which also lack a singular designer.) Hacks creatively undermine those systems. Like all of the hacks of human-created systems, cognitive hacks exploit a vulnerability in order to subvert the intent of cognitive systems.

Cognitive hacking is powerful. Many of the societal systems our society relies on—democracy, market economics, and so on—depend on humans making rational decisions. In the previous chapters, we've seen hack after hack that successfully limited one of the three aspects of that: information, choice, and agency. In these upcoming chapters, we'll see them hacked directly—in our own minds.

For example, disinformation is a hack that subverts our system of free-dom of speech and freedom of the press. This isn't a new notion. Goebbels, Hitler's propaganda minister, once said: "This will always remain one of the best jokes of democracy, that it gave its deadly enemies the means by which it was destroyed." Disinformation is also a hack that subverts many of the cognitive systems we will talk about: attention, persuasion, trust, authority, tribalism, and sometimes fear.

Unlike other hacks, cognitive hacks lie at a higher level of generality. In fact, they are the most general hacks of all. While laws govern basi-cally all economic transactions and many other areas of society, legisla-tures and courts govern the creation and revision of laws, and a nation's constitution (or similar document) establishes the legislative process and the court system. But our social systems—and all technological systems, insofar as they interact with human users—rely on people thinking or, more often, using cognitive shortcuts to muddle through. If you can hack a mind, you can hack any system that is governed by human action.

Cognitive hacks are as old as our species, and many were normalized so long ago that we don't even think twice about them—let alone think of them as hacks. Because humans are intelligent and conscious, because we have a theory of mind and an ability to plan far into the future, we have taken hacking to a level of sophistication beyond any other creature in the natural world. And, like many of the hacks in the previous chapters, cognitive hacks tend to target the information, choice, or agency humans need so they can make deliberative and effective decisions.

What has changed over the past half-century is the extent to which computers and computer interfaces provide greater opportunities to manipulate the perceptions of others. Combined with computer algo-rithms and behavioral science, they change the speed and sophistication of mind-meddling, and those differences in degree lead to differences in kind.

Not always, though. Writer and activist Cory Doctorow cautions us from blindly believing "the thesis that Big Tech used Big Data to create a mind-control ray to sell us fidget spinners." At best, what I'll be talk-ing about in the next few chapters are cognitive nudges that push us one way or the other to varying degrees. But I think we need to be equally reluctant to ignore these techniques. Paired with AI, they're going to get more effective.

Patching generally doesn't work with cognitive systems, although conscious awareness of a hack is itself a patch. Security against cognitive hacks requires prevention and damage mitigation. Many con games work by hacking our emotions of greed, trust, fear, and so on. There's no way to patch our brains, but we can use a different system to declare specific hacks illegal—that is, outside the bounds of acceptable social behavior— and educate potential victims on how to avoid them.

One more caveat: hacks of cognitive systems aren't as cleanly delineated as the hacks described in previous chapters. For example, consider the various webpage interface design tricks that the Trump campaign used to trick people into donating far more money than they had intended, and for purposes other than political campaigning: pre-checked boxes authorizing recurring weekly withdrawals from a donor's checking or credit card account, donation amounts hidden in small print, more small print stating that the donation could be used for the candidate's personal expenses, and the like. These are clearly hacks: they're examples of a "dark pattern" that we'll talk about later. But are they hacks of our perceptual, emotional, or executive decision-making systems? The answer is, kind of all three. I'm okay with this ambiguity. Humans are complicated. Cognitive systems are messy. Any discussion of them will be messy as well.

44

Attention and Addiction

Everyone hates pop-up ads. Even their inventor, Ethan Zuckerman, has publicly apologized for creating them. But they have proliferated because they are profitable, and they are profitable because they successfully hack the attention of enough people to increase advertisers' sales.

Unlike banner ads, which we are generally able to tune out, pop-up ads force you to devote at least grudging attention to them, even if only to swat them away. They usually appear right in front of you, blocking whatever you were actually watching. Many include images, sounds, and video. You have to take action to close them—and sometimes that action is hard to figure out, or takes several tries to accomplish. And they work. Holding our attention, even for a relatively short period of time, can have a long-term effect.

As a cognitive system, attention enables us to focus on important things. At any given time, countless events are occurring around and within us. Although our brains are powerful, their processing capacity is limited. We can't pay attention to everything.

Given this limitation, we deploy attention selectively. We prioritize things and events that promote our survival, and pay less attention to things we already trust. Our attention is most readily captured by phenomena that could indicate the presence of a predator or other threat: sudden movements, loud noises, bright lights. We also prioritize phenom-

ena that affect our social survival, like our security and position within
a group, or phenomena that involve attracting and maintaining sexual
partners. Similarly, we generally focus our attention on phenomena that
promote our well-being and our level of comfort. That's why anything
that gives us a reward—whether that be food, money, drugs, a Kinder Egg
prize, or even a "like" on our digital profile—will capture our attention.
We can't always consciously choose how or where we focus our attention,
because so much of the attentional system is hardwired into our brains.

Advertising doesn't naturally capture our attention, so advertisers
have to hack our cognitive systems. In the 1860s, French lithographer
Jules Chéret invented a new form of advertising poster: bright, contrast-
ing colors, beautiful half-dressed women, scenes in motion—all impossible to ignore. Later, Leonetto Cappiello helped to promote all manner
of consumer products with stunning, larger-than-life images specifically
designed to be recognized at high speed by passengers on the newly built
Paris Metro.

Advertisers are always looking to hack our attention more effectively. It's why supermarkets, and even stores like Staples and Bed Bath
& Beyond, stock candy in the checkout aisles, a hack known as "point-
of-purchase placement." It's also why television commercials used to be
slightly louder than the shows they punctuated, until the FCC banned
the practice in 2012. And it's why we have pop-up ads.

While data-driven endeavors took off with the market research and
psychology-driven campaigns of the 1950s (and onward), contemporary
ad campaigns can use microtargeting to hack each of us personally. In
doing so, advertisers and data brokers amass and monetize vast hoards of
personal information, threatening our personal privacy in an attempt to
better capture our attention.

One more hack of our attention circuits that occurs on modern social
networks: manufacturing outrage. Facebook uses algorithms to optimize
your feed. Its goal is to keep you on the platform—the more you're on Facebook, the more ads you see, and the more money the company makes—
so it tries to show you content that engages you on which to display ads.
(Don't forget this: the whole point of these systems is to sell advertising,
whose whole point is to manipulate you into making purchases.)

Similarly, Google wants to keep you watching YouTube videos. (You-Tube is a Google subsidiary.) The YouTube algorithm figured out that increasingly polarizing and fringe content engages users. This is an unanticipated hack and very profitable for Google. Facebook and YouTube are polarizing not because they were originally intended to be, but because (1) the algorithm optimized itself to serve up ever more specialized content on the basis of a user's interests, and (2) management chose to disregard the potential problems that this created. Applied to politics, such schemes tend to polarize users by making it easier for them to occupy an ideological bubble with others who share their worldview, and by prioritizing material that provokes the most excitement. By accelerating and fine-tuning the task of finding and displaying specialized, polarizing content, automated content recommendation systems reduce the less filtered interactions that force us to consider and reconsider our beliefs and opinions.

One solution to the advertising part of this problem is to regulate the information utilized by advertisers for microtargeting. After the 2020 election, Google implemented a policy in which it decided to limit the targeting of election ads to general categories: age, gender, and location at the postal code level. These sorts of simple defenses are likely to be effective—assuming, of course, that Google sticks with them. Members of both parties will do their best to subvert them, though, as microtargeting has become essential to modern politics.

A better solution is to enforce antitrust laws. With so much content in one place, this sort of hyper-specialization becomes both easy and problematic. In contrast, a proliferation of smaller social media sites—each with less content—would limit the amount of specialization that's possible. Note that the hyperconservative social media sites that sprang up when Donald Trump was banned from Twitter have nowhere near the power that the large multinational social media companies do.

The logical extreme of attention hacking is addiction, the most effective form of lock-in there is. The hack isn't the physiological process of addiction, but the process of getting someone addicted. By designing their products to be addictive, manufacturers and developers ensure that their customers and users continue to use them. Sometimes the addition is physiological, but most of the time it starts as a behavioral fixation, then becomes entrenched with the help of endorphins, adrenaline, and other neurochemicals that the behavior elicits.

The basic methodology of behavioral addiction is nicely illustrated with a slot machine. We know that variable rewards are more addictive than fixed rewards, and by its nature gambling provides them. It's worth going through the system in detail. Step one consists of a trigger that sparks our attention. Slot machines are deliberately bright and noisy. They make noise when no one is using them, and they make a racket when someone wins. Step two consists of an action that brings with it an anticipation of a reward. That's the bet—once a coin in a slot, now a push of a button. Step three consists of the variable reward; you win some, you lose some. Step four consists of the emotional investment, which increases the player's propensity to re-enter the loop; everyone loves a winner. All it takes is another push of the button and—who knows?—there might be a jackpot, and you might be a winner again.

Online games are getting in on the variable-reward addictive action, particularly with digital goods known as "loot boxes." Players pay—sometimes using in-game currency but mostly real money—for a random assortment of in-game items. Valuable items are rare, sometimes extremely rare, mimicking the addictive characteristics of a slot machine. Video games in general are usually engineered with dozens of behaviorist tweaks intended to keep players online as long as possible, to the point that their addictive nature is an open secret in the industry.

Information products, like smartphone apps and social networking sites, are deliberately designed to work in a similar manner and become addictive. The triggers are the alerts that grab our attention: beeps, dings, vibrations, push notifications. (Very Pavlovian, I know.) The action is the click that brings with it an anticipation of a reward. The variable rewards are the wins, posts, comments, images, and whatever else appears in our feed.

None of this is accidental. Digital platforms can update and refresh their pages automatically, with no user intervention, if their designers choose to do so. But forcing users to click or swipe to see more posts mimics the behavior of the slot machine and provides an addicting smidgen of control that will habituate you to do it repeatedly. Similarly, offering any sort of batch notification—show me all of my new notifications once per day—reduces the variable reward feature and its addictiveness. And that's why this otherwise convenient, simple feature has never been offered by any advertising-based social media platform.

For all of the tendency of people to regard addiction as a moral failing, it's much better thought of as a hack—a reliable and highly effective one. We know the properties that make behaviors and experiences addictive. Companies can and do deploy them everywhere, often so subtly that consumers never notice. And as we'll see, algorithms and rapid testing are making digital platforms more addictive with less and less human intervention.

45

Persuasion

In 2014, bots posing as females on the Tinder dating app would text male users, make trivial small talk, mention a phone game they were playing—Castle Clash—then supply a link. As cognitive hacks go, it was kind of lame. It played on a variety of male emotions, including trust and sexual desire, but the new "friend" was pretty obviously a bot if you were the least bit suspicious. We don't know how successful those accounts were at persuading people to download and play the game before Tinder removed them.

This sort of scam isn't unique. Chatbots have regularly been used to manipulate human emotions and persuade people to do things for commercial and governmental benefit. In 2006, the US Army deployed SGT STAR, a chatbot designed to persuade people to enlist. AI and robotics technologies make efforts like these all much more effective.

In the 1970s, the Federal Trade Commission asked advertising executives to explain marketing to them. Before then, they had a pretty basic view of the industry, that advertisements were vehicles for companies to explain the benefits of their products to prospective consumers. Of course, advertising is much more than that, and today's techniques are more about hacking cognitive systems.

Persuasion isn't easy. Out of fear of manipulation or just fear of change, people often resist attempts to change their minds or behavior.

But despite our conscious and unconscious resistance, countless tricks subtly but reliably change our minds. Many are deviously simple, like the "illusory truth" effect: people are more likely to believe what they've heard repeatedly. (Yes, the Big Lie technique works: if you repeat a lie often enough, your listeners will begin to believe it.) Smarter and more analytical people aren't any better at resisting the illusory truth effect, either. In fact, repetitions of lies and half-truths by elites and media might actually explain the persistence of false beliefs. Either way, it's clear that simple tricks like repetition can slip below our radar and persuade us more powerfully than we might expect.

Drip pricing is another example. It's common in the airline and hotel industries, since price is regularly the first attribute people look at when choosing a travel service. The trick is to display a low price initially, then pile on fees and hope that the buyer isn't paying close attention. One study with StubHub, an online ticket marketplace, showed that drip pricing resulted in people spending about 21% more than they otherwise might.

Some sellers use decoy prices to influence buyers. If you are choosing between two products, a cheaper one and more expensive one, you'll try to evaluate them on their merits—and you might select the cheaper one because the more expensive one isn't worth it. But if the seller adds a third decoy item, one even more luxurious and expensive, you're more likely to choose the middle option.

Online, persuasion is often accomplished by means of "dark patterns." Much user interface design consists of norms and metaphors that we humans use to make sense of what computers do under the hood. The metaphors are just that: files, folders, and directories are all to some extent abstractions and representations. And they're not always accurate. When we move a file into a folder, we're not actually moving anything, just changing a pointer designating where the file is stored. Deleting a file isn't the same thing as destroying the physical object, something that criminal defendants learn over and over again as files they thought they'd deleted are recovered and used against them by prosecutors. But they're close enough for most purposes. And the norms are taken from the real world as much as possible.

"Dark patterns" is a term given to subversive user-design tricks that co-opt common designs to nudge users towards certain ends. Normally, standardized design guides us through our interactions online; it's a visual language that we trust. In habitual behaviors like driving, for example, green means go, and red means stop. Those same colors are similarly used as guides in user experience design all the time. They become a dark pattern when a series of green "continue" buttons is suddenly subverted to sell an in-app purchase, as in the mobile game "Two Dots." Or when ads for other software place a green "click here to download" button as they interrupt a series of "continue" buttons in a sequence of webpages. Way too often those buttons get you something other than what you're expecting—you have to be constantly vigilant.

Intuit has a free tax-filing program called Free File, but it's intentionally hard to find, and tries to trick users into paying for the tax-filing features in its TurboTax product. (A 2022 multistate plea agreement forced Intuit to pay $141 million in restitution over this; we'll see if it changes Intuit's future behavior in any meaningful way.) A banner ad from a company called Chatmost has what looks like a speck of dust on a touchscreen, tricking users into clicking on the ad as they try to swipe away the dirty spot.

In 2019, US senators Mark Warner and Deb Fischer introduced legislation banning dark patterns. It didn't pass. But if a future version does, the sponsors had better get their definition right, because that definition itself will be subject to all sorts of hacks, as programmers and apps that use dark patterns to hack us try to get around the rules.

46

Trust and Authority

On March 19, 2016, John Podesta, then chair of Senator Hillary Clinton's presidential campaign, received an email purporting to come from Google. It was a security alert, and included a link to what looked like a Google log-in page. Podesta entered his credentials on the page, which wasn't Google at all. It was actually run by the GRU, the Russian military intelligence agency. Once operatives on the other side of the screen had Podesta's Gmail password, they grabbed at least 20,000 of his old emails—then sent them to WikiLeaks to publish. This was a social engineering hack.

Social engineering is a common way to hack computer systems. Basically, it involves convincing someone with some specialized access to a system to use it in a way that they shouldn't. Over twenty years ago, I wrote "Only amateurs attack machines; professionals target people." It's still true today, and much of it relies on hacking trust.

One social engineering attack involves calling a cell phone tech-support line, pretending to be someone else, and convincing the operator to transfer that person's cell phone number to a phone that you control. This is known as SIM swapping, and is a particularly nasty attack because controlling your phone number is a gateway to a variety of other frauds—and often results in losses in the thousands of dollars. One victim lost $24 million; aggregate losses are huge.

There are a gazillion variations on social engineering. They can involve telephoning an employee—that's how the 2020 Twitter hackers were able to access the company's network and take over 130 accounts—and they can also involve email. "Phishing" is the term for sending fake emails trying to entice the recipient to click on a link, open an attachment, or otherwise do something that might compromise the recipient's computer or bank account. They're not that effective; mostly their perpetrators cast a wide net and necessarily keep their appeals fairly generic. "Spear phishing" is the term used when these emails are personalized. It takes a lot of research to craft a persuasive message, but it can be a very effective hacking technique. Podesta fell for it. So did former secretary of state Colin Powell.

In Chapter 12, I discussed business email compromise. A hacker gains access to the email account of a company executive, then writes to a subordinate something like: "Hi. I'm Mr. CEO. Yes, this is unusual, but I'm traveling and don't have my normal network access. I need you to transfer $20 million to this foreign account right now. It's important. A big deal depends on this. I'll send you the various forms when I'm back in my hotel." Depending on how good the hacker is at making the details plausible, how distracted and trusting the employee is, and how this all fits into whatever situation is actually going on, it can be a very successful fraud. Toyota lost $37 million to this scam in 2019, one of many victims, big and small.

In 2015, Syrian agents posing as beautiful women on Skype were used to steal battle plans from gullible rebels, as well as the identities and personal details of senior leaders. Russian agents have used this same tactic to try to glean classified information from US service members.

Technology is making this kind of chicanery easier. Criminals are now using deep-fake technology to commit social engineering attacks. In 2019, the CEO of a UK energy company was tricked into wiring €220,000 to an account because he thought the chief executive of his parent company was telling him to do so in a phone call and then in an email. That hack only used fake audio, but video is next. Already one scam artist has used a silicone mask to record videos and trick people into wiring him millions of dollars.

This kind of fraud can have geopolitical effects, too. Researchers have produced deep-fake videos of politicians saying things they didn't say and doing things they didn't do. In 2022, a video of Ukrainian president Volodymyr Zelenskyy telling Ukrainian troops to surrender to their Russian invaders was debunked by Zelenskyy himself. Although the video was of poor quality, and easily identified as a fraud, it is inevitable that these will get better with time and technological advancement.

The very existence of such technology is enough to degrade our trust in audio and video in general. In 2019, a video of Gabon's long-missing president Ali Bongo, who was believed to be in poor health or already dead, was labeled as a deep fake by his opponents and served as the trigger for an unsuccessful coup by the Gabonese military. It was a real video, but how could a non-expert be sure what was true?

Combine these techniques with existing and near-future AI technologies that enable bots to produce realistic text—essays, messages, and conversations—and we will soon have some very persuasive technologies that hack our perception of what is and isn't human.

We saw this sort of fakery in action in the 2016 US presidential election. BuzzFeed found 140 fake news websites with American-sounding domain names and sensationalistic headlines that got high traction on Facebook. That marked the beginning of a plethora of newly hatched websites disguised as authoritative sources of information. Domain names like BostonTribune.com, KMT11.com, and ABCNews.com.co looked official and tricked many readers into believing their content. Sites like The Tennessee Star, the Arizona Monitor, and the Maine Examiner were designed to look like traditional newspapers, but instead delivered partisan propaganda.

Many historical indicators of trust no longer work. Print books and television news were both seen as authoritative, because the publishing and broadcast industries acted as gatekeepers. That sort of naive trust doesn't translate well to the Internet. Now anyone can publish anything as a book. It's still hard to fake a paper newspaper, but it's easy for a website to mimic a trusted newspaper. An impressive bank building used to send a message of solvency and trustworthiness; now it's easy to have that iconography on a website.

I can offer more examples of trust hacking. "Sponsored content" matches the form and function of the platform that features it but is in fact paid advertising. (Most platforms do, however, identify sponsored content as such at the beginning of an article.) Customer reviews, now ubiquitous on Internet commerce sites, may appear authentic but are easily faked. People routinely claimed false or dubious professional credentials: goons pretending to be immigration authorities in order to extort money from recent newcomers, mail-order PhDs pretending to be medical doctors in order to hawk quack remedies, fraudsters pretending to be tax authorities in order to gain access to honest taxpayers' computers and passwords.

One final thing: our cognitive systems of trust are based on trusting individuals. We're not hardwired to evaluate the trustworthiness of organizations, brands, corporations, and the like. Hence the lovable mascot and celebrity endorsement; advertisers have been giving brands a human face and triggering all of our cognitive trust systems for decades.

Brands have even acquired distinct social media personalities, from the fast-food chain Wendy's Twitter persona as a sarcastic troll to Amazon's furious pushback on critics in government, all to mimic intimacy and gain trust in the same manner that influencers and politicians do. As businesses and political movements increasingly employ AI to optimize their social media presence—and grow tempted to make and run fake accounts to create perceptions of grassroots support—even cynics and skeptics may soon have their trust hacked as they never have before.

47

Fear and Risk

Our human sense of fear is innate; it evolved over millennia as our ancestors learned how to evade predators who wanted to turn us into food and—more recently—members of our own species who wanted to harm us for their own advantage. Like the systems of attention we just reviewed, our fear system consists of cognitive shortcuts. It too is optimized for the circumstances of our evolutionary past.

These are very basic brain functions, largely controlled by the amygdala in the brain stem. Our brains aren't very good at probability and risk analysis. We tend to exaggerate spectacular, strange, and rare events, and downplay ordinary, familiar, and common ones. We think rare risks are more common than they are. We fear them more than probability indicates we should.

Many psychological researchers have sought to explain this, and one of their key findings is that people react to risk more on the basis of stories than data. Stories engage us at a visceral level, especially if they're vivid, exciting, or personally involving. A friend's story about getting mugged in a foreign country is more likely to affect how safe you feel traveling to that country than will a page of abstract crime statistics. Novelty plus dread plus a good story equals overreaction.

The effects of this are everywhere. We fear being murdered, kidnapped, raped, or assaulted by strangers, when it's far more likely that any perpetrator of such offenses will be a relative or a friend. We worry about airplane crashes and rampaging shooters instead of automobile crashes and domestic violence—both of which are far more common and deadly. We initially had, and some of us still have, no idea how to react to the risks of COVID-19, which are individually small, collectively huge, extremely sensitive to small changes in social conditions, and continually mutating.

Terrorism directly hacks these cognitive shortcuts. As an actual risk, it's minor. The 9/11 attacks killed about 3,000 people, and about 300 more have died from terrorist attacks in the US in the two decades since then. On the other hand, 38,000 people die every year in car accidents; that's about 750,000 deaths in the same span of time. Over a million people died in the US from COVID-19. But terrorism is designed to override any logic. It's horrifying, vivid, spectacular, random, and malicious: the very things that cause us to exaggerate risk and overreact. Fear takes hold, and we make security trade-offs we might have never considered before. These are society's anxieties and instincts collectively being hacked.

Politicians hack fear as well. If you can argue that your political program can provide security and resolve whatever threat may be most in the news, you'll attract support. People can acquire fears from party leadership or their peers, even in the absence of relevant personal experience. A voter living in northern New Hampshire may be extremely fearful of immigrants at the southern border of the US, even though that person has no experiences with people from Central America. As Bill Clinton said, "When people are insecure, they'd rather have somebody who is strong and wrong than someone who's weak and right."

Tribalism is a system of collective group identity. We are wired to form groups and to exclude nonmembers. The vulnerability lies in the fact that we will form groups at the slightest provocation, even if it makes no real sense to do so. When I was a kid at summer camp, the counselors organized something called "color war." Basically, the whole camp was randomly divided into two groups for a week: reds and golds. We no longer ate together. We no longer played together. The effects were immediate. We were the good guys, and they were the enemy. Of course, I can no longer remember what color I was, but I remember well the feeling of being polarized against other campers who used to be my friends.

There are three basic ways to exploit our tribalism vulnerability. The first is to reinforce existing group identity and group divisions. This is what the Russian Internet Research Agency did in the US in the months leading up to the 2016 election, with tactics like donating money to partisan organizations and provoking conflict on online forums. "Find the cracks," I've heard it called. That is, find existing societal fissures that can be magnified into tribal divisions.

The second is to deliberately create tribal groups for some ulterior purpose. Colonial governments in the nineteenth and twentieth centuries were infamous for this. In Rwanda, the Germans and Belgians who ruled the region turned an economic distinction between Hutus (farmers) and Tutsis (herders) into a major ethnic and class distinction, ultimately leading to genocide decades later. Today, brands use similar strategies—albeit at a much lower intensity—to sell us everything from sneakers to soda to cars.

The third is to create conditions for tribalism to naturally arise. That is, take existing affinity groups and make that affinity tribal in nature. Sports teams do this. Increasingly, political parties and partisan actors also do this.

Fox News must certainly understand the research demonstrating that an amplified sense of threat is associated with increased support for in-groups and fear of out-groups. When Fox runs stories with themes like "immigrants are going to take your jobs," "[this or that city] is crime-ridden and dangerous," "ISIS is a threat to Americans," and "Democrats are going to take your guns," they aren't only building support for those issues. They're also creating the conditions under which groups become more polarized.

Data analytics and automation are only getting smarter at hacking people's sense of group identity to achieve some goal. And tribalism is so powerful and divisive that hacking it—especially with digital speed and precision—can have disastrous social effects, whether that's the goal of a computer-assisted social hacker (like the Russians) or a side effect of an AI that neither knows nor cares about the costs of its actions (like social media recommendation engines).

48

Defending against Cognitive Hacks

The "pick-up artist" community is a movement of men who develop and share manipulative techniques to seduce women. It predates the popular Internet but thrives there today. A lot of their techniques resemble cognitive hacks. "Negging" is one of their techniques. Basically, it's a backhanded compliment deliberately designed to undermine the recipient's confidence and increase their need to seek emotional approval by the manipulator. Yeah, I know. Gross.

I have no idea if negging, or any of their other hacks, reliably work. The men who discuss this online offer plenty of self-aggrandizing anecdotal evidence, but it's hard to separate the lies from the bad scientific methodology. Reading stories by women who are on the receiving end of these attempted hacks, one thing is clear: foreknowledge is the best defense. If you know that negging is a tactic, you can see it coming.

Foreknowledge accelerates regression to the mean. That is, many cognitive hacks work well in the beginning but less so as people adapt to them. Banner ads had a 49% click-through rate when they first appeared in 1994; now their success rate is less than 1%. Pop-up ads exhibited a similar decline as they became annoyingly ubiquitous. We're likely to see the same effect with microtargeting, drip pricing, fake Facebook accounts, and everything else I talked about in the past several chapters. As we become inured to these tactics, they become less effective.

Foreknowledge only goes so far, though. Many cognitive hacks work even when we know we're being manipulated. If you can manipulate a person into believing something, they often maintain or strengthen their beliefs when confronted with clear evidence that they are wrong. More concretely, companies often use free introductory trials followed by recurring monthly subscriptions to hack consumers' willingness to pay, counting on humans' systematic overconfidence in their memory and time management skills to charge them monthly for services they keep meaning to cancel—and knowing that even if they are aware of their tendency to lose track of time, they won't stop doing it.

Another defense is to declare particular manipulative practices illegal. For instance, Australia has mandated that the full price of goods be disclosed up front to prevent drip pricing, and the FTC requires that advertised claims be "reasonably substantiated." We can render some of these hacks less effective, and therefore less dangerous, by reducing the ability to microtarget these hacks at particular individuals. If paid messaging, particularly political advertising, must be broadly targeted, it would be more difficult to exploit many classes of cognitive hacks for nefarious means.

However, any new rules will be hacked. So, while we need robust, flexible oversight and transparency to ensure that cognitive hacks can't be used to mislead, these alone are unlikely to be sufficient to stop people from deploying them. It's even harder because it's difficult to explain what's "wrong" with many of these hacks, whose harms can be abstract or long-term and challenging to prove.

Cognitive hacks play on the most basic and pervasive aspects of the human mind, from our survival instincts to our craving for social status. They can be used against anyone. Protecting ourselves from cognitive hacks requires society-wide defense-in-depth: spanning education, regulation and—especially online—technical solutions. As digital technology occupies ever more of our attention, cognitive hacking is increasingly taking place by means of machines. And as computer programs evolve from tools of human hackers into ever faster, more powerful, and more autonomous hackers, understanding how our digital products can hack *us* will become increasingly critical to protecting ourselves from manipulation.

49

A Hierarchy of Hacking

No system exists in isolation. It's always part of a hierarchy.

Imagine someone who wants to steal money via an online banking transaction. They can hack the bank's website. They can hack a bank customer's Internet browser. They can hack the customer's computer operating system or its hardware. All of those hacks could potentially achieve their goal of free money and their objective of thievery.

Now imagine someone who wants to pay less tax. Most obviously, they can hack the tax code and find new loopholes. But if they have the power and influence, they can also go up a level and hack the legislative process used to create the tax code. Or they can go up another level and hack the rule-making process used to implement the legislation, or the appropriations process, so the taxation authorities don't have enough staff to conduct tax audits. (Hacking the enforcement process is another way to subvert the intent of a system.) They can go up three levels and hack the political process used to elect the legislators. They can go up four levels and hack the media ecosystem used to discuss the political processes. Or they can go up five levels and hack the cognitive processes provoked by the media ecosystem used to discuss the political processes that elect the legislators that create the tax code that opens or closes loopholes. They can even go *down* one level and find vulnerabilities and exploits in a tax preparation program.

My point here is that systems occupy a hierarchy of increasing generality whereby the system above governs the system beneath it—and hacks can target any level. Hacking works by exploiting a hierarchy of mutually entangled systems. One system may be hard to breach or manipulate on its own, but the higher-level systems that govern it or the lower-level systems that implement system commands can be a powerful source of exploits for targets that would be secure in themselves.

In the technological context, moving up levels is difficult. The fact that Microsoft Windows has vulnerabilities doesn't guarantee that someone can hack the Microsoft Corporation's hiring process to put himself in a position to insert more vulnerabilities into the operating system. In social systems, it's easier, especially for those with money and influence. Jeff Bezos had no problem buying the largest home in DC to entertain and influence lawmakers. Or buying the *Washington Post*, one of the most respected news sources in the US. He can also easily hire programmers to write any sort of software he wants.

Some hacks work at multiple levels simultaneously. In 2020, we learned about Ghostwriter, a collective—probably Russian in origin—that breached the content management systems of several Eastern European news sites and posted fake stories. This is a conventional hack of computer systems connected to the Internet, combined with a trust hack: the reputation for legitimacy of those news sites.

Patching is also easier lower down than higher up. A vulnerability in TurboTax can be fixed in days. A vulnerability in the tax code might take years to fix. Cognitive vulnerabilities can easily last generations (although the particular exploitation tactics may have to change regularly).

This makes cognitive hacks the most dangerous exploits of all. They govern all of our actions, both individual and collective, and thus all of our social systems. If you can hack the human mind, you can use those techniques on voters, employees, businessmen, regulators, politicians, and other hackers alike, and nudge them to reshape the systems they inhabit as you see fit.

The danger of cognitive hacking is spreading. Human minds are not the only cognitive systems we need to worry about anymore. Public services, business transactions, and even basic social interactions are now mediated by digital systems that make predictions and decisions just like humans do, but they do it faster, more consistently, and less accountably than humans. Our machines increasingly make decisions for us, but they don't think like we do, and the interaction of our minds with these artificial intelligences points the way to an exciting and dangerous future for hacking: in the economy, the law, and beyond.

PART 7

HACKING AI SYSTEMS

50

Artificial Intelligence and Robotics

Artificial intelligence—AI—is an information technology. It consists of software, it runs on computers, and it is already deeply embedded into our social fabric, both in ways we understand and in ways we don't. It will hack our society in a way that nothing heretofore has done.

I mean this in two very different ways. One, AI systems will be used to hack us. And two, AI systems will themselves become hackers: finding vulnerabilities in all sorts of social, economic, and political systems, and then exploiting them at an unprecedented speed, scale, scope, and sophistication. It's not just a difference in degree; it's a difference in kind. We risk a future of AI systems hacking other AI systems, with the effects on humans being little more than collateral damage.

This may seem somewhat hyperbolic, but none of what I describe requires far-future science-fiction technology. I'm not postulating any "singularity," where the AI-learning feedback loop becomes so fast that it outstrips human understanding. My scenarios don't require evil geniuses. I'm not assuming intelligent androids like Data from Star Trek, R2-D2 from Star Wars, or Marvin from The Hitchhiker's Guide to the Galaxy series. We don't need malicious AI systems like Skynet from Terminator, Ultron from the Avengers works, or the agents from the Matrix movies. Some of the hacks I will discuss don't even require major research breakthroughs. They'll improve as AI techniques grow in sophistication, but we can see hints of them in operation today. This hacking will arise naturally, as AIs become more advanced at learning, understanding, and problem-solving.

> Def: **AI** / ā-ī/ (noun) -
>
> 1. (abbrev.) Artificial intelligence.
>
> 2. A computer that can (generally) sense, think, and act.
>
> 3. An umbrella term encompassing a broad array of decision-making technologies that simulate human thinking.

This definition isn't canonical, but defining AI is hard. In 1968, the pioneering computer scientist Marvin Minsky described AI as "the science of making machines do things that would require intelligence if done by men." Patrick Winston, another AI pioneer, defined it as "computations that make it possible to perceive, reason, and act." The 1950 version of the Turing test—called the "imitation game" in the original discussion—focused on a hypothetical computer program that humans couldn't distinguish from an actual human.

I need to differentiate between specialized—sometimes called "narrow"—AI and general AI. General AI is what you see in the movies, the AI that can sense, think, and act in a very general and human way. If it's smarter than humans, it's called "artificial superintelligence." Combine it with robotics and you have an android, one that may look more or less like a human. The movie robots that try to destroy humanity are all general AI.

A lot of practical research has been conducted into how to create general AI, as well as theoretical research about how to design these systems so they don't do things we don't want them to, like destroy humanity. While this is fascinating work, encompassing fields from computer science to sociology to philosophy, its practical applications are probably decades away. I want to focus instead on specialized AI, because that's what's under development now.

Specialized AI is designed for a specific task, such as the system that controls a self-driving car. It knows how to steer the vehicle, how to follow traffic laws, how to avoid getting into accidents, and what to do when something unexpected happens—like a child's ball suddenly bouncing into the road. Specialized AI knows a lot and can make decisions based on that knowledge, but only in the limited domain of driving.

One common joke among AI researchers is that as soon as something works, it's no longer AI. It's just software. That might make AI research depressing, since by definition the only advances that count are failures, but the joke hides a grain of truth. AI is inherently a mystifying science-fictional term, but once it becomes reality, it's no longer all mystifying. We used to assume that reading chest X-rays required a radiologist: that is, an intelligent human with appropriate training and professional credentials. We've learned that it's a rote task that can also be performed by a computer.

Here's how to think about it: there is a continuum of decision-making technologies and systems, ranging from a simple electromechanical thermostat that operates a furnace in response to changing temperatures to a science-fictional android. What makes something AI often depends on the complexity of both the tasks performed and the environment in which this occurs. The thermostat performs a very simple task that only has to take into account that one aspect of the environment. It doesn't even require a computer. A modern digital thermostat might be able to sense who is in the room and make predictions about future heat needs on the basis of both usage and weather forecast, as well as citywide power consumption and second-by-second energy costs. A futuristic AI thermostat might act like a thoughtful and caring butler, whatever that might mean in the context of adjusting the ambient temperature.

I would rather avoid preoccupation with definitions, because they largely don't matter for the purpose of this discussion. In addition to decision-making, the relevant qualities of the AI systems I'll be discussing are autonomy (the ability to act independently), automation (the ability to act on preset responses to specific triggers), and physical agency (the ability to alter the physical environment). A thermostat has limited automation and physical agency, and no autonomy. A system that predicts

criminal recidivism has no physical agency; it just makes recommendations to a judge. A driverless car has some of all three. R2-D2 has a lot of
all three, although for some reason its designers left out English speech
synthesis.

> Def: **Robot** /'rō-,bät/ (noun) -
>
> 1. Physically embodied objects that can sense, think, and act on their en-
> vironments through physical motion.

Robotics also has developed a popular mythology and a less-flashy
reality. Like AI, there are many different definitions of the term. In film
and television, robots are often represented as artificial people: androids.
But like AI, robotics encompasses a spectrum of reasoning and physical
abilities. Again, I prefer to focus on technologies that are more prosaic and
near term. For our purposes, robotics is autonomy, automation, and physical agency dialed way up. It's "cyber-physical autonomy": AI technology
inside objects that can interact with the world in a direct, physical manner.

51

Hacking AI

A I systems are computer programs, running on computers, almost certainly on large-scale computer networks. As such, they are vulnerable to all the same types of hacking to which other computer systems are vulnerable. But there are also hacks to which AI systems are uniquely vulnerable—machine learning (ML) systems in particular. ML is a subfield of AI, but has come to dominate practical AI systems. In ML systems, blank "models" are fed an enormous amount of data and given instructions to figure solutions out for themselves. Some ML attacks involve stealing the "training data" used to teach the ML system, or stealing the ML model upon which the system is based. Others involve configuring the ML system to make bad—or wrong—decisions.

This last category, known as "adversarial machine-learning," is essentially a collection of hacks. Sometimes, they involve studying the ML system in detail in order to develop enough understanding about its functioning and its blind spots to craft inputs that target those blind spots. For example, an ML system can be fooled with carefully constructed inputs. In 2017, MIT researchers designed a toy turtle such that an AI image classifier would decide it was a rifle. Other examples include carefully placed, seemingly innocuous stickers affixed to a stop sign that fool an AI classifier into thinking it's a speed-limit sign, or placement of stickers on a road that fool a self-driving car into swerving into oncoming traffic. These are all theoretical examples, and while researchers have succeeded in causing cars to fail in this manner in tests, as far as we know no one has actually crashed a self-driving car through adversarial ML.

Adversarial ML doesn't have to be malevolent, and it isn't restricted to laboratory settings. Right now, there are adversarial ML projects trying to hack facial recognition systems so that protesters and others can congregate publicly without fear of being identified by police. Similarly, you can imagine a future where insurance companies use AI systems to make claims-authorization decisions. A doctor might resort to a known hack to guarantee insurance approval for a patient who needs a particular drug or procedure.

Other successful hacks involve feeding an ML system specific inputs designed to elicit changes in the system. In 2016, Microsoft introduced a chatbot, Tay, on Twitter. Its conversational style was modeled on the speech patterns of a teenage girl, and was supposed to grow more sophisticated as it interacted with people and learned their conversational style. Within twenty-four hours, a group on the 4Chan discussion forum coordinated their responses to Tay. They flooded the system with racist, misogynistic, and anti-Semitic tweets, thereby transforming Tay into a racist, misogynistic anti-Semite. Tay learned from them, and—with no actual understanding—parroted their ugliness back to the world.

AI systems are computer programs, so there's no reason to believe that they won't be vulnerable to the same hacks to which other computer programs are vulnerable. Research into adversarial ML is still in its early stages of development, so we can't say definitively whether any of the adversarial attacks I have described will be easy or difficult, or how effective security countermeasures will be. If the history of computer hacking is any guide, there will be exploitable vulnerabilities in AI systems for the foreseeable future. AI systems are embedded in the same sorts of sociotechnical systems that I've discussed throughout the book, so there will always be people who want to hack them for their personal gain.

The thing about the hacks I just described is that the results are obvious. Cars crash. A turtle is misclassified as a rifle. Tay acts like a racist misogynistic Nazi. We'll see it happening, and—hopefully—patch the ML systems and restore their functioning to a more reasonable state.

There is a continuum of imaginable hacks, from the obvious to the invisible. I am more worried about attacks the results of which are subtler and less obvious. Cars may not crash, but they may drive slightly erratically. Chatbots may not turn into full-fledged Nazis, but they may become slightly more inclined to validate the positions of one particular political party. Hackers may figure out a phrase to add to college applications that will bump them up into a better category. As long as the results are subtle and the algorithms are unknown to us, how would anyone know that they're happening?

52

The Explainability Problem

In *The Hitchhiker's Guide to the Galaxy*, a race of hyper-intelligent, pan-dimensional beings build the universe's most powerful computer, Deep Thought, to answer the ultimate question to life, the universe, and everything. After 7.5 million years of computation, Deep Thought informs them that the answer is 42. But it's unable to explain its answer, or even what the question was.

That, in a nutshell, is the explainability problem. Modern AI systems are essentially black boxes. Data goes in at one end, and an answer comes out the other. It can be impossible to understand how the system reached its conclusion, even if you are the system's designer and can examine the code. Researchers don't know precisely how an AI image-classification system differentiates turtles from rifles, let alone why one of them mistook one for the other.

In 2016, the AI program AlphaGo won a five-game match against one of the world's best Go players, Lee Sedol—something that shocked both the AI and the Go-playing worlds. AlphaGo's most famous move was in game two: move thirty-seven. It's hard to explain without diving deep into Go strategy, but it was a move that no human would ever have chosen to make. It was an instance of an AI thinking differently.

AIs don't solve problems like humans do. Their limitations are different from ours. They'll consider more possible solutions than we might. More importantly, they'll look at more *types* of solutions. They'll explore paths that we simply have not considered, paths more complex than the sorts of things we generally keep in mind. (Our cognitive limits on the amount of simultaneous data we can mentally juggle has long been described as "the magical number seven plus or minus two." An AI system has nothing even remotely like that limitation.)

In 2015, a research group fed an AI system called Deep Patient health and medical data from approximately 700,000 individuals, and tested whether or not the system could predict diseases. The result was an across-the-board success. Unexpectedly, Deep Patient performed well at anticipating the onset of psychiatric disorders like schizophrenia, even though a first psychotic episode is nearly impossible for physicians to predict. It sounds great, but Deep Patient provides no explanation for the basis of its diagnoses and predictions, and the researchers have no idea how it comes to its conclusions. A doctor either can trust or ignore the computer, but can't query it for more info.

That's not ideal. The AI system should not only spit out an answer but also provide some explanation of its reasoning in a format that humans can understand. We need this both to be comfortable trusting the AI system's decisions and to ensure that our AI systems haven't been hacked to make biased decisions. Providing a reasoned explanation has intrinsic value apart from whether it improves the likelihood of accuracy; it is regarded as a basic component of the idea of due process under the law.

Researchers are working on explainable AI; in 2017, the Defense Advanced Research Projects Agency (DARPA) launched a $75 million research fund for a dozen programs in the area. While there will be advances in this field, there seems to be a trade-off between efficacy and explainability—and other trade-offs between efficacy and security, and explainability and privacy. Explanations are a form of cognitive shorthand used by humans, suited for the way humans make decisions. AI decisions simply might not be conducive to humanly understandable explanations, and forcing AI systems to make those explanations might pose an additional constraint that could affect the quality of their decisions. It's unclear where all this research will lead to. In the near term, AI is becoming more and more opaque, as systems become more complex, less human-like, and less explainable.

In some contexts, we might not care about explainability. I might feel confident being diagnosed by Deep Patient—even though it couldn't explain its actions—if the data demonstrated that it was more accurate than a human doctor. I might also feel the same way about an AI system that decided where to drill for oil or predicted which airplane parts were more likely to fail. I might not be as comfortable with an AI system that made college admission decisions by predicting the likelihood that an applicant would succeed academically, a system that made loan decisions by factoring racial stereotypes into its predictions of the possibility of default, or a system that made parole decisions by predicting recidivism. Some people may eventually be comfortable with AI systems making even high-stakes decisions without an explanation. This is all highly subjective and will likely change over time as we become more inculcated in AI decision-making.

Others disagree, and strongly oppose unexplainable AI. The Future of Life Institute and other AI researchers note that explainability is especially important for systems that might "cause harm," have "a significant effect on individuals," or affect "a person's life, quality of life or reputation." The report "AI in the UK" suggests that if an AI system has a "substantial impact on an individual's life" and cannot provide "full and satisfactory explanation" for its decisions, then the system should not be deployed.

To me, the difference between an AI that needs to offer an explanation and an AI that doesn't is one of fairness. We need to ensure that AI systems aren't racist, sexist, ableist, or discriminatory in some way that we haven't even dreamed up yet. Without explainability, we could easily obtain the results similar to those generated by Amazon's internal AI system to screen job applications. That system was trained on ten years of the company's hiring data, and because the tech industry is male dominated, the AI system taught itself to be sexist, ranking resumes lower if they included the word "women's" or if the applicant graduated from an all-women's college. (There are times when we don't want the future to look like the past.)

That was obviously biased and unfair, and Amazon executives lost enthusiasm for the project and scrapped the system once they realized what was going on. They faced a difficult, maybe even insurmountable problem, because there are multiple contradictory definitions of fairness; "fair" in one context isn't necessarily fair in another. Is a fair system for determining admission one that is gender blind, one that deliberately corrects for previous gender biases, one that awards admission to genders in the proportion they apply, or one that provides for equal opportunity between the genders as well as for transgender or non-binary people?

If an AI system can explain its reasoning for making a particular hiring recommendation or a particular parole decision, we will be better able to scrutinize its decision-making process. This means we are more likely to trust that system in situations that are more socially nuanced than "Does this X-ray indicate a tumor?"

On the other hand, human decisions aren't necessarily very explainable. Sure, we can give them, but the research indicates that they are more after-the-fact justifications than actual explanations. So maybe the answer is to simply look at the results. When courts decide if a particular police department's behavior is racist, they don't open up the skulls of the police officers or ask them for explanations of their behavior. They look at the results and make a determination from that.

53

Humanizing AI

Artificial intelligence systems will affect us at the personal level as well as the social level. Previously, I mentioned social engineering. The most effective phishing attempts—the ones that result in people and companies losing lots of money—are personalized. An email impersonating the CEO to someone in the finance department, asking for a particular wire transfer, can be especially effective, voice or video even more so. The laborious task of customizing phishing attacks could be automated by AI techniques, enabling scammers to fine-tune their individually targeted emails or voice messages from authority figures to make them more believable.

Being deceived by an AI isn't necessarily more problematic than being deceived by another human; the greater danger lies in the fact that AIs will be capable of persuasion at computer speed and scale. Today's cognitive hacks are crude: a fake newspaper article or provocative nudge capable of fooling only the most gullible or desperate. AI has the potential for cognitive hacks to be microtargeted: personalized, optimized, and individually delivered. Old-style con games like the pigeon drop are individually crafted person-to-person cognitive hacks. Advertising messages are bulk-broadcast cognitive hacks. AI techniques have the potential to blend aspects of both of those techniques.

People have long ascribed human-like qualities to computer programs. In the 1960s, programmer Joseph Weizenbaum created a primitive conversational program called ELIZA that mimicked the manner of a psychotherapist. Weizenbaum was amazed that people would confide deeply personal secrets to what they knew was a dumb computer program. Weizenbaum's secretary would even ask him to leave the room so that she could talk to ELIZA in private. Today, people are often polite to voice assistants like Alexa and Siri as if they would actually care about tone. Siri even complains when you're mean to it: "That's not very nice," it says—because it's programmed to, of course.

Numerous experiments bear similar results. Research subjects would rate a computer's performance less critically if they gave the rating on the computer they were criticizing, indicating that they didn't want to hurt its feelings. In another experiment, if a computer told a research subject some obviously fictional piece of "personal information," the subject was likely to reciprocate by sharing actual personal information. The power of reciprocation is something that psychologists study. It's a hack that people use, too—yet another cognitive hack that the scale and personalization of AI can supercharge.

The addition of robotics makes AI hacks more effective. We humans have developed some pretty efficient cognitive shortcuts to recognize other people. We see faces everywhere; two dots over a horizontal line registers as a face. This is why even minimalist illustrations are so effective. If something has a face, then it's a creature of some sort, with intentions, feelings, and everything else that comes with real-world faces. If that something speaks or, even better, converses, then we may believe it has intentions, desires, and agency. If it has eyebrows, we're even more likely to do so.

Robots are no exception. Many people have quasi-social relationships with their robot vacuums, even complaining if the company offers to replace rather than repair "their" Roomba. A US Army–developed anti-landmine robot ran into problems when a colonel refused to allow the insect-shaped device to continue to harm itself by stepping on mines. A Harvard robot could convince students to buzz it into dorms by pretending to be a food-delivery robot. And Boxie, a childlike talking robot developed by researchers at MIT, could persuade people to answer personal questions just by asking nicely.

At least some of our response to robots is similar to our response to the appearance and behavior of children. Children have large heads in proportion to their bodies, large eyes in proportion to their heads, and large lashes in proportion to their eyes. They have high-pitched voices. We respond to these characteristics with a sense of protectiveness.

Artists have taken advantage of this phenomenon for generations to make their creations appear more sympathetic. Children's dolls are designed to evoke a loving, protective response. Cartoon characters are drawn this way, including Betty Boop in the 1930s and Bambi in 1942. The main character of the 2019 live-action movie *Alita: Battle Angel* had her eyes computer-enhanced so that they would appear larger.

In 2016, the Georgia Institute of Technology published a study on human trust in robots that employed a non-anthropomorphic robot to assist participants in navigating through a building, providing directions such as "This way to the exit." First, participants interacted with the robot in a normal setting to experience its performance, which was deliberately poor. Then, they had to decide whether or not to follow the robot's commands in a simulated emergency. In the latter situation, all twenty-six participants obeyed the robot's directional advice, despite having observed just moments before that it had lousy navigational skills. The degree of trust they placed in this machine was striking: when the robot pointed to a dark room with no clear exit, the majority of people obeyed it, rather than safely exiting by the door through which they had entered. The researchers conducted similar experiments with other robots that seemed to malfunction. Again, subjects followed these robots' emergency directions, apparently abandoning their common sense. It seems that robots can naturally hack our trust.

Anthropomorphic robots are an emotionally persuasive technology, and AI will only amplify their attractiveness. As AI mimics humans, or even animals, it will hijack all the mechanisms that humans use to evaluate each other and come up with new ways to hack those mechanisms. As psychologist Sherry Turkle wrote in 2010: "When robots make eye contact, recognize faces, mirror human gestures, they push our Darwinian buttons, exhibiting the kind of behavior people associate with sentience, intentions, and emotions." That is, they hack our brains.

We won't just treat AIs as people. They'll also act like people in ways that will be deliberately designed to fool us. They'll employ cognitive hacks.

54

AI and Robots Hacking Us

During the 2016 US election, about a fifth of all political tweets were posted by bots. For the UK Brexit vote of the same year, a third. An Oxford Internet Institute report from 2019 found evidence of bots being used to spread propaganda in fifty countries. These tended to be simple programs mindlessly repeating slogans. For example, a quarter-million pro-Saudi "We all have trust in [crown prince] Mohammed bin Salman" tweets were posted following the 2018 murder of Jamal Khashoggi.

In 2017, the Federal Communications Commission announced an online period of public comment regarding its plans to repeal net neutrality. A staggering 22 million comments were received. Many of them—maybe half—were submitted using stolen identities. These fake comments were crude; 1.3 million were generated from the same template, with some words altered to make them appear unique. They didn't stand up to even cursory scrutiny.

Efforts like these will only grow in sophistication. For years, AI programs have composed news stories about sports and finance for real news organizations like the Associated Press. The constrained nature of much reporting on those topics has made them easier to adapt to AI. AI is now being used to write more general stories. Modern text-creation systems like Open AI's GPT-3 can be fed facts and write true stories, but they can just as easily be fed untruths and write fake news.

It doesn't take much imagination to see how AI will degrade political discourse. Already, AI-driven personas can write personalized letters to newspapers and elected officials, leave intelligible comments on news sites and message boards, and intelligently debate politics on social media. As these systems become more articulate and personal and harder to distinguish from real people, tactics that were once obvious may become much harder to detect.

In a recent experiment, researchers used a text-generation program to submit 1,000 comments in response to a government request for public input on a Medicaid issue. They all sounded unique, like real people advocating a specific policy position. They fooled the Medicaid.gov administrators, who accepted the submissions as genuine concerns from actual human beings. The researchers subsequently identified the comments and asked for them to be removed, so that no actual policy debate would be unfairly biased. Others won't be as ethical.

These techniques are already being used to influence policy in the real world. An online propaganda campaign has used AI-generated headshots to create fake journalists. China disseminated AI-generated text messages designed to influence the 2020 Taiwanese election. Deep-fake technology—AI techniques to create real videos of fake events, often with actual people saying things they didn't actually say—are being used politically in countries such as Malaysia, Belgium, and the US.

One example of an extension of this technology is the "persona bot," an AI posing as an individual on social media and other online groups. Persona bots have histories, personalities, and communication styles. They don't constantly spew propaganda. They hang out in various interest groups: gardening, knitting, model railroading, whatever. They act as normal members of those communities, posting and commenting and discussing. Systems like GPT-3 will make it easy for those AIs to mine previous conversations and related Internet content and to appear knowledgeable. Then, once in a while, the AI might post something relevant to a political issue, maybe an article about a healthcare worker having an allergic reaction to the COVID-19 vaccine, with worried commentary. Or maybe it might offer its developer's opinions about a recent election, or racial justice, or any other polarizing subject. One persona bot can't move public opinion, but what if there were thousands of them? Millions?

This has been called "computational propaganda," and will change the way we view communication. AI has the potential to make the future supply of disinformation spreaders infinite. It may also break community discourse. In 2012, robotics ethicist Kate Darling conducted an experiment with an animatronic plastic dinosaur named Cleo, a toy that responded to touch in various ways. After having participants at a science conference play with Cleo, she tried to persuade them to "hurt" it in various ways. People felt such strong empathy after only a short time playing with Cleo that they refused to do so, even though it felt no pain. This is a fundamentally human response. We might intuitively know that Cleo is just a plastic green dinosaur. But a large face paired with a small body makes us regard it as a child. It has a name that tells us it's a she! And she reacts to our touch! Suddenly we're thinking of her as a creature with feelings, and feel compelled to protect her from harm. And while that reaction may be benign, what happens when that sweet little robot looks up at her human owners with her big, sad eyes and pleads with them to buy her a software upgrade?

Because we humans are prone to making category errors and treating robots as living creatures with feelings and intentions, we are vulnerable to being manipulated by them. Robots could persuade us to do things we might not do otherwise. They could scare us into not doing things we might otherwise do. In one experiment, a robot was able to exert "peer pressure" on subjects, encouraging them to take more risks. How soon before a sex robot suggests in-app purchases in the heat of the moment?

AIs will get better at this sort of persuasion. Researchers are already designing AIs that detect emotions by analyzing our writing, reading our facial expressions, or monitoring our breathing and heart rate. They get it wrong a lot of the time, but this will change as technology advances. And AIs will eventually surpass people in capability. This will allow more precise manipulation, with the caveat about adaptability that I mentioned earlier.

AIBO is a robot dog introduced by Sony in 1999. The company released new and improved models every year through 2005, then over the next few years slowly discontinued support for older AIBOs. AIBO was pretty primitive by computing standards, but that didn't stop people from becoming emotionally attached to their AIBOs. In Japan, people held funerals for their "dead" AIBOs.

In 2018, Sony started selling a new generation of AIBO. What's particularly interesting here aren't the software advances that make it more pet-like, but the fact that AIBO now requires cloud data storage to function. This means that, unlike previous generations, Sony can modify or even remotely "kill" any AIBO. Cloud storage costs $300 per year. If Sony had wanted to maximize its revenue, it should have made the first three years free and then—when owners had become emotionally attached to their pets—charged a lot more for subsequent years. One might call this tactic "emotional lock-in."

As AIs and autonomous robots take on more real-world tasks, human trust in autonomous systems will be hacked with dangerous and costly results. But never forget that humans control AIs. All AI systems are designed and bankrolled by humans who want to manipulate other humans in a particular way for a particular purpose.

Corporations like Sony, and other powerful actors, think long and hard about how to hack our emotions for power and profit. They invest heavily in research and technology to do it. And without an active effort to establish norms and regulations limiting these hacks, we'll soon find the literally inhuman capabilities of AI turned against ordinary people on behalf of their powerful masters.

55

Computers and AI Are
Accelerating Societal Hacking

Hacking is as old as humanity. We humans have been hacking systems for as long as there have been systems, and we've seen computer systems hacked for as long as there have been computers. Thanks to their complexity and programmable interfaces, computers are uniquely hackable. And today, many consumer products—such as cars, appliances, and phones—are controlled by computers. All of our social systems—finance, taxation, regulatory compliance, elections—are complex sociotechnical systems involving computers, networks, people, and institutions. This makes all of these products and systems more susceptible to hacking.

Computerization changes hacking, though. Especially when combined with techniques of AI, it accelerates hacking across four dimensions: speed, scale, scope, and sophistication.

Speed is easy to explain; computers are much faster than people. They don't need to sleep, and don't get bored or distracted. Properly programmed, they make mistakes far less often than humans do. This means computers scale rote tasks much more efficiently than humans are capable of doing; a smartphone takes a fraction of the energy and a minute percentage of the time a person would take to make a correct mathematical calculation. By vastly reducing the labor required to perform rote tasks, computers turn certain hacks from practically impossible to impossibly practical.

We're already seeing evidence of these new capabilities. A free AI-driven service called Donotpay.com automates the process of contesting parking tickets, helping to overturn hundreds of thousands of citations issued in cities like London and New York. The service has expanded into other domains, helping users receive compensation for delayed airline flights and cancel a variety of services and subscriptions.

AI speed also enables fast experimentation: computers can quickly try and discard countless variations of a product element to find the best one. A/B testing, in which different users are randomly shown different versions of a product, is frequently employed by web developers to test the effectiveness of their webpage designs. For example, users may be randomly shown a "version A" with a bigger "click here" button and a "version B" with a smaller one, with the website automatically collecting data on which version results in more clicks. Automated A/B testing enables developers to simultaneously test complex combinations of variables (like button size, color, placement, and font), allowing an unprecedented variety of hacks that can be further personalized to fit specific users' preferences and habits through the power of big data. The ability to simulate thousands of variations of a hack also widens the scope of the hacks that can be performed, both by commercial enterprises and by criminals.

The next dimension to consider is the scale of AI. A human activity with a long history, like stock trading, becomes something different, with unintended and unanticipated qualities, when magnified through computer automation. AI systems may engage in the same activities as their human creators, but they do so at an unprecedented scale.

It is more than possible that the persona bots discussed previously will be deployed in bulk across social media. They will be able to engage on the issues around the clock, sending unlimited numbers of messages, long and short. If allowed to run rampant, they have the potential to overwhelm any actual online debate. They'll artificially influence what we think is normal, and what we think others think, and their influence will be felt not just on social media but also in every public square and every living room. This sort of manipulation is not healthy for the marketplace of ideas or any democratic political process. Recall that to function properly, democracy requires information, choice, and agency. Artificial personas can starve citizens of both information and agency.

The scope of AIs is inevitably going to grow. As computer systems become more capable, society will delegate more—and more important—decisions to them. This means that hacks of these systems will cause more widespread damage and will have greater potential to destroy underlying sociotechnical systems, even if that isn't the intent of those who deploy them.

AI will exacerbate these trends. AI systems already make decisions that affect our lives, from the mundane to the life-defining. They give us turn-by-turn driving directions. They decide whether you stay in jail and whether you get a bank loan. They screen job candidates, applicants for college admission, and people who apply for government services. They make investment decisions and help shape decisions in criminal cases. They decide the news we see on social media, which candidates' ads we see, and what people and topics are brought to our attention again and again. They make military targeting decisions. In the future, AIs might recommend politicians for a wealthy political donor to support. They might decide who is eligible to vote. They might translate desired social outcomes into tax policies or tweak the details of entitlement programs.

Hacks of these increasingly critical systems will become more damaging. (We've seen early examples of this with "flash crashes" of the stock market.) And for the most part, we have little insight into how the systems are designed, made, or used.

Finally, the sophistication of AIs means that they will increasingly replace humans, since computers can often execute more complex and unanticipated strategies than humans can. This capability will also only increase as computers grow faster and more powerful, and networking grows more complex.

Many algorithms are already beyond human understanding, whether they recommend what movies we want to watch, which investments to purchase, or what move to make in the game of Go. This trend will only increase, potentially exponentially once algorithms begin to design other algorithms.

With the ascendance of AI, computer hacking becomes one of the most powerful ways to hack our social systems. When everything is a computer, software controls it all. Imagine a hacker inside a financial network, altering how money flows. Or inside legal databases—making small, substantive changes in laws and court rulings. (Will people notice, or know enough to verify the original wording?) Imagine a hacker altering Facebook's algorithms from the inside, changing the rules that govern whose post rises to the top of the feed, whose voice is amplified, and who else hears it. When computer programs operate the everyday systems we use to work, spend, talk, organize, and live, technology becomes the new policymaker. And for all the freedom that tech's capabilities can offer us, in the hands of a hacker they can transform into an unparalleled architecture for social control.

All of these systems are vulnerable to hacking; in fact, current research indicates that all machine-learning systems can be undetectably compromised. And those hacks will have increasingly large societal effects.

56

When AIs Become Hackers

Hacker "Capture the Flag" is basically the outdoor game played on computers. Teams defend their own networks while attacking those of the other teams. Played in a controlled setting, the game mirrors what computer hackers do in real life: finding and fixing vulnerabilities in their own systems, and exploiting them in others'.

The competition has been a mainstay at hacker conventions since the mid-1990s. These days, dozens of teams from around the world compete in weekend-long marathon events held all over the world. People train for months, and winning is a big deal. If you're into this sort of thing, it's pretty much the most fun you can possibly have on the Internet without committing multiple felonies.

The DARPA Cyber Grand Challenge was a similarly styled event for AI, run in 2016. One hundred teams entered. After completing qualifying rounds, seven finalists competed at the DEF CON convention in Las Vegas. The competition occurred in a specially designed test environment filled with custom software that had never been analyzed or tested. The AIs were given ten hours to find vulnerabilities to exploit against the other AIs in the competition and to patch themselves against exploitation. A system called Mayhem, created by a team of Pittsburgh computer security researchers, won. The researchers have since commercialized the technology, which is now busily defending networks for customers like the Department of Defense.

There was a human-team capture-the-flag event at DEF CON that same year. Mayhem was invited to participate as the only non-human team. It finished last overall, but it didn't come in last in every category all the time. You can easily imagine how this mixed competition might unfold in the future. We saw the trajectory with the game of chess, and then the game of Go. AI entrants will improve every year, because the core technologies are all improving. The human teams will largely stay the same, because humans remain humans even as our tools and facility with using them improves. Eventually, it's likely that the AIs will routinely beat the humans. My guess is that it'll take less than a decade.

DARPA inexplicably never repeated its AI capture-the-flag event, but China has been holding them regularly ever since. They also host hybrid events, with human–computer teams competing against each other. Details are few because these events are domestic only and increasingly hosted by the military, but—just as expected—Chinese AI systems are improving.

It will be years before we have entirely autonomous AI cyberattack capabilities, but AI technologies are already transforming the nature of cyberattacks in several dimensions. One area that seems particularly fruitful for AI systems is that of finding vulnerabilities. Plowing through software code line by line is exactly the sort of tedious problem at which AIs excel, if they can only be taught how to recognize a vulnerability. Many domain-specific challenges will need to be addressed, of course, but there is a healthy amount of academic literature on the topic, and research is continuing. There's every reason to expect AI systems will improve over time, and some reason to expect them to eventually become very accomplished.

The implications of this potential extend far beyond computer networks. There's no reason that AIs can't find thousands of new vulnerabilities in many of the systems I discussed in this book: the tax code, banking regulations, political processes. Whenever many rules interact with each other, we should expect AIs to eventually be finding their vulnerabilities

and creating exploits to compromise them. AIs are already at work looking for loopholes in contracts.

This capability will improve with time. Hackers of any kind are only
as good as their understanding of the system that they're targeting and its
interactions with the rest of the world. AIs initially capture this understanding through the data with which they're trained, and they continue
to improve as they are used. Modern AIs are constantly evolving as they
acquire new data and adjust their own internal workings accordingly. The
constant flow of data continues to train the AI as it operates and adds to
its expertise. This is why designers of driverless car systems brag about
the number of road hours their creations have clocked.

The development of AIs capable of hacking other systems gives rise
to two different but related problems. First, an AI might be instructed to
hack a system. Someone might feed an AI the world's tax codes or the
world's financial regulations, in order to create a slew of profitable hacks.
Second, an AI might inadvertently hack a system during the course of its
operations. Both scenarios are dangerous, but the second is more dangerous because we might never know it happened.

57

Reward Hacking

As I've noted previously, AIs don't solve problems in the same way that people do. They will inevitably stumble on solutions that we humans might never have anticipated, and some will subvert the intent of the system they're analyzing, because AIs don't think in terms of the implications, context, norms, and values that humans share and take for granted.

Reward hacking involves an AI achieving a goal in a way the AI's designers neither wanted nor intended. Here are some great examples:

- In a one-on-one soccer simulation, a player was supposed to score against the goalie. Instead of trying to directly kick the ball into the goal, the AI system figured out that if it kicked the ball out of bounds instead, the opponent goalie would have to throw it back in, leaving the goal undefended.
- An AI was instructed to stack blocks. Height was measured by the position of the bottom face of one particular block. The AI learned to flip that block upside down so that its bottom faced up, rather than stack it on top of another block with its bottom pointing downward. (Obviously, the rules failed to explicitly state how the blocks should be oriented.)
- In a simulated environment for "evolved" creatures, an AI was allowed to modify its own physical characteristics in order to better fulfill its

objectives. Given a goal of crossing a distant finish line as quickly as possible, you would expect that the AI would grow longer legs, or stronger muscles, or greater lung capacity. Instead, the AI grew tall enough to cross the finish line immediately by falling over it.

These are all hacks. You can blame them on poorly specified goals or rewards, and you would be correct. You can point out that they all occurred in simulated environments, and you would also be correct. But the problem they illustrate is more general: AIs are designed to optimize their function in order to achieve a goal. In so doing, they will naturally and inadvertently implement unexpected hacks.

Imagine a robotic vacuum assigned the task of cleaning up any mess it sees. Unless the goal is more precisely specified, it might disable its visual sensors so that it doesn't see any messes—or just cover them up with opaque materials. In 2018, an entrepreneurial—or perhaps just bored—programmer wanted his robot vacuum to stop bumping into furniture. He trained it by rewarding it for not hitting the bumper sensors. Instead of learning not to bump into things, the AI learned to drive the vacuum backwards because there were no bumper sensors on the back of the device.

If problems, inconsistencies, or loopholes exist in a set of rules, and if those properties lead to an acceptable solution as defined by the rules, then AIs will find them. We might look at the results and say, "Well, technically, the AI followed the rules." Yet we humans nonetheless sense a deviation, a cheat, a hack—because we understand the social context of the problem in a way AIs don't, and we have different expectations. AI researchers call this problem "goal alignment."

This problem is well illustrated by the King Midas story. When the god Dionysus grants him a single wish, Midas asks that everything he touches turn to gold. Midas ends up starving and miserable when his food, his drink, and his daughter all turn to inedible, unpotable, unlovable gold. That's a goal alignment problem: Midas programmed the wrong goal into his system of desires.

Genies, too, are very precise about the wording of wishes, and can be maliciously pedantic when granting them. But here's the thing: there is no way to outsmart the genie. Whatever you wish for, the genie will always be able to fulfill it in a way that you wish he hadn't. The genie will always be able to hack your wish.

More generally, in human language and thought, goals and desires are always underspecified. We never conceive of all of the options. We never delineate all of the caveats and exceptions and provisos. We never close off all the avenues for hacking. We can't. Any goal we specify will necessarily be incomplete.

This is largely acceptable in human interactions, because people understand context and usually act in good faith. We are all socialized, and in the process of becoming so, we generally acquire common sense about the way people and the world works. We fill any gaps in our understanding with both context and goodwill.

Philosopher Abby Everett Jaques, then head of the Ethics of AI Project at MIT, explained it something like this: If I asked you to get me some coffee, you would probably go to the nearest coffeepot and pour me a cup, or maybe walk to the corner coffee shop and buy one. You would not bring me a truckload of raw beans. You would not buy a coffee plantation in Costa Rica. You would also not look for the person closest to you holding a cup of coffee and rip it out of their hands. You wouldn't bring me week-old cold coffee, or a used paper towel that had wiped up a coffee spill. I wouldn't have to specify any of that. You would just know.

Similarly, if I ask you to develop a technology that would turn things to gold on touch, you wouldn't build it so that it starved the person using it. I wouldn't have to specify that; you would just know.

We can't completely specify goals to an AI, and AIs won't be able to completely understand context. In a TED talk, AI researcher Stuart Russell joked about a fictional AI assistant causing an airplane delay in order to delay someone's arrival at a dinner engagement. The audience laughed, but how would a computer program know that causing an airplane computer malfunction is not an appropriate response to someone who wants to get out of dinner? Perhaps it learned its lesson from reports of airline passengers who engaged in similar behavior. (Internet joke from 2017: Jeff Bezos: "Alexa, buy me something at Whole Foods." Alexa: "Okay, buying Whole Foods.")

In 2015, Volkswagen was caught cheating on emissions control tests. The company didn't forge test results; instead, it designed its cars' onboard computers to do the cheating for it. Engineers programmed the software to detect when the car was undergoing an emissions test. The computer activated the car's emissions control system for the duration of the test, then deactivated it once the test was over. Volkswagen's cars demonstrated superior performance on the road; they also emitted up to forty times the permissible amount of nitrogen oxide pollutants, but only when the US Environmental Protection Agency (EPA) wasn't watching.

The Volkswagen story doesn't involve AI—human engineers programmed a regular computer system to cheat—but it illustrates the problem nonetheless. Volkswagen got away with the fraud for over ten years because computer code is complex and difficult to analyze. It's hard to figure out exactly what it's doing, and it's similarly hard to look at a car and figure out what it's doing. As long as the programmers keep their secret, a hack like that is likely to remain undetected for a long time. In this case, the reason we now know about Volkswagen's actions is that a group of scientists at West Virginia University tested the performance of Volkswagens on the road using an onboard emissions testing system different from the EPA's. Since the software was specifically designed to evade the EPA's testing systems, the scientists succeeded in accurately measuring the cars' emissions without the software realizing it.

If I asked you to design a car's engine control software to maximize performance while still passing emissions control tests, you wouldn't design the software to cheat without comprehending that you were cheating. This simply isn't true for an AI. It doesn't instinctively understand the abstract concept of cheating. It will think "outside the box" simply because it won't have a conception of the box, or of the limitations of existing human solutions. It also doesn't understand abstract ethical concepts. It won't understand that Volkswagen's solution harmed others, that it undermined the intent of the emissions control tests, or that the company's solution was illegal, unless the data upon which the AI relies includes the laws that pertain to emissions. The AI won't even realize that it's hacking the system. And thanks to the explainability problem, we humans might never realize it, either.

Unless AI programmers specify that the system must not change its behavior when being tested, an AI might come up with the same cheat. The programmers will be satisfied. The accountants will be ecstatic. And no one is likely to catch on. And yes, now that the Volkswagen scandal has been extensively documented, the programmers can set the explicit goal of avoiding that particular hack. However, there will inevitably be other unanticipated actions that the programmers will not anticipate. The lesson of the genie is that this will always be the case.

58

Defending against AI Hackers

Obvious hacks aren't the only problem. If your driverless car navigation system satisfies the goal of maintaining a high speed by spinning in circles, programmers will notice this behavior and modify the AI's goal accordingly. We'll never see this behavior on the road. The greatest concern lies in the less obvious hacks that we won't even notice because their effects are subtle.

Much has been written about recommendation engines—the first generation of subtle AI hacks—and how they push people towards extreme content. They weren't programmed to do this; it's a property that naturally emerged as the systems continually tried things, saw the results, then modified themselves to do more of what increased user engagement and less of what didn't. YouTube's and Facebook's recommendation algorithms learned to push more extreme content to users because it provokes strong emotional reactions, and that's what gets people to spend more time on the platform. It didn't take a bad actor to create this hack: a pretty basic automated system found it on its own. And most of us didn't realize that it was happening at the time.

Similarly, in 2015, an AI taught itself to play the 1970s arcade video game Breakout. The AI wasn't told anything about the game's rules or strategy. It was just given the controls and was rewarded for maximizing its score. That it learned how to play isn't interesting; everyone expected that. But it independently discovered, and optimized to a degree not seen in human players, the tactic of "tunneling" through one column of bricks to bounce the ball off the back wall.

Nothing I'm saying here will be news to AI researchers, and many are currently considering ways to defend against goal and reward hacking. One solution is to teach AIs context. Just as researchers must consider the problem of goal alignment, so too must they must consider the challenge of "value alignment," to create AIs that mirror human values. Solutions to this challenge can be framed as two extremes. First, we can explicitly specify values pertinent to the endeavor. That can be done today, more or less, but is vulnerable to all of the hacking I just described. Alternatively, we can create AIs that learn our values, possibly by observing humans in action, or by taking as input all of humanity's writings: our history, our literature, our philosophy, and so on. That is many years out, and probably a feature of general AI. Most current research oscillates between these two extremes.

One can easily imagine the problems that might arise by having AIs align themselves to historical or observed human values. Whose values should an AI mirror? A Somali man? A Singaporean woman? The average of the two, whatever that means? We humans hold contradictory values, and we're also not consistent about living up to them. Any individual person's values might be irrational, immoral, or based on false information. History, literature, and philosophy are full of irrationality, immorality, and error. Humans are often not very good examples of our ideals.

The most effective hacking defenses rely on identifying vulnerabilities: finding and patching hacks before they're used to subvert systems. This is something that AI technologies can substantially aid, especially since they can operate at superhuman speeds.

Think back to computer systems. Once AIs become capable of discovering new software vulnerabilities, government, criminal, and hobbyist hackers will all benefit. They'll be able to use those newly discovered vulnerabilities to compromise computer networks around the world to great effect. It will put us all at risk.

The same technology will be more useful for defense, because once a vulnerability is discovered, it can be patched forever. Imagine how a software company might deploy an AI vulnerability detector on the company's code. It could locate, then patch, all of the vulnerabilities it finds before the software is generally released. This testing might occur automatically as part of the development process. So while both the offense and defense would have access to the same technology, the defense could use it to permanently improve the security of its systems. We can imagine a future when software vulnerabilities are a thing of the past. "Remember the early decades of computing, when hackers would use software vulnerabilities to hack systems? Wow, was that a crazy time."

Of course, the transition period will be fraught. New code might be secure, but legacy code will still be vulnerable. AI tools will examine code that's already released and that in many cases can't be patched. In such cases, attackers will use automatic vulnerability finding to their advantage. However, over the long run, an AI technology that finds software vulnerabilities favors those who defend systems from intrusion and corruption.

This will also hold true when AIs start finding hacks in broader social systems. Political, economic, and social vulnerabilities will be exposed, then exploited. What's more, all of these hacks will further the interests of those who control the AI systems. Not only will individually tailored advertisements persuade more successfully; someone will pay for that added persuasive power because it works to their benefit. When the AI figures out a novel tax loophole, it will do so because someone with access to the AI system wants to exploit it in order to reduce their tax liability. Hacking largely reinforces existing power structures, and AIs will further reinforce them, unless we learn to overcome the imbalance better than we have so far.

The same technology can also benefit the defense. While AI hackers might find thousands of vulnerabilities in the existing tax code, the same technology can be used to evaluate potential vulnerabilities in any proposed tax law or tax ruling. The implications are game changing. Imagine a new tax law being tested in this manner. A legislator, watchdog organization, journalist, or any concerned citizen could analyze the text of a bill using AI to find *all* the exploitable vulnerabilities. This doesn't mean that they'll get fixed (remember, patching vulnerabilities is its own separate problem), but it does mean that they can be publicly debated. In theory, they could also be patched before someone finds and exploits them. Here, too, the transition period will be dangerous because of all of our legacy laws and rules. But again, over the long run, AI vulnerability-finding technology favors the defense.

This is both good and bad. It could be used by society to prevent the powerful from hacking systems, but it is more likely to be used by the powerful to prevent others from hacking systems as a way to resist social control and accelerate social change. Again, the structure of power matters.

59

A Future of AI Hackers

How realistic is a future of AI hacking?
Its feasibility depends on the specific system being modeled and hacked. For an AI to even begin optimizing a solution, let alone developing a completely novel one, all of the rules of the environment must be formalized in a way the computer can understand. Goals—known in AI as objective functions—need to be established. The AI needs some sort of feedback on how well it is doing so that it can improve its performance.

Sometimes this is a trivial matter. For a game like Go, it's easy. The rules, objective, and feedback—did you win or lose?—are all precisely specified, and there's nothing outside of those things to muddy the waters. The GPT-3 AI can write coherent essays because its "world" is just text. This is why most of the current examples of goal and reward hacking come from simulated environments. Those are artificial and constrained, with all of the rules specified to the AI.

What matters is the amount of ambiguity in a system. We can imagine feeding the world's tax laws into an AI, because the tax code consists of formulas that determine the amount of tax owed. There is even a programming language, Catala, that is optimized to encode law. Even so, all law contains some ambiguity. That ambiguity is difficult to translate into code, so an AI will have trouble dealing with it. AI notwithstanding, there will be full employment for tax lawyers for the foreseeable future.

Most human systems are even more ambiguous. It's hard to imagine an AI coming up with a real-world sports hack like curving a hockey stick. An AI would have to understand not just the rules of the game but also human physiology, the aerodynamics of the stick and the puck, and so on. It's not impossible, but it would be a lot more difficult than coming up with a novel Go move.

This latent ambiguity in complex societal systems offers a near-term security defense against AI hacking. We won't have AI-generated sports hacks until androids actually play those sports, or until a generalized AI is developed that is capable of understanding the world broadly in all its intersecting dimensions. A similar challenge exists with casino game hacks or hacks of the legislative process. (Could an AI independently discover gerrymandering?) It will be a long time before AIs are capable of modeling and simulating the ways that people work, individually and in groups, before they are as capable as humans are of devising novel ways to hack legislative processes.

But while a world filled with AI hackers is still a science-fiction problem, it's not a stupid science-fiction problem. Advances in AI are coming fast and furious, and jumps in capability are erratic and discontinuous. Things we thought were hard turned out to be easy, and things we think should be easy turn out to be hard. When I was a college student in the early 1980s, we were taught that the game of Go would never be mastered by a computer because of its enormous complexity: not the rules, but the number of possible moves. Today, AIs are Go grandmasters.

So while AI may primarily be tomorrow's problem, we're seeing precursors of it today. We need to start thinking about enforceable, understandable, and ethical solutions, because if we can expect anything with AI, it's that we'll need those solutions sooner than we might expect.

Probably the first place to look for AI-generated hacks is in financial systems, since those rules are designed to be algorithmically tractable. High-frequency trading algorithms are a primitive example of this, and will become much more sophisticated in the future. We can imagine equipping an AI with all the world's financial information in real time, plus all of the world's laws and regulations, plus news feeds and anything else we think might be relevant, then assigning it the goal of "maximum legal profit" or maybe "maximum profit we can get away with." My guess is that this isn't very far off, and that the result will be all sorts of novel and completely unexpected hacks. And there will probably be some hacks that are simply beyond human comprehension, which means we'll never realize they're happening.

In the short term, we're more likely to see collaborative AI–human hacks. An AI could identify an exploitable vulnerability that would potentially be a hack, and then an experienced accountant or tax attorney would use their experience and judgment to figure out if that vulnerability could be profitably exploited.

For almost all of history, hacking has exclusively been a human activity. Searching for new hacks requires expertise, time, creativity, and luck. When AIs start hacking, that will change. AIs won't be constrained in the same ways or have the same limits as people. They won't need to sleep. They'll think like aliens. And they'll hack systems in ways we can't anticipate.

As I said in Chapter 55, computers have accelerated hacking across four dimensions: speed, scale, scope, and sophistication. AI will exacerbate these trends even more.

First, speed: The human process of hacking, which sometimes takes months or years, could become compressed to days, hours, or even seconds. What might happen when you feed an AI the entire US tax code and command it to figure out all of the ways one can minimize one's tax liability? Or, in the case of a multinational corporation, analyze and optimize the entire planet's tax codes? Could an AI figure out, without being prompted, that it's smart to incorporate in Delaware and register a ship in Panama? How many vulnerabilities—loopholes—will it find that we don't already know about? Dozens? Hundreds? Thousands? We have no idea, but we'll probably find out within the next decade.

Next, scale: Once AI systems begin to discover hacks, they'll be capable of exploiting them at a scale for which we're simply not prepared. So when AIs begin to crunch financial systems, they will come to dominate that space. Already our credit markets, tax codes, and laws in general are biased towards the wealthy. AI will accelerate that inequity. The first AIs to hack finance in pursuit of profit won't be developed by equality-minded researchers; they'll be developed by global banks and hedge funds and management consultants.

Now, scope: We have societal systems that deal with hacks, but those were developed when hackers were humans, and hacks unfolded at a human pace. We have no system of governance that could quickly and efficiently adjudicate an onslaught of hundreds—let alone thousands—of newly discovered tax loopholes. We simply can't patch the tax code that quickly. We haven't been able to prevent humans' use of Facebook to hack democracy; it's a challenge to imagine what could happen when an AI does it. If AIs begin to figure out unanticipated but legal hacks of financial systems, then take the world's economy for a wild ride, recovery will be long and painful.

And finally—sophistication: AI-assisted hacks open the door to complex strategies beyond those that can be devised by the unaided human mind. The sophisticated statistical analyses of AIs can reveal relationships between variables, and thus possible exploits, that the best strategists and experts might never have recognized. That sophistication may allow AIs to deploy strategies that subvert multiple levels of the target system. For example, an AI designed to maximize a political party's vote share may determine a precise combination of economic variables, campaign messages, and procedural voting tweaks that could make the difference between election victory and defeat, extending the revolution that mapping software brought to gerrymandering into all aspects of democracy. And that's not even getting into the hard-to-detect tricks an AI could suggest for manipulating the stock market, legislative systems, or public opinion.

At computer speed, scale, scope, and sophistication, hacking will become a problem that we as a society can no longer manage.

I'm reminded of a scene in the movie *Terminator*, in which Kyle Reese describes to Sarah Connor the cyborg that is hunting her: "It can't be bargained with. It can't be reasoned with. It doesn't feel pity, or remorse, or fear. And it absolutely will not stop, ever . . ." We're not dealing with *literal* cyborg assassins, but as AI becomes our adversary in the world of social hacking, we might find it just as hard to keep up with its inhuman ability to hunt for our vulnerabilities.

Some AI researchers do worry about the extent to which powerful AIs might overcome their human-imposed constraints and—potentially—

come to dominate society. Although this may seem like wild speculation, it's a scenario worth at least passing consideration and prevention.

Today and in the near future, though, the hacking described in this book will be perpetrated by the powerful against the rest of us. All of the AIs out there, whether on your laptop, online, or embodied in a robot, are programmed by other people, usually in their interests and not yours. Although an Internet-connected device like Alexa can mimic being your trusted friend, never forget that it is designed to sell Amazon's products. And just as Amazon's website nudges you to buy its house brands instead of competitors' higher-quality goods, it won't always be acting in your best interest. It will hack your trust in Amazon for the goals of its shareholders.

In the absence of any meaningful regulation, there really isn't anything we can do to prevent AI hacking from unfolding. We need to accept that it is inevitable, and build robust governing structures that can quickly and effectively respond by normalizing beneficial hacks into the system and neutralizing the malicious or inadvertently damaging ones.

This challenge raises deeper, harder questions than how AI will evolve or how institutions can respond to it: What hacks count as beneficial? Which are damaging? And who decides? If you think government should be small enough to drown in a bathtub, then you probably think hacks that reduce government's ability to control its citizens are usually good. But you still might not want to substitute technological overlords for political ones. If you believe in the precautionary principle, you want as many experts testing and judging hacks as possible before they're incorporated into our social systems. And you might want to apply that principle further upstream, to the institutions and structures that make those hacks possible.

The questions continue. Should AI-created hacks be governed locally or globally? By administrators or by referendum? Or is there some way we can let the market or civil society groups decide? (The current efforts to apply governance models to algorithms are an early indicator of how this will go.) The governing structures we design will grant some people and organizations power to determine the hacks that will shape the future. We'll need to make sure that that power is exercised wisely.

60

Governance Systems for Hacking

Defensive AI is a potential response to AI hacking, but it's not sufficiently developed yet to be feasible. Today, we need humans working
together to establish governance structures to guide the development and
deployment of this technology.

How those governance structures should look isn't entirely clear yet,
but a variety of proposals have been forwarded for new models of regulation that might effectively address the problems posed by the speed, scale,
scope, and sophistication of artificial intelligences. AI technologists and
industry leaders like Nick Grossman have proposed that the Internet and
big data enterprises switch from a "Regulation 1.0" paradigm, where new
ventures are deemed permissible and require no after-the-fact review or
accountability, to a "Regulation 2.0" regime in which new ventures are
subject to rigorous, data-driven review and constraint. In Chapter 33,
we saw the best governance system we have for general societal hacks:
our common-law system of courtrooms, judges, juries, and continually
evolving precedent. In the future, any system of governance to handle AI
developments would need to be fast, inclusive, transparent, and agile—
like any good system of modern governance.

We can try to sketch what sort of governance system can defend society
from the potential effects of both intentional and inadvertent AI hacking.
(And while I tend to hate randomly invented acronyms, let me use "HGS" as

an abbreviation for "hacking governance system" in the next few paragraphs. It's an abstraction that will make talking about that sort of thing easier.)

- *Speed:* Most fundamentally, with the pace of technological and social change accelerating, **any HGS would need to work with speed and precision to be effective**. The Collingridge dilemma is an old observation of technological change: by the time something new and disruptive is widespread enough for its social consequences to be clear, it's too late to regulate it. By then, too many lives and livelihoods are built around the new technology to put the genie back in the bottle. This is nonsense—building trades, railroads, food, medicine, factories, chemicals, nuclear energy all demonstrate otherwise—but it is definitely harder to regulate something already established. Hacks will move faster than most governments can change their laws or rulings, and governments will struggle to regulate them even when they could theoretically implement a response in time. Ideally, an HGS should be able to act faster than a hack can proliferate, and know quickly whether a new hack needs to be nurtured to maturity or nipped in the bud.

- *Inclusivity:* In order to identify whether a hack is good or bad, especially in its early stages, **any HGS must be inclusive of as many perspectives as possible** to ensure that no potential threat or advantage of a hack is overlooked. That means, at a minimum, that it includes a diverse multidisciplinary team that can examine hacks and their effects from every angle, from sociology and law to economics, design thinking, and ecology. The HGS would also need to proactively seek and incorporate input from outside groups, particularly affected communities underrepresented by its professional staff, but also from independent researchers and experts, academics, unions, trade associations, local governments, and civic groups. These groups and individuals would not only offer their opinion at the occasional meeting; they would ideally be in continual dialogue with HGS staffers and with each other, so that the HGS assessment both evolves through deliberation with the public and helps the public clarify its views on major hacks, setting up activism and lobbying to change how politicians and other officials beyond the HGS control hacks.

- *Transparency:* Because the HGS needs to incorporate a wide range of both experts and lay citizenry into its decision-making, **its processes and rulings must be publicly transparent**. An opaque HGS that can only be followed by insiders and people with advanced degrees would close itself off to the whole-of-society feedback critical to fully understanding social hacks and their side effects. An HGS with more transparent processes, and transparency about the rationales for its decisions, will also earn more trust from citizens. That extra trust will be critical in maintaining political support for new and untested agencies managing tough trade-offs between innovation, system stability, and contested values like equity and fairness.

- *Agility:* Lastly, as citizens' political support shifts, or permitted hacks go horribly wrong, or as academics and government learn more about how to effectively regulate hacks, **any HGS needs mechanisms to rapidly evolve its structure, capabilities, decisions, and approaches** to succeed in a changing world. Even with all the best information and input, social systems are complex and hard to predict, and attempts to block harmful social hacks will sometimes fail. And when the HGS finds an effective patch or other defense against a social hack, hackers will immediately begin working to undermine it. So to succeed, an HGS needs to be iterative: to rapidly learn from its mistakes, test which approaches work best for controlling and incorporating each social hack, and continually improve its ability to implement those newly discovered best practices.

The overarching solution here is for all of us as citizens to think more deliberately about the proper role of technology in our lives. To date, we have largely been okay with allowing programmers to code the world as they see fit. We've done this for several reasons: we didn't want to unduly constrain the nascent technologies, legislators (limitedly) didn't understand the technologies well enough to regulate them, and—largely—it didn't matter enough to worry about. That's changed. Computer systems affect more than computers, and when engineers make decisions about them, they are literally designing the world's future.

The common-law system of judicial decisions is a good place to start.

I don't want to minimize the tension between democracy and technology here. It simply isn't true that everyone has the ability to understand or contribute to regulating AI. On the other hand, how do we find techno-crats who can be trusted, and how do we ensure that that trust is shared? This is a more general, and very hard, problem of modern governance of our deeply information-rich, connected, and otherwise technologically powerful world: one that is well beyond the scope of this book. It also isn't a substantially different problem than building governing structures that can operate at the speed of, and in the face of the complexity of, the information age. Legal scholars like Gillian Hadfield, Julie Cohen, Joshua Fairfield, and Jamie Susskind are writing about this more general prob-lem, and much more work needs to be done.

Again, these solutions require us first to solve some larger problems in society. To put it another way: pervasive, predatory hacking is a symp-tom of a flawed system. Money is power, and there is different justice for rule breakers who are powerful than for those who are not. If enforcement agencies don't act equitably—consider that corporate crime is seldom prosecuted—then there's no incentive for those who are powerful to follow the rules. That undermines societal trust in both the systems and the rules.

The stakes of inequitable enforcement are actually very high. Mini-mal regulation of the most privileged individuals or enterprises means that they get to set policy: they become de facto governments. This means that we the people no longer have a voice, which means that democracy dies. Yes, this is an extreme formulation of the problem, but it's an end state that we can't lose sight of.

I've been describing the interplay between human and computer sys-tems, and the risks inherent when the computers begin to play the part of humans. This, too, is a more general problem than the use and misuse of AI. It's also one that technologists and futurists are writing about. And while it's easy to let technology lead us into the future, we're much better off if citi-zens collectively decide what technology's role in our future should be—especially in a world where so much technology is available to everyone.

There isn't an HGS anywhere in the world right now, and there really isn't any government that is thinking about building one. It's time we did.

Concluding Thoughts

While finishing up this book manuscript in the summer of 2022, I came across an article in the *Wall Street Journal* describing a new financial hack. Importers have to pay government tariffs—often considerable—on foreign goods. But there's a loophole, called the *de minimis* rule, which is intended to exempt American tourists bringing back souvenirs from overseas trips. But it's now being abused by importers, who are having items shipped from overseas sellers directly to customers. "As a result, more than a tenth of Chinese imports by value now arrives as *de minimis* shipments, up from under 1% a decade ago." Total lost tax revenue from this hack: $67 billion annually.

It's hard not to be depressed about all of this societal hacking. It feels inevitable. It's how systems are subverted to achieve the ends of a few, and it has been going on since forever. The defenses we have are barely able to keep up today, and are woefully inadequate for the future—because societal hacking is going to get worse.

At its core, hacking is a balancing act. On the one hand, it's an engine of innovation. On the other, it subverts systems, reinforces existing inequitable power structures, and can be damaging to society. For most of our history, it was easy to argue that the innovation was worth the risk. Sure, privileged individuals hacked systems for their own benefit. But most of society was already skewed in their favor. A little hacking didn't make that much difference.

Today, that balance is changing for two reasons: one cultural and the other technological. And it's worth laying them out in detail.

Here's the cultural reason. Over the long term—and by that I mean over the centuries—our societal systems have typically become fairer, more democratic, and more just. And as systems evolve in this way, hacking becomes a more attractive means for privileged individuals and groups to subvert systems to their advantage. Very broadly, it's easier to get what you want when you're in charge in an autocratic system. If you can make and break the rules with impunity, there's no need to hack. If, instead, you're just as constrained by the law as everyone else, it's harder. Your best option may be to hack the economic, social, and political systems that limit your behavior.

I don't have any proof, but I believe hacking has become more common in recent decades because of this dynamic. It's my personal explanation of "late-stage capitalism" and all the problems it brings: finding loopholes in the rules is now regularly the path of least resistance. When those with means or technical ability realized that they could profitably hack systems, they quickly developed the resources and expertise to do so. They learned to exploit vulnerabilities. They learned to move up and down the hacking hierarchy to achieve their goals. They learned how to get their hacks normalized, declared legal, and adopted into the system.

This is being made even worse by income inequality. The economist Thomas Piketty explains that inequality produces surplus resources for the winners, and that that surplus can be mobilized to create even more inequality. Much of that mobilization is hacking.

Now we have more people with more knowledge of hacking and more resources to hack with than ever before, and with that knowledge and resources comes power. Our social systems are becoming overwhelmed by the kludged-together hacks resulting from generations of tussles over power and prestige. And as cloud computing, viral media, and AI make new hacks more accessible and powerful than ever, the instability and innovation they breed seems set to grow exponentially—to the benefit of those who design or control them, even as more people in general use them.

Societal systems rely on trust, and hacking undermines that. It might not matter at small scales, but when it's pervasive, trust breaks down—and eventually society ceases to function as it should. A tax loophole only available to the wealthy will generate resentment and erode trust in the entire system of taxation. The tsunami of hacks in our society reflects an absence of trust, social cohesion, and civic engagement.

The second reason is technological. Our societal systems, in general, may have grown fairer and more just over the centuries, but progress isn't linear or equitable. The trajectory may appear to be upwards when viewed in hindsight, but from a more granular point of view there are a lot of ups and downs. It's a "noisy" process.

Technology changes the amplitude of the noise. Those near-term ups and downs are getting more severe. And while that might not affect the long-term trajectories, they drastically affect all of us living in the short term. This is how the twentieth century could—statistically—both be the most peaceful in human history and also contain the most deadly wars.

Ignoring this noise was only possible when the damage wasn't potentially fatal on a global scale; that is, if a world war didn't have the potential to kill everybody or destroy society, or occur in places and to people that the West wasn't especially worried about. We can't be sure of that anymore. The risks we face today are existential in a way they never have been before. The magnifying effects of technology enable short-term damage to cause long-term planet-wide systemic damage. We've lived for half a century under the potential specter of nuclear war and the life-ending catastrophe that could have been. Fast global travel allowed local outbreaks to quickly become the COVID-19 pandemic, costing millions of lives and billions of dollars while increasing political and social instability. Our rapid, technologically enabled changes to the atmosphere, compounded through feedback loops and tipping points, may make Earth much less hospitable for the coming centuries. Today, individual hacking decisions can have planet-wide effects. Sociobiologist Edward O. Wilson once described the fundamental problem with humanity is that "we have Paleolithic emotions, medieval institutions, and godlike technology."

Imagine a Volkswagen-like hack to receive credit for more carbon emissions reductions than are actually being realized. If too many companies were to do that, then we would promptly barrel over a two degrees Celsius global temperature increase, and life on Earth could become impossible. Or imagine an apocalyptic terrorist group hacking the nuclear command structure and launching missiles—or biohacking and releasing a new disease. We could see mass death and worldwide government breakdowns that could lead to downward spirals more rapidly and more permanently than the slow and painful upwards struggles humanity has seen so far.

For those two reasons, hacking now poses an existential risk. We can hack more, faster, better. Our social and technical systems are evolving rapidly into battlefields of constant subversion and countersubversion, mutating into entirely new forms in the process. And between its bias in favor of the top of the food chain and the instability it breeds, all this hacking will come at the expense of the rest of us, and maybe all of us.

At the same time, I think there is cause for optimism. The technological advances that will exacerbate hacking also have the potential to make things better, by defending against bad hacks while finding and promoting the good ones. The trick is going to be getting the governance systems right. The hard part of the trick is that we need to figure it out soon.

To turn hacks—both today's human-generated hacks and tomorrow's AI-generated hacks—into social innovation means separating the good hacks from the bad ones, scaling up the former, and containing the effects of the latter. This is a lot more than the hacking defenses I talked about in Part 2. It also means governance systems that can keep pace with rapid change, and weigh the conflicting interests and interpretations of each hack's risks, benefits, and potential.

We must build resilient governing structures that can quickly and effectively respond to hacks. It won't do any good if it takes years to patch the tax code, or if a legislative hack becomes so entrenched that it can't be patched for political reasons. We need society's rules and laws to be as patchable as your computers and phones.

Unless we can hack the process of hacking itself, keeping its benefits and mitigating its costs and inequities, we may struggle to survive this technological future.

Acknowledgments

This book was born during a global pandemic and a personal life upheaval, and suffered from the effects of both. After writing 86,000 words in 2020, I largely ignored the manuscript in 2021—missing a deadline—and didn't pick it up again until the spring of 2022. Then, with the help of Evelyn Duffy at Open Boat Editing, I trimmed 20,000 words and reorganized the book into the sixty-plus small chapters you've (hopefully) just read.

A lot of people helped with this book during those two years. I would like to thank my research assistants: Nicholas Anway, Justin DeShazor, Simon Dickson, Derrick Flakoll, David Leftwich, and Vandinika Shukla. These were all Harvard Kennedy School students who worked with me for a few months, either over a summer or a semester. Ross Anderson, Steve Bass, Ben Buchanan, Nick Couldry, Kate Darling, Jessica Dawson, Cory Doctorow, Tim Edgar, FC (aka freakyclown), Amy Forsyth, Brett Frischmann, Bill Herdle, Trey Herr, Campbell Howe, David S. Isenberg, Dariusz Jemielniak, Richard Mallah, Will Marks, Aleecia McDonald, Roger McNamee, Jerry Michalski, Peter Neumann, Craig Newmark, Cirsten Paine, David Perry, Nathan Sanders, Marietje Schaake, Martin Schneier, James Shires, Erik Sobel, Jamie Susskind, Rahul Tongia, Arun Vishwanath, Jim Waldo, Rick Wash, Sara M. Watson, Tarah Wheeler, Josephine Wolff, and Ben Wizner all read the book somewhere in the draft stage, and all made helpful comments that I—mostly—listened to. Kathleen Seidel gave the book a very close edit. As did my longtime assistant and copyeditor, Beth Friedman.

Thank you to my editor, Brendan Curry, and everyone else at Norton who had a hand in turning my manuscript into a finished product. Also my agent, Sue Rabiner. Also to my new community here in Cambridge: the Harvard Kennedy School, the Berkman Klein Center, Inrupt (and the Solid project), and my many colleagues and friends. And Tammy: thank you for everything.

Notes

INTRODUCTION

1 **"They say that water":** Massimo Materni (1 May 2012), "Water never runs uphill / Session Americana," YouTube, https://www.youtube.com/watch?v=0Pe9XdFr_Eo.

2 **I announce a surprise quiz:** I did not invent this exercise. Gregory Conti and James Caroland (Jul-Aug 2011), "Embracing the Kobayashi Maru: Why you should teach your students to cheat," *IEEE Security & Privacy* 9, https://www.computer.org/csdl/magazine/sp/2011/04/msp2011040048/13rRUwbs1Z3.

3 **But billionaire Peter Thiel found a hack:** Justin Elliott, Patricia Callahan, and James Bandler (24 Jun 2021), "Lord of the Roths: How tech mogul Peter Thiel turned a retirement account for the middle class into a $5 billion tax-free piggy bank," *ProPublica*, https://www.propublica.org/article/lord-of-the-roths-how-tech-mogul-peter-thiel-turned-a-retirement-account-for-the-middle-class-into-a-5-billion-dollar-tax-free-piggy-bank.

5 **I wish I could remember where:** If anyone knows, please email me.

1. WHAT IS HACKING?

9 **these terms are overloaded:** Finn Brunton has assembled a list of "significant meanings" of the term. Finn Brunton (2021), "Hacking," in Leah Lievrouw and Brian Loader, eds., *Routledge Handbook of Digital Media and Communication*, Routledge, pp. 75–86, http://finnb.net/writing/hacking.pdf.

9 **Def: Hack /hak/ (noun):** The late hacker Jude Mihon (St. Jude) liked this definition: "Hacking is the clever circumvention of imposed limits, whether those limits are imposed by your government, your own personality, or the laws of Physics." Jude Mihon (1996), *Hackers Conference*, Santa Rosa, CA.

10 **In my 2003 book:** Bruce Schneier (2003), *Beyond Fear: Thinking Sensibly About Security in an Uncertain World*, Copernicus Books.

11 **someone used a drone:** Lauren M. Johnson (26 Sep 2019), "A drone was caught on camera delivering contraband to an Ohio prison yard," *CNN*, https://www.cnn.com/2019/09/26/us/contraband-delivered-by-drone-trnd/index.html.

11 **someone using a fishing rod:** Selina Sykes (2 Nov 2015), "Drug dealer uses fishing rod to smuggle cocaine, alcohol and McDonald's into jail," *Express*, https://www.express.co.uk/news/uk/616494/Drug-dealer-used-fishing-rod-to-smuggle-cocaine-alcohol-and-McDonald-s-into-jail.

11 **also about a cat:** Telegraph staff (3 Aug 2020), "Detained 'drug smuggler' cat

escapes Sri Lanka prison," *Telegraph*, https://www.telegraph.co.uk/news/2020/08/03/
detained-drug-smuggler-cat-escapes-sri-lanka-prison.

12 **traces its origins:** Jay London (6 Apr 2015), "Happy 60th birthday to the word 'hack,'"
Slice of MIT, https://alum.mit.edu/slice/happy-60th-birthday-word-hack.

2. HACKING SYSTEMS

13 **The tax laws themselves:** Dylan Matthews (29 Mar 2017), "The myth of the 70,000-
page federal tax code," *Vox*, https://www.vox.com/policy-and-politics/2017/3/29/1510
9214/tax-code-page-count-complexity-simplification-reform-ways-means.

13 **Microsoft Windows 10:** Microsoft (12 Jan 2020), "Windows 10 lines of code," https://
answers.microsoft.com/en-us/windows/forum/all/windows-10-lines-of-code/
a8f77f5c-0661-4895-9c77-2efd42429409.

14 **surprise tax bills:** Naomi Jagoda (14 Nov 2019), "Lawmakers under pressure to
pass benefits fix for military families," *The Hill*, https://thehill.com/policy/national
-security/470393-lawmakers-under-pressure-to-pass-benefits-fix-for-military
-families.

15 **Here's how it worked:** *New York Times* (28 Apr 2012), "Double Irish with a Dutch Sandwich"
(infographic), https://archive.nytimes.com/www.nytimes.com/interactive/2012/04/28/
business/Double-Irish-With-A-Dutch-Sandwich.html.

15 **US companies avoided paying:** Niall McCarthy (23 Mar 2017), "Tax avoidance
costs the U.S. nearly $200 billion every year" (infographic), *Forbes,* https://www.forbes
.com/sites/niallmccarthy/2017/03/23/tax-avoidance-coststhe-u-s-nearly-200-billion
-every-year-infographic.

15 **income tax deductions for property taxes:** US Internal Revenue Services (27 Dec
2017), "IRS Advisory: Prepaid real property taxes may be deductible in 2017 if assessed
and paid in 2017," https://www.irs.gov/newsroom/irs-advisory-prepaid-real-property
-taxes-may-be-deductible-in-2017-if-assessed-and-paid-in-2017.

16 **its fix won't be complete:** Jim Absher (29 Jan 2021), "After years of fighting, the military has started phasing out 'Widow's Tax,'" *Military.com*, https://www.military.com/
daily-news/2021/01/19/after-years-of-fighting-military-has-started-phasing-out-widows
-tax.html.

4. THE HACKING LIFE CYCLE

23 **selling their knowledge:** I remember reading about one tax loophole that was only
shown to prospective investors after they signed an NDA, and even then, they weren't
given all the details. I would love to have a reference to that story.

5. THE UBIQUITY OF HACKING

26 **Kids have hacked them all:** Stephanie M. Reich, Rebecca W. Black, and Ksenia Korob-
kova (Oct 2016), "Connections and communities in virtual worlds designed for children," *Journal of Community Psychology* 42, no. 3, https://sites.uci.edu/disc/files/2016/10/
Reich-Black-Korobkova-2014-JCOP-community-in-virtual-worlds.pdf.

26 **foldering:** Steven Melendez (16 Jun 2018), "Manafort allegedly used 'foldering' to hide
emails. Here's how it works," *Fast Company*, https://www.fastcompany.com/40586130/
manafort-allegedly-used-foldering-to-hide-emails-heres-how-it-works.

27 **In Nigeria, it's called "flashing":** Cara Titilayo Harshman (22 Dec 2010), "Please
don't flash me: Cell phones in Nigeria," *North of Lagos*, https://northoflagos.wordpress
.com/2010/12/22/please-dont-flash-me-cell-phones-in-nigeria.

27 **also huge in India:** Atul Bhattarai (5 April 2021), "Don't pick up! The rise and fall of

a massive industry based on missed call," *Rest of World*, https://restofworld.org/2021/the-rise-and-fall-of-missed-calls-in-india/.

27 **Homeschooling during the:** Tribune Web Desk (14 May 2020), "Students find 'creative' hacks to get out of their Zoom classes, video goes viral," *Tribune of India*, https://www.tribuneindia.com/news/lifestyle/students-find-creative-hacks-to-get-out-of-their-zoom-classes-video-goes-viral-84706.

27 **one-star reviews:** Anthony Cuthbertson (9 Mar 2020), "Coronavirus: Quarantined school children in China spam homework app with 1-star reviews to get it off app store," *Independent*, https://www.independent.co.uk/life-style/gadgets-and-tech/news/coronavirus-quarantine-children-china-homework-app-dingtalk-a9387741.html.

27 **Recall Gödel:** Kimberly D. Krawiec and Scott Baker (2006), "Incomplete contracts in a complete contract world," *Florida State University Law Review* 33, https://scholarship.law.duke.edu/faculty_scholarship/2038.

27 **systems of trust:** Bruce Schneier (2012), *Liars and Outliers: Enabling the Trust that Society Needs to Thrive,* John Wiley & Sons.

28 **complexity is the worst enemy of security:** Bruce Schneier (19 Nov 1999), "A plea for simplicity: You can't secure what you don't understand," *Information Security*, https://www.schneier.com/essays/archives/1999/11/a_plea_for_simplicit.html.

6. ATM HACKS

31 **Saunders withdrew $1.6 million:** Jack Dutton (7 Apr 2020), "This Australian bartender found an ATM glitch and blew $1.6 million," *Vice*, https://www.vice.com/en_au/article/pa5kgg/this-australian-bartender-dan-saunders-found-an-atm-bank-glitch-hack-and-blew-16-million-dollars.

33 **changes in ATM design:** Z. Sanusi, Mohd Nor Firdaus Rameli, and Yusarina Mat Isa (13 Apr 2015), "Fraud schemes in the banking institutions: Prevention measures to avoid severe financial loss," *Procedia Economics and Finance*, https://www.semanticscholar.org/paper/Fraud-Schemes-in-the-Banking-Institutions%3A-Measures-Sanusi-Rameli/681c06a647cfef1e90e52ccbf829438016966c44.

33 **this is known as "jackpotting":** Joseph Cox (14 Oct 2019), "Malware that spits cash out of ATMs has spread across the world," *Vice Motherboard*, https://www.vice.com/en_us/article/7x5ddg/malware-that-spits-cash-out-of-atms-has-spread-across-the-world.

33 **Another attack:** Dan Goodin (22 Jul 2020), "Thieves are emptying ATMs using a new form of jackpotting," *Wired*, https://www.wired.com/story/thieves-are-emptying-atms-using-a-new-form-of-jackpotting.

34 **US Secret Service began warning:** Brian Krebs (27 Jan 2018), "First 'jackpotting' attacks hit U.S. ATMs," *Krebs on Security*, https://krebsonsecurity.com/2018/01/first-jackpotting-attacks-hit-u-s-atms.

34 **Barnaby Jack demonstrated:** Kim Zetter (28 Jul 2010), "Researcher demonstrates ATM 'jackpotting' at Black Hat conference," *Wired*, https://www.wired.com/2010/07/atms-jackpotted.

7. CASINO HACKS

35 **He modified over thirty machines:** *Las Vegas Sun* (21 Feb 1997), "Slot cheat, former casino regulator, reputed mob figure added to Black Book," https://lasvegassun.com/news/1997/feb/21/slot-cheat-former-casino-regulator-reputed-mob-fig.

36 **wearable computer with toe switches:** Paul Halpern (23 May 2017), "Isaac Newton vs. Las Vegas: How physicists used science to beat the odds at roulette," *Forbes*, https://www.forbes.com/sites/startswithabang/2017/05/23/how-physicists-used-science-to-beat-the-odds-at-roulette.

36   **Nevada banned the use of devices:** Don Melanson (18 Sep 2013), "Gaming the system: Edward Thorp and the wearable computer that beat Vegas," Engadget, https://www .engadget.com/2013-09-18-edward-thorp-father-of-wearable-computing.html.

36   **Casinos have responded:** Grant Uline (1 Oct 2016), "Card counting and the casino's reaction," *Gaming Law Review and Economics*, https://www.liebertpub.com/doi/10.1089/ glre.2016.2088.

37   **Laws were passed banning:** David W. Schnell-Davis (Fall 2012), "High-tech casino advantage play: Legislative approaches to the threat of predictive devices," *UNLV Gaming Law Journal* 3, https://scholars.law.unlv.edu/cgi/viewcontent.cgi?article=1045 &context=glj.

37   **casinos are private business:** New Jersey is an exception to this. Atlantic City casinos cannot ban card counters. Donald Janson (6 May 1982), "Court rules casinos cannot bar card counters," *New York Times*, https://www.nytimes.com/1982/05/06/nyregion/ court-rules-casinos-may-not-bar-card-counters.html.

37   **MIT and Harvard academics invented:** Ben Mezrich (Dec 2002), *Bringing Down the House: The Inside Story of Six MIT Students Who Took Vegas for Millions*, Atria Books.

37   **an estimated $10 million:** Janet Ball (26 May 2014), "How a team of students beat the casinos," *BBC World Service*, https://www.bbc.com/news/magazine-27519748.

8. AIRLINE FREQUENT-FLIER HACKS

39   **airlines started changing:** Josh Barro (12 Sep 2014), "The fadeout of the mileage run," *New York Times*, https://www.nytimes.com/2014/09/14/upshot/the-fadeout-of-the-mile ag-run.html.

39   **ways to accrue points:** Darius Rafieyan (23 Sep 2019), "How one man used miles to fulfill his dream to visit every country before turning 40," *NPR*, https://www.npr .org/2019/09/23/762259297/meet-the-credit-card-obsessives-who-travel-the-world-on -points.

39   **Chase instituted a rule:** Gina Zakaria (25 Feb 2020), "If you're interested in a Chase card like the Sapphire Preferred you need to know about the 5/24 rule that affects whether you'll be approved," *Business Insider*, https://www.businessinsider.com/ personal-finance/what-is-chase-524-rule.

39   **American Express now revokes:** Nicole Dieker (2 Aug 2019), "How to make sure you don't lose your credit card rewards when you close the card," *Life Hacker*, https://twocents.life hacker.com/how-to-make-sure-you-dont-lose-your-credit-card-rewards-1836913367.

39   **back to the Pudding Guy:** Carla Herreria Russo (3 Oct 2016), "Meet David Phillips, the guy who earned 1.2 million airline miles with chocolate pudding," *Huffington Post*, https:// www.huffpost.com/entry/david-philipps-pudding-guy-travel-deals_n_577c9397e4b0 a629c1ab35a7.

9. SPORTS HACKS

41   **St. Louis Browns:** Associated Press (20 Aug 1951), "Brownies hit all-time low; Use 3-foot 7-inch player," *Spokesman-Review*, https://news.google.com/newspapers?id=rS5WA AAAIBAJ&sjid=3uUDAAAAIBAJ&pg=4920%2C3803143.

41   **the Suns would get the ball:** Presh Talwalkar (6 Jun 2017), "Genius strategic think-ing in the 1976 NBA Finals," *Mind Your Decisions*, https://mindyourdecisions.com/ blog/2017/06/06/genius-strategic-thinking-in-the-1976-nba-finals-game-theory -tuesdays. Secret Base (5 Feb 2019), "The infinite timeout loophole that almost broke the 1976 NBA Finals," YouTube, https://www.youtube.com/watch?v=Od2wgHLq69U.

42   **hacked the backstroke:** John Lohn (24 Sep 2021), "Seoul Anniversary: When the backstroke went rogue: How David Berkoff and underwater power changed the event,"

Swimming World, https://www.swimmingworldmagazine.com/news/seoul-anniversary
-when-the-backstroke-went-rogue-how-david-berkoff-and-underwater-power
-changed-the-event.

42   **New England Patriots used:** Rodger Sherman (10 Jan 2015), "The Patriots' trick play that got John Harbaugh mad," *SB Nation*, https://www.sbnation.com/nfl/2015/1/10/7526841/ the-patriots-trick-play-that-got-john-harbaugh-mad-ravens.

42   **the league amended its rules:** Ben Volin (26 Mar 2015), "NFL passes rule aimed at Patriots' ineligible receiver tactic," *Boston Globe*, https://www.bostonglobe.com/ sports/2015/03/25/nfl-passes-rule-change-aimed-patriots-ineligible-receiver-tactic/ uBqPWS5dKYdMYMcIiJ3sKO/story.html.

42   **dunking was once a hack:** The plot of the 1997 movie *Air Bud* involves hacking the rules to pro basketball. In the movie, at least, there is no rule preventing a dog from playing on a basketball team. (No, the movie isn't any good.)

42   **a few cricketers realized:** Manish Verma (7 Jan 2016), "How Tillakaratne Dilshan invented the 'Dilscoop,'" *SportsKeeda*, https://www.sportskeeda.com/cricket/how-tilla karatne-dilshan-invented-dilscoop.

43   **Tyrell team built a six-wheeled:** Jordan Golson (17 Dec 2014), "Well that didn't work: The crazy plan to bring 6-wheeled cars to F1," *Wired*, https://www.wired.com/2014/12/ well-didnt-work-crazy-plan-bring-6-wheeled-cars-f1.

43   **Brabham team skirted the rule:** Gordon Murray (23 Jul 2019), "Gordon Murray looks back at the notorious Brabham fan car," *Motor Sport*, https://www.motorsportmagazine .com/articles/single-seaters/f1/gordon-murray-looks-back-notorious-brabham-fan-car.

43   **two brake pedals:** McLaren (1 Nov 2017), "The search for the extra pedal," https:// www.mclaren.com/racing/inside-the-mtc/mclaren-extra-pedal-3153421.

44   **a hole in the cockpit:** Matt Somerfield (20 Apr 2020), "Banned: The 2010 Formula 1 season's F-duct," *AutoSport*, https://www.autosport.com/f1/news/149090/banned-the -f1-2010-season-fduct.

44   **its Formula One engine's turbo charger:** Laurence Edmondson (6 Feb 2016), "Mercedes F1 engine producing over 900bhp with more to come in 2016," *ESPN*, https://www.espn .com/f1/story/_/id/14724923/mercedes-f1-engine-producing-900bhp-more-come-2016.

44   **a feature to the steering wheel:** Laurence Edmondson (21 Feb 2020), "Mercedes' DAS system: What is it? And is it a 2020 game-changer?" *ESPN*, https://www.espn.com/f1/ story/_/id/28749957/mercedes-das-device-and-2020-game-changer.

44   **illegally curved stick:** Dave Stubbs (2 Jun 2017), "Marty McSorley's illegal stick still part of Stanley Cup Final lore," National Hockey League, https://www.nhl.com/news/ marty-mcsorleys-illegal-stick-still-part-of-stanley-cup-final-lore/c-289749406.

12. MORE SUBTLE HACKING DEFENSES

56   **red team was the pretend enemy:** University of Foreign Military and Cultural Studies Center for Applied Critical Thinking (5 Oct 2018), *The Red Team Handbook: The Army's Guide to Making Better Decisions*, US Army Combined Arms Center, https://usacac.army .mil/sites/default/files/documents/ufmcs/The_Red_Team_Handbook.pdf.

56   **"We argue that red teaming":** Defense Science Board (Sep 2003), "Defense Science Board Task Force on the Role and Status of DoD Red Teaming Activities," Office of the Under Secretary of Defense for Acquisition, Technology, and Logistics, https://apps .dtic.mil/dtic/tr/fulltext/u2/a430100.pdf.

13. REMOVING POTENTIAL HACKS IN THE DESIGN PHASE

61   **my 2000 book:** Bruce Schneier (2000), *Secrets and Lies: Digital Security in a Networked World*, John Wiley & Sons.

14. THE ECONOMICS OF DEFENSE

62 **all the threats to a system:** Adam Shostack (2014), *Threat Modeling: Designing for Security*, John Wiley & Sons.

16. HACKING HEAVEN

71 **What started as a system of redemption:** R. N. Swanson (2011), *Indulgences in Late Medieval England: Passports to Paradise?* Cambridge University Press.

72 **Johann Tetzel, a Dominican friar:** Ray Cavanaugh (31 Oct 2017), "Peddling purgatory relief: Johann Tetzel," *National Catholic Reporter*, https://www.ncronline.org/news/people/peddling-purgatory-relief-johann-tetzel.

72 **indulgences for deceased friends:** He supposedly even had an advertising jingle: "As soon as the gold in the casket rings / The rescued soul to heaven springs."

72 **a "get out of hell free" card:** Totally unrelated, but the "get out of jail free" card can be used in the game of Monopoly to hack the rule that players are not allowed to lend money to each other. It's not worth much, but players can sell it to each other for any amount of money—making it a useful cash transfer device. Jay Walker and Jeff Lehman (1975), *1000 Ways to Win Monopoly Games*, Dell Publishing, http://www.lehman-intl.com/jeffreylehman/1000-ways-to-win-monopoly.html.

17. HACKING BANKING

74 **Regulation Q is a security measure:** R. Alton Gilbert (Feb 1986), "Requiem for Regulation Q: What it did and why it passed away," Federal Reserve Bank of St. Louis, https://files.stlouisfed.org/files/htdocs/publications/review/86/02/Requiem_Feb1986.pdf.

75 **NOW accounts were legalized:** Joanna H. Frodin and Richart Startz (Jun 1982), "The NOW account experiment and the demand for money," *Journal of Banking and Finance* 6, no. 2, https://www.sciencedirect.com/science/article/abs/pii/0378426682900322. Paul Watro (10 Aug 1981), "The battle for NOWs," Federal Reserve Bank of Cleveland, https://www.clevelandfed.org/en/newsroom-and-events/publications/economic-commentary/economic-commentary-archives/1981-economic-commentaries/ec-19810810-the-battle-for-nows.aspx.

76 **we'll see it again and again:** Although he never used the word "hacking," Hyman Minsky discussed this. Hyman Minsky (May 1992), "The financial instability hypothesis," Working Paper No. 74, The Jerome Levy Economics Institute of Bard College, https://www.levyinstitute.org/pubs/wp74.pdf.

76 **banks had moved 95%:** Charles Levinson (21 Aug 2015), "U.S. banks moved billions of dollars in trades beyond Washington's reach," Reuters, https://www.reuters.com/investigates/special-report/usa-swaps. Marcus Baram (29 Jun 2018), "Big banks are exploiting a risky Dodd-Frank loophole that could cause a repeat of 2008," *Fast Company*, https://www.fastcompany.com/90178556/big-banks-are-exploiting-a-risky-dodd-frank-loophole-that-could-cause-a-repeat-of-2008.

77 **financial services industry spent $7.4 billion:** Deniz O. Igan and Thomas Lambert (9 Aug 2019), "Bank lobbying: Regulatory capture and beyond," IMF Working Paper No. 19/171, International Monetary Fund, https://www.imf.org/en/Publications/WP/Issues/2019/08/09/Bank-Lobbying-Regulatory-Capture-and-Beyond-45735.

77 **Some countries:** Several banking regulators, including the Office of the Comptroller of the Currency and the Consumer Financial Protection Bureau, offer opportunities to comment, at least on some occasions, see https://www.occ.treas.gov/about/connect-with-us/public-comments/index-public-comments.html. Consumer Finan-

cial Protection Bureau (last updated 7 Apr 2022), "Notice and opportunities to comment," https://www.consumerfinance.gov/rules-policy/notice-opportunities-comment.

18. HACKING FINANCIAL EXCHANGES

80   **three people were charged:** US Securities and Exchange Commission (9 Jul 2021), "SEC charges three individuals with insider trading," https://www.sec.gov/news/press-release/2021-121.

80   **"want these laws purposely vague":** Knowledge at Wharton staff (11 May 2011), "Insider trading 2011: How technology and social networks have 'friended' access to confidential information," *Knowledge at Wharton,* https://knowledge.wharton.upenn.edu/article/insider-trading-2011-how-technology-and-social-networks-have-friended-access-to-confidential-information.

80   **the SEC indicted two Ukrainian hackers:** US Securities and Exchange Commission (11 Aug 2015), "SEC charges 32 defendants in scheme to trade on hacked news releases," https://www.sec.gov/news/pressrelease/2015-163.html.

19. HACKING COMPUTERIZED FINANCIAL EXCHANGES

83   **the rise of computerization:** Atlantic Re:think (21 Apr 2015), "The day social media schooled Wall Street," *Atlantic,* https://www.theatlantic.com/sponsored/etrade-social-stocks/the-day-social-media-schooled-wall-street/327. Jon Bateman (8 Jul 2020), "Deepfakes and synthetic media in the financial system: Assessing threat scenarios," Carnegie Endowment, https://carnegieendowment.org/2020/07/08/deepfakes-and-synthetic-media-in-financial-system-assessing-threat-scenarios-pub-82237.

20. LUXURY REAL ESTATE

87   **160 UK properties:** Matteo de Simone et al. (Mar 2015), "Corruption on your doorstep: How corrupt capital is used to buy property in the U.K.," Transparency International, https://www.transparency.org.uk/sites/default/files/pdf/publications/2016Corruptio nOnYourDoorstepWeb.pdf.

87   **owned by shell corporations:** Louise Story and Stephanie Saul (7 Feb 2015), "Stream of foreign wealth flows to elite New York real estate," *New York Times,* https://www.nytimes.com/2015/02/08/nyregion/stream-of-foreign-wealth-flows-to-time-warner-condos.html.

88   **geographic targeting orders:** Michael T. Gershberg, Janice Mac Avoy, and Gregory Bernstein (2 May 2022), "FinCEN renews and expands geographic targeting orders for residential real estate deals," *Lexology,* https://www.lexology.com/library/detail.aspx?g=065ffb4d-f737-42dc-b759-ef5c4d010404.

88   **could get rid of:** Max de Haldevang (22 Jun 2019), "The surprisingly effective pilot program stopping real estate money laundering in the US," *Quartz,* https://qz.com/1635394/how-the-us-can-stop-real-estate-money-laundering.

21. SOCIETAL HACKS ARE OFTEN NORMALIZED

89   **Cisco announced multiple vulnerabilities:** Michael Cooney (5 May 2022), "Cisco warns of critical vulnerability in virtualized network software," *Network World,* https://www.networkworld.com/article/3659872/cisco-warns-of-critical-vulnerability-in-virtualized-network-software.html.

89   **F5 warned its customers:** Harold Bell (5 May 2022), "F5 warns of BIG-IP iCon-

trol REST vulnerability," *Security Boulevard*, https://securityboulevard.com/2022/05/ f5-warns-of-big-ip-icontrol-rest-vulnerability.

89   **AVG Corporation announced:** Charlie Osborne (5 May 2022), "Decade-old bugs discovered in Avast, AVG antivirus software," *ZD Net*, https://www.zdnet.com/article/ decade-old-bugs-discovered-in-avast-avg-antivirus-software.

90   **a history of normalization:** I could have written much the same story about index funds. Annie Lowrey (Apr 2021), "Could index funds be 'worse than Marxism'?" *Atlantic*, https://www.theatlantic.com/ideas/archive/2021/04/the-autopilot-economy/618497.

91   **Normalization isn't a new phenomenon:** Robert Sabatino Lopez and Irving W. Raymond (2001), *Medieval Trade in the Mediterranean World: Illustrative Documents*, Columbia University Press.

22. HACKING THE MARKET

92   **trucks would shuffle:** David Kocieniewski (20 Jun 2013), "A shuffle of aluminum, but to banks, pure gold," *New York Times*, https://www.nytimes.com/2013/07/21/ business/a-shuffle-of-aluminum-but-to-banks-pure-gold.html.

93   **the economic interests of businessmen:** Adam Smith (1776), *The Wealth of Nations*, William Strahan, pp. 138, 219–220.

23. "TOO BIG TO FAIL"

98   **bail them out again if needed:** Michael Greenberger (Jun 2018), "Too big to fail U.S. banks' regulatory alchemy: Converting an obscure agency footnote into an 'at will' nullification of Dodd-Frank's regulation of the multi-trillion dollar financial swaps market," Institute for New Economic Thinking, https://www.ineteconomics.org/uploads/ papers/WP_74.pdf.

24. VENTURE CAPITAL AND PRIVATE EQUITY

100   **We don't want some central planner:** Eric Levitz (3 Dec 2020), "America has central planners. We just call them 'venture capitalists,'" *New York Magazine*, https://nymag .com/intelligencer/2020/12/wework-venture-capital-central-planning.html.

102   **the case of Greensill Capital:** Eshe Nelson, Jack Ewing, and Liz Alderman (28 March 2021), "The swift collapse of a company built on debt," *New York Times*, https://www .nytimes.com/2021/03/28/business/greensill-capital-collapse.html.

25. HACKING AND WEALTH

104   *cum-ex* **trading:** David Segal (23 Jan 2020), "It may be the biggest tax heist ever. And Europe wants justice," *New York Times*, https://www.nytimes.com/2020/01/23/ business/cum-ex.html.

104   **Germany recently sentenced:** Karin Matussek (1 Jun 2021), "A banker's long prison sentence puts industry on alert," Bloomberg, https://www.bloomberg.com/news/ articles/2021-06-01/prosecutors-seek-10-years-for-banker-in-398-million-cum-ex-case.

104   **Two London bankers:** Olaf Storbeck (19 Mar 2020), "Two former London bankers convicted in first cum-ex scandal trial," *Financial Times*, https://www.ft.com/ content/550121de-69b3-11ea-800d-da70cff6e4d3.

104   **A former senior German tax inspector:** Olaf Storbeck (4 Apr 2022), "Former German tax inspector charged with €279mn tax fraud," *Financial Times*, https://www.ft.com/ content/e123a255-bc52-48c4-9022-ac9c4be06daa.

104   **Frankfurt offices of Morgan Stanley bank:** Agence France-Presse (3 May 2022), "Ger-

man prosecutors raid Morgan Stanley in cum-ex probe," *Barron's*, https://www.barrons
.com/news/german-prosecutors-raid-morgan-stanley-in-cum-ex-probe-01651575308.

105 **Donald Trump famously said:** Daniella Diaz (27 Sep 2016), "Trump: 'I'm
smart' for not paying taxes," *CNN*, https://www.cnn.com/2016/09/26/politics/
donald-trump-federal-income-taxes-smart-debate/index.html.

105 **if he only exploited legal loopholes:** A 1935 US Supreme Court ruling confirmed
this: "Anyone may so arrange his affairs that his taxes shall be as low as possible; he is
not bound to choose that pattern which will best pay the Treasury; there is not even a
patriotic duty to increase one's taxes." US Supreme Court (7 Jan 1935), *Gregory v. Helvering*, 293 US 465, https://www.courtlistener.com/opinion/102356/gregory-v-helvering.

26. HACKING LAWS

110 **the turducken was originally:** That's a turkey stuffed with a duck stuffed with a
chicken. The particulars are modern, dreamed up by chef Paul Prudhomme. I tried
making it once; it's not worth the work.

110 **emergency loan program:** Jeanna Smialek (30 Jul 2020), "How Pimco's Cayman-based
hedge fund can profit from the Fed's rescue," *New York Times*, https://www.nytimes
.com/2020/07/30/business/economy/fed-talf-wall-street.html.

27. LEGAL LOOPHOLES

112 **"Zone of Death":** Brian C. Kalt (2005), "The perfect crime," *Georgetown Law Journal* 93,
no. 2, https://fliphtml5.com/ukos/hbsu/basic.

113 **his lawyers used this hack:** Clark Corbin (3 Feb 2022), "Idaho legislator asks
U.S. Congress to close Yellowstone's 'zone of death' loophole," *Idaho Capital Sun*,
https://idahocapitalsun.com/2022/02/03/idaho-legislator-asks-u-s-congress-to-close
-yellowstones-zone-of-death-loophole.

113 **A more sinister version of this hack:** Louise Erdrich (26 Feb 2013), "Rape on the
reservation," *New York Times*, https://www.nytimes.com/2013/02/27/opinion/
native-americans-and-the-violence-against-women-act.html.

113 **state taxes being applied:** US Supreme Court (6 Dec 1937), *James v. Dravo Contracting
Co.* (Case No. 190), 302 U.S. 134, https://tile.loc.gov/storage-services/service/ll/usrep/
usrep302/usrep302134/usrep302134.pdf.

113 **residents of federal enclaves:** US Supreme Court (15 Jun 1970), *Evans v. Cornman* (Case No. 236), 398 U.S. 419, https://www.justice.gov/sites/default/files/osg/
briefs/2000/01/01/1999-2062.resp.pdf.

114 **owners of a San Francisco restaurant:** Andrew Lu (16 Jul 2012), "Foie gras ban doesn't
apply to SF Social Club?" *Law and Daily Life*, FindLaw, https://www.findlaw.com/
legalblogs/small-business/foie-gras-ban-doesnt-apply-to-sf-social-club.

114 **a 2019 reauthorization was derailed:** Indian Law Resource Center (Apr 2019),
"VAWA reauthorization bill with strengthened tribal provisions advances out of the
House," https://indianlaw.org/swsn/VAWA_Bill_2019. Indian Law Resource Center (2019), "Ending violence against Native women," https://indianlaw.org/issue/
ending-violence-against-native-women.

28. HACKING BUREAUCRACY

115 **those who must comply with them:** C. A. E. Goodhart (1984), *Monetary Theory and Practice:
The UK Experience*, Springer, https://link.springer.com/book/10.1007/978-1-349-17295-5.

115 **more, and cheaper, space probes:** Howard E. McCurdy (2001), *Faster, Better, Cheaper:
Low-Cost Innovation in the U.S. Space Program*, Johns Hopkins University Press.

116 **rents were collected after the harvest:** James C. Scott (1985), *Weapons of the Weak: Everyday Forms of Peasant Resistance,* Yale University Press.

116 **paying for rat tails:** Michael G. Vann (2003), "Of rats, rice, and race: The Great Hanoi Rat Massacre, an episode in French colonial history," *French Colonial History* 4, https://muse.jhu.edu/article/42110/pdf.

116 **cars with even and odd license plates:** Lucas W. Davis (2 Feb 2017), "Saturday driving restrictions fail to improve air quality in Mexico City," *Scientific Reports* 7, article 41652, https://www.nature.com/articles/srep41652.

116 **Uber drivers in Nairobi:** Sean Cole (7 Aug 2020), "Made to be broken," *This American Life,* https://www.thisamericanlife.org/713/made-to-be-broken. Gianluca Iazzolino (19 Jun 2019), "Going Karura. Labour subjectivities and contestation in Nairobi's gig economy," DSA2019: Opening Up Development, Open University, Milton Keynes, https://www.devstud.org.uk/past-conferences/2019-opening-up-development-conference.

117 **FAA managers took Boeing's side:** Natalie Kitroeff, David Gelles, and Jack Nicas (27 Jun 2019), "The roots of Boeing's 737 Max crisis: A regulator relaxes its oversight," *New York Times,* https://www.nytimes.com/2019/07/27/business/boeing-737-max-faa.html.

117 **The FAA even waived:** Gary Coglianese, Gabriel Scheffler, and Daniel E. Walters (30 Oct 2020), "The government's hidden superpower: 'Unrules,'" *Fortune,* https://fortune.com/2020/10/30/federal-law-regulations-loopholes-waivers-unrules.

29. HACKING AND POWER

121 **"power interprets regulation as damage":** Julie Cohen and Chris Bavitz (21 Nov 2019), "Between truth and power: The legal constructions of informational capitalism," Berkman Klein Center for Internet and Society at Harvard University, https://cyber.harvard.edu/sites/default/files/2019-12/2019_11_21_Berkman_Julie_Cohen_NS.pdf.

30. UNDERMINING REGULATIONS

123 **Uber is a taxi service:** The company was initially named UberCab but changed it for precisely this reason.

123 **a hack of the taxi industry:** Ruth Berens Collier, Veena Dubal, and Christopher Carter (Mar 2017), "The regulation of labor platforms: The politics of the Uber economy," University of California Berkeley, https://brie.berkeley.edu/sites/default/files/reg-of-labor-platforms.pdf.

123 **Uber has since leveraged:** Uber Technologies, Inc. (2021), "2021 Form 10-K Annual Report," US Securities and Exchange Commission, https://www.sec.gov/ix?doc=/Archives/edgar/data/1543151/000154315122000008/uber-20211231.htm.

124 **It has 3.5 million drivers:** Brian Dean (23 Mar 2021), "Uber statistics 2022: How many people ride with Uber?" *Backlinko,* https://backlinko.com/uber-users.

124 **Airbnb is a similar hack:** Paris Martineau (20 Mar 2019), "Inside Airbnb's 'guerilla war' against local governments," *Wired,* https://www.wired.com/story/inside-Airbnbs-guerrilla-war-against-local-governments.

125 **Payday loans are short-term loans:** Carter Dougherty (29 May 2013), "Payday lenders evading rules pivot to installment loans," Bloomberg, https://www.bloomberg.com/news/articles/2013-05-29/payday-lenders-evading-rules-pivot-to-installmant-loans.

126 **They also operate as loan brokers:** S. Lu (22 Aug 2018), "How payday lenders get around interest rate regulations," WRAL (originally from the MagnifyMoney blog), https://www.wral.com/how-payday-lenders-get-around-interest-rate-regulations/17788314.

126 **moved to Indian reservations:** Liz Farmer (4 May 2015), "After payday lenders skirt

state regulations, Feds step in," *Governing*, https://www.governing.com/topics/finance/
gov-payday-lending-consumer-crackdown.html.

126 **there was a loophole:** Dave McKinley and Scott May (30 Nov 2020), "Canadians
buzz through Buffalo as a way to beat border closure," WGRZ, https://www.wgrz
.com/article/news/local/canadians-buzz-through-buffalo-as-a-way-to-beat-border
-closure/71-07c93156-1365-46ab-80c1-613e5b1d7938.

126 **the industry needs to constantly work:** Carter Dougherty (29 May 2013), "Payday lenders evading rules pivot to installment loans," Bloomberg, https://www.bloomberg.com/
news/articles/2013-05-29/payday-lenders-evading-rules-pivot-to-installmant-loans.

31. JURISDICTIONAL INTERACTIONS

128 **Global tax avoidance:** Alex Cobham and Petr Jansky (Mar 2017), "Global distribution
of revenue loss from tax avoidance," United Nations University WIDER Working Paper
2017/55, https://www.wider.unu.edu/sites/default/files/wp2017-55.pdf.

128 **Total cost to global tax revenue:** Ernesto Crivelli, Ruud A. de Mooij, and Michael Keen
(29 May 2015), "Base erosion, profit shifting and developing countries," International
Monetary Fund Working Paper 2015118, https://www.imf.org/en/Publications/WP/
Issues/2016/12/31/Base-Erosion-Profit-Shifting-and-Developing-Countries-42973.

128 **Combined Reporting Systems:** Center for Budget and Policy Priorities (2019),
"28 states plus D.C. require combined reporting for the state corporate income tax,"
https://www.cbpp.org/27-states-plus-dc-require-combined-reporting-for-the-state
-corporate-income-tax.

130 **the "Delaware Loophole":** The Institute on Taxation and Economic Policy (Dec 2015),
"Delaware: An onshore tax haven," https://itep.org/delaware-an-onshore-tax-haven/.

130 **This allows companies to shift:** Patricia Cohen (7 Apr 2016), "Need to hide some
income? You don't have to go to Panama," *New York Times*, https://www.nytimes
.com/2016/04/08/business/need-to-hide-some-income-you-dont-have-to-go
-to-panama.html.

130 **the other forty-nine states:** Leslie Wayne (30 Jun 2012), "How Delaware thrives as a
corporate tax haven," *New York Times*, https://www.nytimes.com/2012/07/01/business/
how-delaware-thrives-as-a-corporate-tax-haven.html.

32. ADMINISTRATIVE BURDENS

132 **named this phenomenon:** Pamela Herd and Donald P. Moynihan (2019), *Administrative
Burden: Policymaking by Other Means*, Russell Sage Foundation.

132 **Florida's unemployment insurance scheme:** Rebecca Vallas (15 Apr 2020), "Republicans wrapped the safety net in red tape. Now we're all suffering." *Washington Post*, https://
www.washingtonpost.com/outlook/2020/04/15/republicans-harder-access-safety-net.

133 **prevent the submission:** Vox staff (10 Jun 2020), "Why it's so hard to get unemployment
benefits," *Vox*, https://www.youtube.com/watch?v=ualUPur6iks.

133 **only accessible at specific hours:** Emily Stewart (13 May 2020), "The American unemployment system is broken by design," *Vox*, https://www.vox.com/
policy-and-politics/2020/5/13/21255894/unemployment-insurance-system-problems-florida
-claims-pua-new-york.

133 **many people spent hours:** Palm Beach Post Editorial Board (30 Nov 2020), "Where
is that probe of the broken Florida unemployment system, Governor?" *Florida Today*,
https://www.floridatoday.com/story/opinion/2020/11/30/where-probe-broken
-florida-unemployment-system-governor/6439594002.

134 **The biggest offender was Louisiana:** Elizabeth Nash (11 Feb 2020), "Louisiana has

passed 89 abortion restrictions since Roe: It's about control, not health," Guttmacher Institute, https://www.guttmacher.org/article/2020/02/louisiana-has-passed-89-abortion-restrictions-roe-its-about-control-not-health.

134 **When the US Supreme Court ruled:** US Supreme Court (29 Jun 1992), *Planned Parenthood of Southern Pennsylvania v. Casey*, 505 U.S. 833 (1992), https://www.oyez.org/cases/1991/91-744.

134 **less than half of families:** L. V. Anderson (17 Feb 2015), "The Federal Nutrition Program for Pregnant Women is a bureaucratic nightmare," *Slate*, https://slate.com/human-interest/2015/02/the-wic-potato-report-a-symptom-of-the-bureaucratic-nightmare-that-is-americas-welfare-system.html.

33. HACKING COMMON LAW

135 **too complex for traditional analysis:** Jon Kolko (6 Mar 2012), "Wicked problems: Problems worth solving," *Stanford Social Innovation Review*, https://ssir.org/books/excerpts/entry/wicked_problems_problems_worth_solving.

136 **The English courts decided:** England and Wales High Court (King's Bench), *Entick v. Carrington* (1765), EWHC KB J98 1066.

137 **patent injunction hack was adjudicated:** US Supreme Court (15 May 2006), *eBay Inc. v. MercExchange, LLC*, 547 U.S. 388, https://www.supremecourt.gov/opinions/05pdf/05-130.pdf.

34. HACKING AS EVOLUTION

139 **an unbroken piece of wire:** M. Olin (2019), "The *Eruv*: From the Talmud to Contemporary Art," in S. Fine, ed., *Jewish Religious Architecture: From Biblical Israel to Modern Judaism*, Koninklijke Brill NV.

140 **just automatically stop:** Elizabeth A. Harris (5 Mar 2012), "For Jewish Sabbath, elevators do all the work," *New York Times*, https://www.nytimes.com/2012/03/06/nyregion/on-jewish-sabbath-elevators-that-do-all-the-work.html.

140 **there's a Bluetooth device:** JC staff (12 Aug 2010), "Israeli soldiers get Shabbat Bluetooth phone," https://www.thejc.com/news/israel/israeli-soldiers-get-shabbat-bluetooth-phone-1.17376.

140 **states and institutions are developed:** Francis Fukuyama (2014), *Political Order and Political Decay: From the Industrial Revolution to the Globalization of Democracy*, Farrar, Straus & Giroux.

140 **when conservative groups:** Yoni Appelbaum (Dec 2019), "How America ends," *Atlantic*, https://www.theatlantic.com/magazine/archive/2019/12/how-america-ends/600757. Uri Friedman (14 Jun 2017), "Why conservative parties are central to democracy," *Atlantic*, https://www.theatlantic.com/international/archive/2017/06/ziblatt-democracy-conservative-parties/530118. David Frum (20 Jun 2017), "Why do democracies fail?" *Atlantic*, https://www.theatlantic.com/international/archive/2017/06/why-do-democracies-fail/530949.

141 **concept of corporate personhood:** Adam Winkler (5 Mar 2018), "'Corporations are people' is built on an incredible 19th-century lie," *Atlantic*, https://www.theatlantic.com/business/archive/2018/03/corporations-people-adam-winkler/554852.

35. HIDDEN PROVISIONS IN LEGISLATION

145 **intercepting network equipment:** S. Silbert (16 May 2014), "Latest Snowden leak reveals the NSA intercepted and bugged Cisco routers," Engadget, https://www.engadget.com/2014-05-16-nsa-bugged-cisco-routers.html.

146   **lobbied for by Starbucks:** Ben Hallman and Chris Kirkham (15 Feb 2013), "As Obama confronts corporate tax reform, past lessons suggest lobbyists will fight for loopholes," *Huffington Post*, https://www.huffpost.com/entry/obama-corporate-tax-reform_n_2680880.

146   **exemptions for "natural monopolies":** Leah Farzin (1 Jan 2015), "On the antitrust exemption for professional sports in the United States and Europe," *Jeffrey S. Moorad Sports Law Journal* 75, https://digitalcommons.law.villanova.edu/cgi/viewcontent.cgi?article=1321&context=mslj.

146   **over 6,000 lobbyists:** Taylor Lincoln (1 Dec 2017), "Swamped: More than half the members of Washington's lobbying corps have plunged into the tax debate," Public Citizen, https://www.citizen.org/wp-content/uploads/migration/swamped-tax-lobbying-report.pdf.

146   **gift for Teach For America:** Valerie Strauss (16 Oct 2013), "The debt deal's gift to Teach For America (yes, TFA)," *Washington Post*, https://www.washingtonpost.com/news/answer-sheet/wp/2013/10/16/the-debt-deals-gift-to-teach-for-america-yes-tfa.

147   **how real estate investors could offset:** Jesse Drucker (26 Mar 2020), "Bonanza for rich real estate investors, tucked into stimulus package," *New York Times*, https://www.nytimes.com/2020/03/26/business/coronavirus-real-estate-investors-stimulus.html. Nicholas Kristof (23 May 2020), "Crumbs for the hungry but windfalls for the rich," *New York Times*, https://www.nytimes.com/2020/05/23/opinion/sunday/coronavirus-economic-response.html.

147   **Republican staffers added the provision:** Akela Lacy (19 Apr 2020), "Senate Finance Committee Democrats tried to strike millionaire tax break from coronavirus stimulus—then failed to warn others about it," *Intercept*, https://theintercept.com/2020/04/19/coronavirus-cares-act-millionaire-tax-break.

147   **This kind of thing is so common:** GOP congressional aide Billy Pitts said in 2017: "What got snuck into there? What got airdropped into there in conference or whatever? That's always the threat of a big, fat bill—there's always something hidden inside of it." https://www.npr.org/2017/03/11/519700465/when-it-comes-to-legislation-sometimes-bigger-is-better.

147   **Krusty the Clown gets elected to Congress:** Matt Groening and J. L. Brooks (11 Feb 1996), "Bart the fink," *The Simpsons*, Season 7, episode 15, Fox Broadcasting Company/YouTube, https://www.youtube.com/watch?v=hNeIkS9EMV0.

148   **part of its ninety-seven recommendations:** Select Committee on the Modernization of Congress (2019), "116th Congress recommendations," https://modernizecongress.house.gov/116th-recommendations.

148   **goal would be to make it easier:** Select Committee on the Modernization of Congress (2019), "Finalize a new system that allows the American people to easily track how amendments change legislation and the impact of proposed legislation to current law," Final Report, https://modernizecongress.house.gov/final-report-116th/chapter/recommendation/finalize-a-new-system-that-allows-the-american-people-to-easily-track-how-amendments-change-legislation-and-the-impact-of-proposed-legislation-to-current-law.

149   **the CARES Act was released:** Mia Jankowicz (22 Dec 2020), "'It's hostage-taking.' AOC lashed out after lawmakers got only hours to read and pass the huge 5,593-page bill to secure COVID-19 relief," *Business Insider*, https://www.businessinsider.com/aoc-angry-representatives-2-hours-read-covid-19-stimulus-bill-2020-12.

149   **The measure contained $110 billion:** Yeganeh Torbati (22 Dec 2020), "Tucked into Congress's massive stimulus bill: Tens of billions in special-interest tax giveaways," *Washington Post*, https://www.washingtonpost.com/business/2020/12/22/congress-tax-breaks-stimulus.

149   **Many lawmakers were unaware:** Akela Lacy (19 Apr 2020), "Senate Finance Com-

mittee Democrats tried to strike millionaire tax break from coronavirus stimulus—then failed to warn others about it," *Intercept*, https://theintercept.com/2020/04/19/coronavirus-cares-act-millionaire-tax-break.

36. MUST-PASS LEGISLATION

151   **the logic behind single-subject laws:** US Congress (10 Apr 2019; latest action 20 May 2019), H.R. 2240: One Subject at a Time Act, 116th Congress, https://www.congress.gov/bill/116th-congress/house-bill/2240.

151   **Minnesota's constitution:** State of Minnesota (13 Oct 1857; revised 5 Nov 1974), Constitution of the State of Minnesota, Article IV: Legislative Department, https://www.revisor.mn.gov/constitution/#article_4.

152   **an older Pennsylvania Supreme Court case:** Richard Briffault (2019), "The single-subject rule: A state constitutional dilemma," *Albany Law Review* 82, https://scholarship.law.columbia.edu/cgi/viewcontent.cgi?article=3593&context=faculty_scholarship.

152   **several organizations have proposed:** Committee for a Responsible Federal Budget (17 Sep 2020), "Better Budget Process Initiative: Automatic CRs can improve the appropriations process," http://www.crfb.org/papers/better-budget-process-initiative-automatic-crs-can-improve-appropriations-process.

37. DELEGATING AND DELAYING LEGISLATION

154   **between 3,000 and 4,000 new administrative rules:** Clyde Wayne Crews and Kent Lassman (30 Jun 2021), "New Ten Thousand Commandments report evaluates the sweeping hidden tax of regulation; Provides definitive assessment of Trump deregulatory legacy," Competitive Enterprise Institute, https://cei.org/studies/ten-thousand-commandments-2020.

155   **filibuster was most often used:** Zack Beauchamp (25 Mar 2021), "The filibuster's racist history, explained," *Vox*, https://www.vox.com/policy-and-politics/2021/3/25/22348308/filibuster-racism-jim-crow-mitch-mcconnell.

156   **misused as a delaying tactic:** Lauren C. Bell (14 Nov 2018), "Obstruction in parliaments: A cross-national perspective," *Journal of Legislative Studies*, https://www.tandfonline.com/doi/full/10.1080/13572334.2018.1544694.

156   **In the Japanese Diet:** Michael Macarthur Bosack (31 Jan 2020), "Ox walking, heckling and other strange Diet practices," *Japan Times*, https://www.japantimes.co.jp/opinion/2020/01/31/commentary/japan-commentary/ox-walking-heckling-strange-diet-practices.

156   **a 2016 constitutional reform bill:** Gazetta del Sud staff (11 April 2016), "Democracy doesn't mean obstructionism says Renzi," https://www.ansa.it/english/news/2016/04/11/democracy-doesnt-mean-obstructionism-says-renzi-2_e16b1463-aa10-432a-b40e-28a00354b182.html.

38. THE CONTEXT OF A HACK

157   **Loose language in the:** Natalie Kitroeff (27 Dec 2017), "In a complex tax bill, let the hunt for loopholes begin," *New York Times*, https://www.nytimes.com/2017/12/27/business/economy/tax-loopholes.html.

158   **It's impossible to know for sure:** Edmund L. Andrews (13 Oct 2004), "How tax bill gave business more and more," *New York Times*, https://www.nytimes.com/2004/10/13/business/how-tax-bill-gave-business-more-and-more.html.

158   **Curved sticks make for a faster puck:** National Hockey League (accessed 11 May 2022), "Historical rule changes," https://records.nhl.com/history/historical-rule-changes.

158 **opposition to private ownership:** Donald Clarke (19 Jan 2017), "The paradox at the heart of China's property regime," *Foreign Policy*, https://foreignpolicy.com/2017/01/19/the-paradox-at-the-heart-of-chinas-property-regime-wenzhou-lease-renewal-problems. Sebastian Heilmann (2008), "Policy experimentation in China's economic rise," *Studies in Comparative International Development* 43, https://link.springer.com/article/10.1007/s12116-007-9014-4.

160 **Trump withdrew his nomination:** Lara Seligman (2 Aug 2020), "Trump skirts Senate to install nominee under fire for Islamaphobic tweets in Pentagon post," *Politico*, https://www.politico.com/news/2020/08/02/donald-trump-anthony-tata-pentagon-390851.

160 **It depends on your opinion:** Kevin Drum (3 Aug 2020), "Do we really need Senate confirmation of 1,200 positions?" *Mother Jones*, https://www.motherjones.com/kevin-drum/2020/08/do-we-really-need-senate-confirmation-of-1200-positions.

39. HACKING VOTING ELIGIBILITY

161 **a coalition of conservative Democrats:** Joshua Shiver (16 Apr 2020), "Alabama Constitution of 1875," *Encyclopedia of Alabama*, http://encyclopediaofalabama.org/article/h-4195.

162 **These efforts culminated:** Alabama Legislature (22 May 1901), "Constitutional Convention, second day," http://www.legislature.state.al.us/aliswww/history/constitutions/1901/proceedings/1901_proceedings_vol1/day2.html.

162 **The constitution introduced or entrenched:** John Lewis and Archie E. Allen (1 Oct 1972), "Black voter registration efforts in the South," *Notre Dame Law Review* 48, no. 1, p. 107, https://scholarship.law.nd.edu/cgi/viewcontent.cgi?article=2861&context=ndlr.

162 **In 1903, fewer than 3,000:** Rachel Knowles (10 February 2020), "Alive and well: Voter suppression and election mismanagement in Alabama," *Southern Poverty Law Center*, https://www.splcenter.org/20200210/alive-and-well-voter-suppression-and-election-mismanagement-alabama#Disenfranchisement.

162 **The 1964 Louisiana literacy test:** Open Culture staff (16 Nov 2014), "Watch Harvard students fail the literacy test Louisiana used to suppress the Black vote in 1964," Open Culture, http://www.openculture.com/2014/11/harvard-students-fail-the-literacy-test.html.

40. OTHER ELECTION HACKS

164 **these hacks were only banned:** Constitutional Rights Foundation (n.d., accessed 1 Jun 2022), "Race and voting," https://www.crf-usa.org/brown-v-board-50th-anniversary/race-and-voting.html. US Supreme Court (7 Mar 1966), *South Carolina v. Katzenbach* (Case No. 22), 383 U.S. 301, http://cdn.loc.gov/service/ll/usrep/usrep383/usrep383301/usrep383301.pdf.

165 **people can be denied the right to vote:** Peter Dunphy (5 Nov 2018), "When it comes to voter suppression, don't forget about Alabama," Brennan Center, https://www.brennancenter.org/our-work/analysis-opinion/when-it-comes-voter-suppression-dont-forget-about-alabama.

41. MONEY IN POLITICS

169 **a 1976 ruling excluded money spent:** Yasmin Dawood (30 Mar 2015), "Campaign finance and American democracy," *Annual Review of Political Science*, https://www.annualreviews.org/doi/pdf/10.1146/annurev-polisci-010814-104523.

169 **Lawrence Lessig argues:** Lawrence Lessig (2014), *The USA Is Lesterland*, CreateSpace Independent Publishing Platform.

169 **in the 2012 Republican primary:** Kenneth P. Vogel (12 Jan 2012), "3 billion-

aires who'll drag out the race," *Politico*, https://www.politico.com/story/2012/01/meet-the-3-billionaires-wholl-drag-out-the-race-071358.

170 **take advantage of Green Party candidates:** Sam Howe Verhovek (8 Aug 2001), "Green Party candidate finds he's a Republican pawn," *New York Times*, https://www.nytimes.com/2001/08/08/us/green-party-candidate-finds-he-s-a-republican-pawn.html.

170 **Alex Rodriguez ran against:** Sun-Sentinel Editorial Board (25 Nov 2020), "Evidence of fraud in a Florida election. Where's the outrage?" *South Florida Sun-Sentinel*, https://www.sun-sentinel.com/opinion/editorials/fl-op-edit-florida-election-fraud-20201125-ifg6ssys35bjrp7bes6xzizon4-story.html.

170 **a person with the same name:** Rama Lakshmi (23 Apr 2014), "Sahu vs. Sahu vs. Sahu: Indian politicians run 'clone' candidates to trick voters," *Washington Post*, https://www.washingtonpost.com/world/sahu-vs-sahu-vs-sahu-indian-politicians-run-clone-candidates-to-trick-voters/2014/04/23/613f7465-267e-4a7f-bb95-14eb9a1c6b7a_story.html.

42. HACKING TO DESTRUCTION

172 **he formed a syndicate:** Andy Williamson (16 May 2013), "How Voltaire made a fortune rigging the lottery," Today I Found Out, http://www.todayifoundout.com/index.php/2013/05/how-voltaire-made-a-fortune-rigging-the-lottery.

173 **automatically submitted fake reports:** Janus Rose (8 May 2020), "This script sends junk data to Ohio's website for snitching on workers," *Vice*, https://www.vice.com/en_us/article/wxqemy/this-script-sends-junk-data-to-ohios-website-for-snitching-on-workers.

173 **fake ticket requests:** Taylor Lorenz, Kellen Browning, and Sheera Frenkel (21 Jun 2020), "TikTok teens and K-Pop stans say they sank Trump rally," *New York Times*, https://www.nytimes.com/2020/06/21/style/tiktok-trump-rally-tulsa.html.

174 **Zimbabwe experienced hyperinflation:** Janet Koech (2012), "Hyperinflation in Zimbabwe," *Federal Reserve Bank of Dallas Globalization and Monetary Policy Institute 2011 Annual Report*, https://www.dallasfed.org/~/media/documents/institute/annual/2011/annual11b.pdf.

174 **In Venezuela, hyperinflation began:** Patricia Laya and Fabiola Zerpa (5 Oct 2020), "Venezuela mulls 100,000 Bolivar bill. Guess how much it's worth?," Bloomberg, https://www.bloombergquint.com/onweb/venezuela-planning-new-100-000-bolivar-bills-worth-just-0-23. Gonzalo Huertas (Sep 2019), "Hyperinflation in Venezuela: A stabilization handbook," Peterson Institute for International Economics Policy Brief 19-13, https://www.piie.com/sites/default/files/documents/pb19-13.pdf.

43. COGNITIVE HACKS

181 **Goebbels, Hitler's propaganda minister:** Jason Stanley (2016), *How Propaganda Works*, Princeton University Press, https://press.princeton.edu/books/paperback/9780691173429/how-propaganda-works.

181 **Cory Doctorow cautions us:** Cory Doctorow (26 Aug 2020), "How to destroy surveillance capitalism," *OneZero*, https://onezero.medium.com/how-to-destroy-surveillance-capitalism-8135e6744d59.

44. ATTENTION AND ADDICTION

183 **Everyone hates pop-up ads:** Ethan Zuckerman (14 Aug 2014), "The internet's original sin," *Atlantic*, https://www.theatlantic.com/technology/archive/2014/08/advertising-is-the-internets-original-sin/376041.

184 **Jules Chéret invented a new form:** Richard H. Driehaus Museum (14 Mar 2017), "Jules

Chéret and the history of the artistic poster," http://driehausmuseum.org/blog/view/
jules-cheret-and-the-history-of-the-artistic-poster.

45. PERSUASION

188 **people often resist attempts:** Marieke L. Fransen, Edith G. Smit, and Peeter W. J. Ver-
legh (14 Aug 2015), "Strategies and motives for resistance to persuasion: an integrative
framework," *Frontiers in Psychology* 6, article 1201, https://www.ncbi.nlm.nih.gov/pmc/
articles/PMC4536373.

189 **drip pricing resulted in people spending:** Morgan Foy (9 Feb 2021), "Buyer beware:
Massive experiment shows why ticket sellers hit you with last-second fees," Haas School
of Business, University of California, Berkeley, https://newsroom.haas.berkeley.edu/.
research/buyer-beware-massive-experiment-shows-why-ticket-sellers-hit-you-with
-hidden-fees-drip-pricing.

46. TRUST AND AUTHORITY

191 **"Only amateurs attack machines":** Bruce Schneier (15 Oct 2000), "Semantic
attacks: The third wave of network attacks," *Crypto-Gram*, https://www.schneier.com/
crypto-gram/archives/2000/1015.html#1.

191 **One victim lost $24 million:** Joeri Cant (22 Oct 2019), "Victim of $24 million SIM
swap case writes open letter to FCC chairman," *Cointelegraph*, https://cointelegraph
.com/news/victim-of-24-million-sim-swap-case-writes-open-letter-to-fcc-chairman.

192 **the 2020 Twitter hackers:** Twitter (18 Jul 2020; updated 30 Jul 2020), "An update on our
security incident," Twitter blog, https://blog.twitter.com/en_us/topics/company/2020/
an-update-on-our-security-incident.

192 **the CEO of an unnamed UK energy company:** Nick Statt (5 Sep 2019), "Thieves are
now using AI deepfakes to trick companies into sending them money," *Verge*, https://
www.theverge.com/2019/9/5/20851248/deepfakes-ai-fake-audio-phone-calls-thieves
-trick-companies-stealing-money.

192 **one scam artist has used a silicone mask:** Hugh Schofield (20 Jun 2019), "The fake
French minister in a silicone mask who stole millions," BBC News, https://www.bbc
.com/news/world-europe-48510027.

193 **a video of Gabon's long-missing president:** Drew Harwell (12 Jun 2019), "Top AI
researchers race to detect 'deepfake' videos: 'We are outgunned,'" *Washington Post*,
https://www.washingtonpost.com/technology/2019/06/12/top-ai-researchers-race
-detect-deepfake-videos-we-are-outgunned.

193 **BuzzFeed found 140 fake news websites:** Craig Silverman and Lawrence Alexander
(3 Nov 2016), "How teens in the Balkans are duping Trump supporters with fake news,"
BuzzFeed, https://www.buzzfeednews.com/article/craigsilverman/how-macedonia
-became-a-global-hub-for-pro-trump-misinfo.

47. FEAR AND RISK

195 **very basic brain functions:** Bruce Schneier (3 Apr 2000), "The difference between feeling
and reality in security," *Wired*, https://www.wired.com/2008/04/securitymatters-0403.

196 **Terrorism directly hacks:** Bruce Schneier (17 May 2007), "Virginia Tech lesson: Rare risks breed irrational responses," *Wired*, https://www.wired.com/2007/05/
securitymatters-0517.

196 **"When people are insecure":** Nate Silver (1 Feb 2010), "Better to be strong and wrong—
especially when you're actually right," FiveThirtyEight, https://fivethirtyeight.com/
features/better-to-be-strong-and-wrong.

197 **"immigrants are going to take your jobs"**: Fox News (26 Jan 2017), "The truth about jobs in America," *The O'Reilly Factor* (transcript), https://www.foxnews.com/transcript/the-truth-about-jobs-in-america.

197 **"[this or that city] is crime-ridden"**: Audrey Conklin (21 Feb 2022), "Homicides, rapes in Atlanta soar despite other decreasing violent crime," *Fox News*, https://www.foxnews.com/us/homicides-rapes-atlanta-soar-2022.

197 **"ISIS is a threat to Americans"**: Ronn Blitzer (26 Oct 2021), "Top Pentagon official confirms ISIS-K could have capability to attack US in '6 to 12 months,'" *Fox News*, https://www.foxnews.com/politics/pentagon-official-isis-k-us-attack-6-to-12-months.

197 **"Democrats are going to take your guns"**: Tucker Carlson (9 Apr 2021), "Biden wants to take your guns, but leave criminals with theirs," *Fox News*, https://www.foxnews.com/opinion/tucker-carlson-biden-gun-control-disarm-trump-voters.

48. DEFENDING AGAINST COGNITIVE HACKS

199 **Foreknowledge only goes so far:** Leah Savion (Jan 2009), "Clinging to discredited beliefs: The larger cognitive story," *Journal of the Scholarship of Teaching and Learning* 9, no. 1, https://files.eric.ed.gov/fulltext/EJ854880.pdf.

49. A HIERARCHY OF HACKING

201 **Jeff Bezos had no problem:** Sam Dangremond (4 Apr 2019), "Jeff Bezos is renovating the biggest house in Washington, D.C.," *Town and Country*, https://www.townandcountrymag.com/leisure/real-estate/news/a9234/jeff-bezos-house-washington-dc.

201 **Ghostwriter, a collective:** Lee Foster et al. (28 Jul 2020), "'Ghostwriter' influence campaign: Unknown actors leverage website compromises and fabricated content to push narratives aligned with Russian security interests," Mandiant, https://www.fireeye.com/blog/threat-research/2020/07/ghostwriter-influence-campaign.html.

50. ARTIFICIAL INTELLIGENCE AND ROBOTICS

206 **Marvin Minsky described AI:** Marvin Minsky (1968), "Preface," in *Semantic Information Processing*, MIT Press.

206 **Patrick Winston, another AI pioneer:** Patrick Winston (1984), *Artificial Intelligence*, Addison-Wesley.

206 **probably decades away:** Futurist Martin Ford surveyed twenty-three prominent AI researchers and asked them by what year is there at least a 50% chance of generalized AI being built. The answers ranged between 2029 and 2200, with the average answer being 2099: which I'm guessing is a cop-out "before the end of the century" answer. Martin Ford (2018), *Architects of Intelligence: The Truth About AI from the People Building It*, Packt Publishing.

208 **Def: Robot /'rō-,bät/ (noun):** Kate Darling (2021), *The New Breed: What Our History with Animals Reveals about Our Future with Robots*, Henry Holt.

52. THE EXPLAINABILITY PROBLEM

212 **Deep Thought informs them:** Douglas Adams (1978), *The Hitchhiker's Guide to the Galaxy*, BBC Radio 4.

212 **AlphaGo won a five-game match:** Cade Metz (16 Mar 2016), "In two moves, AlphaGo and Lee Sedol redefined the future," *Wired*, https://www.wired.com/2016/03/two-moves-alphago-lee-sedol-redefined-future.

213 **"the magical number seven":** George A. Miller (1956), "The magical number seven,

plus or minus two: Some limits on our capacity for processing information," *Psychological Review* 63, no. 2, http://psychclassics.yorku.ca/Miller.

214 **explainability is especially important:** J. Fjeld et al. (15 Jan 2020), "Principled artificial intelligence: Mapping consensus in ethical and rights-based approaches to principled AI," Berkman Klein Center for Internet and Society, https://cyber.harvard.edu/publication/2020/principled-ai.

214 **if an AI system:** Select Committee on Artificial Intelligence (16 Apr 2018), "AI in the UK: Ready, willing and able?" House of Lords, https://publications.parliament.uk/pa/ld201719/ldselect/ldai/100/100.pdf.

215 **Amazon executives lost enthusiasm:** Jeffrey Dastin (10 Oct 2018), "Amazon scraps secret AI recruiting tool that shows bias against women," Reuters, https://www.reuters.com/article/us-amazon-com-jobs-automation-insight/amazon-scraps-secret-ai-recruiting-tool-that-showed-bias-against-women-idUSKCN1MK08G.

215 **multiple contradictory definitions of fairness:** David Weinberger (accessed 11 May 2022), "Playing with AI fairness," What-If Tool, https://pair-code.github.io/what-if-tool/ai-fairness.html. David Weinberger (6 Nov 2019), "How machine learning pushes us to define fairness," *Harvard Business Review*, https://hbr.org/2019/11/how-machine-learning-pushes-us-to-define-fairness.

53. HUMANIZING AI

217 **program called ELIZA:** Joseph Weizenbaum (Jan 1966), "ELIZA: A computer program for the study of natural language communication between man and machine," *Communications of the ACM*, https://web.stanford.edu/class/linguist238/p36-weizenabaum.pdf.

217 **voice assistants like Alexa and Siri:** James Vincent (22 Nov 2019), "Women are more likely than men to say 'please' to their smart speaker," *Verge*, https://www.theverge.com/2019/11/22/20977442/ai-politeness-smart-speaker-alexa-siri-please-thank-you-pew-gender-sur.

217 **they didn't want to hurt its feelings:** Clifford Nass, Youngme Moon, and Paul Carney (31 Jul 2006), "Are people polite to computers? Responses to computer-based interviewing systems," *Journal of Applied Social Psychology*, https://onlinelibrary.wiley.com/doi/abs/10.1111/j.1559-1816.1999.tb00142.x.

217 **the subject was likely to reciprocate:** Youngme Moon (Mar 2000), "Intimate exchanges: Using computers to elicit self-disclosure from consumers," *Journal of Consumer Research*, https://www.jstor.org/stable/10.1086/209566?seq=1.

217 **robot ran into problems:** Joel Garreau (6 May 2007), "Bots on the ground," *Washington Post*, https://www.washingtonpost.com/wp-dyn/content/article/2007/05/05/AR2007050501009_pf.html.

218 **a study on human trust in robots:** Paul Robinette et al. (Mar 2016), "Overtrust of robots in emergency evacuation scenarios," 2016 ACM/IEEE International Conference on Human-Robot Interaction, https://www.cc.gatech.edu/~alanwags/pubs/Robinette-HRI-2016.pdf.

218 **"When robots make eye contact":** Sherry Turkle (2010), "In good company," in Yorick Wilks, ed., *Close Engagements with Artificial Companions*, John Benjamin Publishing.

54. AI AND ROBOTS HACKING US

220 **bots being used to spread propaganda:** Samantha Bradshaw and Philip N. Howard (2019), "The global disinformation order: 2019 global inventory of organised social media manipulation," Computational Propaganda Research Project, https://comprop.oii.ox.ac.uk/wp-content/uploads/sites/93/2019/09/CyberTroop-Report19.pdf.

220 **Modern text-creation systems:** Tom Simonite (22 Jul 2020), "Did a person write this

headline, or a machine?" *Wired*, https://www.wired.com/story/ai-text-generator-gpt-3 -learning-language-fitfully.

221 **public input on a Medicaid issue:** Max Weiss (17 Dec 2019), "Deepfake bot submissions to federal public comment websites cannot be distinguished from human submissions," Technology Science, https://techscience.org/a/2019121801.

222 **an animatronic plastic dinosaur named Cleo:** Kate Darling (2021), *The New Breed: What Our History with Animals Reveals about Our Future with Robots*, Henry Holt.

222 **a creature with feelings:** Woodrow Hartzog (4 May 2015), "Unfair and deceptive robots," *Maryland Law Review*, https://papers.ssrn.com/sol3/papers.cfm?abstract_ id=2602452.

222 **a robot was able to exert "peer pressure":** Yaniv Hanoch et al. (17 May 2021), "The robot made me do it: Human–robot interaction and risk-taking behavior," *Cyberpsychology, Behavior, and Social Networking*, https://www.liebertpub.com/doi/10.1089/cyber .2020.0148.

55. COMPUTERS AND AI ARE ACCELERATING SOCIETAL HACKING

224 **computers scale rote tasks:** Karlheinz Meier (31 May 2017), "The brain as computer: Bad at math, good at everything else," *IEEE Spectrum*, https://spectrum.ieee.org/ the-brain-as-computer-bad-at-math-good-at-everything-else.

225 **Donotpay.com automates the process:** Samuel Gibbs (28 Jun 2016), "Chatbot lawyer overturns 160,000 parking tickets in London and New York," *Guardian*, https://www .theguardian.com/technology/2016/jun/28/chatbot-ai-lawyer-donotpay-parking -tickets-london-new-york.

225 **Automated A/B testing:** Amy Gallo (28 Jun 2017), "A refresher on A/B testing," *Harvard Business Review*, https://hbr.org/2017/06/a-refresher-on-ab-testing.

225 **they have the potential to overwhelm:** California has a law requiring bots to identify themselves. Renee DiResta (24 Jul 2019), "A new law makes bots identify themselves—that's the problem," *Wired*, https://www.wired.com/story/law-makes -bots-identify-themselves.

226 **"flash crashes" of the stock market:** Laim Vaughan (2020), *Flash Crash: A Trading Savant, a Global Manhunt, and the Most Mysterious Market Crash in History*, Doubleday.

226 **these systems are vulnerable to hacking:** Shafi Goldwasser et al. (14 Apr 2022), "Planting undetectable backdoors in machine learning models," *arXiv*, https://arxiv.org/ abs/2204.06974.

56. WHEN AIs BECOME HACKERS

228 **a similarly styled event for AI:** Jia Song and Jim Alves-Foss (Nov 2015), "The DARPA Cyber Grand Challenge: A competitor's perspective," *IEEE Security and Privacy Magazine* 13, no. 6, https://www.researchgate.net/publication/286490027_The_DARPA_ cyber_grand_challenge_A_competitor%27s_perspective.

229 **Chinese AI systems are improving:** Dakota Cary (Sep 2021), "Robot hacking games: China's competitions to automate the software vulnerability lifecycle," Center for Security and Emerging Technology, https://cset.georgetown.edu/wp-content/uploads/ CSET-Robot-Hacking-Games.pdf.

229 **research is continuing:** Bruce Schneier (18 Dec 2018) "Machine learning will transform how we detect software vulnerabilities," *Security Intelligence*, https://securityintelligence .com/machine-learning-will-transform-how-we-detect-software-vulnerabilities/.

230 **looking for loopholes in contracts:** Economist staff (12 Jun 2018), "Law firms climb aboard the AI wagon," *Economist*, https://www.economist.com/business/2018/07/12/ law-firms-climb-aboard-the-ai-wagon.

57. REWARD HACKING

231   **AI achieving a goal in a way:** A list of examples is here. Victoria Krakovna (2 Apr 2018), "Specification gaming examples in AI," https://vkrakovna.wordpress.com/2018/04/02/specification-gaming-examples-in-ai.

231   **if it kicked the ball out of bounds:** Karol Kurach et al. (25 Jul 2019), "Google research football: A novel reinforcement learning environment," *arXiv*, https://arxiv.org/abs/1907.11180.

231   **AI was instructed to stack blocks:** Ivaylo Popov et al. (10 Apr 2017), "Data-efficient deep reinforcement learning for dexterous manipulation," *arXiv*, https://arxiv.org/abs/1704.03073.

232   **the AI grew tall enough:** David Ha (10 Oct 2018), "Reinforcement learning for improving agent design," https://designrl.github.io.

232   **Imagine a robotic vacuum:** Dario Amodei et al. (25 Jul 2016), "Concrete problems in AI safety," *arXiv*, https://arxiv.org/pdf/1606.06565.pdf.

232   **robot vacuum to stop bumping:** Custard Smingleigh (@Smingleigh) (7 Nov 2018), Twitter, https://twitter.com/smingleigh/status/1060325665671692288.

233   **goals and desires are always underspecified:** Abby Everett Jaques (2021), "The Underspecification Problem and AI: For the Love of God, Don't Send a Robot Out for Coffee," unpublished manuscript.

233   **a fictional AI assistant:** Stuart Russell (Apr 2017), "3 principles for creating safer AI," TED2017, https://www.ted.com/talks/stuart_russell_3_principles_for_creating_safer_ai.

233   **reports of airline passengers:** Melissa Koenig (9 Sep 2021), "Woman, 46, who missed her JetBlue flight 'falsely claimed she planted a BOMB on board' to delay plane so her son would not be late to school," *Daily Mail*, https://www.dailymail.co.uk/news/article-9973553/Woman-46-falsely-claims-planted-BOMB-board-flight-effort-delay-plane.html. Ella Torres (18 Jan 2020), "London man reports fake bomb threat to delay flight he was running late for: Police," *ABC News*, https://abcnews.go.com/International/london-man-reports-fake-bomb-threat-delay-flight/story?id=68369727. Peter Stubley (16 Aug 2018), "Man makes hoax bomb threat to delay his flight," *Independent*, https://www.independent.co.uk/news/uk/crime/man-late-flight-hoax-bomb-threat-gatwick-airport-los-angeles-jacob-meir-abdellak-hackney-a8494681.html. Reuters (20 Jun 2007), "Woman delays Turkish plane with fake bomb warning," https://www.reuters.com/article/us-turkey-plane-bomb-idUSL2083245120070620.

58. DEFENDING AGAINST AI HACKERS

236   **recommendation engines:** Zeynep Tufekci (10 Mar 2018), "YouTube, the great equalizer," *New York Times*, https://www.nytimes.com/2018/03/10/opinion/sunday/youtube-politics-radical.html. Renee DiResta (11 Apr 2018), "Up next: A better recommendation system," *Wired*, https://www.wired.com/story/creating-ethical-recommendation-engines.

237   **can also benefit the defense:** One example: Gregory Falco et al. (28 Aug 2018), "A master attack methodology for an AI-based automated attack planner for smart cities," *IEEE Access* 6, https://ieeexplore.ieee.org/document/8449268.

59. A FUTURE OF AI HACKERS

242   **novel and completely unexpected hacks:** Hedge funds and investment firms are already using AI to inform investment decisions. Luke Halpin and Doug Dannemiller (2019), "Artificial intelligence: The next frontier for investment management firms," Deloitte,

https://www2.deloitte.com/content/dam/Deloitte/global/Documents/Financial
-Services/fsi-artificial-intelligence-investment-mgmt.pdf. Peter Salvage (March 2019),
"Artificial intelligence sweeps hedge funds," BNY Mellon, https://www.bnymellon.com/
us/en/insights/all-insights/artificial-intelligence-sweeps-hedge-funds.html.

244 **the precautionary principle:** Maciej Kuziemski (1 May 2018), "A precautionary
approach to artificial intelligence," Project Syndicate, https://www.project-syndicate
.org/commentary/precautionary-principle-for-artificial-intelligence-by-maciej
-kuziemski-2018-05.

60. GOVERNANCE SYSTEMS FOR HACKING

245 **AI technologists and industry leaders:** Nick Grossman (8 Apr 2015), "Regulation,
the internet way," Data-Smart City Solutions, Harvard University, https://datasmart
.ash.harvard.edu/news/article/white-paper-regulation-the-internet-way-660.

246 **The Collingridge dilemma:** Adam Thierer (16 Aug 2018), "The pacing problem,
the Collingridge dilemma and technological determinism," Technology Liberation
Front, https://techliberation.com/2018/08/16/the-pacing-problem-the-collingridge
-dilemma-technological-determinism.

247 **its processes and rulings:** Stephan Grimmelikhuijsen et al. (Jan 2021), "Can decision
transparency increase citizen trust in regulatory agencies? Evidence from a representa-
tive survey experiment," *Regulation and Governance* 15, no. 1, https://onlinelibrary.wiley
.com/doi/full/10.1111/rego.12278.

248 **Gillian Hadfield:** Gillian K. Hadfield (2016), *Rules for a Flat World: Why Humans Invented
Law and How to Reinvent It for a Complex Global Economy*, Oxford University Press.

248 **Julie Cohen:** Julie E. Cohen (2019), *Between Truth and Power: The Legal Constructions of
Informational Capitalism*, Oxford University Press.

248 **Joshua Fairfield:** Joshua A. T. Fairfield (2021), *Runaway Technology: Can Law Keep Up?*
Cambridge University Press.

248 **Jamie Susskind:** Jamie Susskind (2022), *The Digital Republic: On Freedom and Democracy in
the 21st Century*, Pegasus.

CONCLUDING THOUGHTS

249 **But there's a loophole:** Josh Zumbrun (25 Apr 2022), "The $67 billion tariff dodge that's
undermining U.S. trade policy," *Wall Street Journal*, https://www.wsj.com/articles/the-67
-billion-tariff-dodge-thats-undermining-u-s-trade-policy-di-minimis-rule-customs
-tourists-11650897161.

250 **inequality produces surplus resources:** Thomas Piketty (2017), *Capital in the Twenty-
First Century*, Harvard University Press.

251 **the fundamental problem with humanity:** Tristan Harris (5 Dec 2019), "Our brains are
no match for our technology," *New York Times*, https://www.nytimes.com/2019/12/05/
opinion/digital-technology-brain.html.

Index